Can't Somebody
Shut Him Up?

DR. MORTON SHULMAN
SUSAN KASTNER

Can't Somebody
Shut Him Up?

Warwick Publishing Inc.
Toronto   Los Angeles

Published by the Warwick Publishing Group
Warwick Publishing Inc., 24 Mercer Street, Toronto, Ontario M5V 1H3
Warwick Publishing Inc., 1300 N. Alexandria, Los Angeles, California 90027

Cover Design: Shaftesbury Books
Text Design: JAQ

ISBN 1-895629-22-5

Distributed in North America by:
Firefly Books Ltd.
250 Sparks Avenue
Willowdale, Ontario
M2H 2S4

Printed and bound in Canada by Best Gagne Book Manufacturers Inc.

To Gloria and Ann for their love
To Geoff and Dianne for their constant delight
To my grandchildren,
Rebecca, David, Carl, Julie, Shoshanna, Allison,
Jaclyn, and Jessie
— MS

For my parents.
For Alan: my best friend and my best editor.
—SK

Author's Note

When Morty Shulman and I sat down to begin work on this book, he left it to me to decide how to tell his story. He didn't care what I wrote or how I wrote it . . . he said. All he wanted was to have what he called "disapproval of inaccuracy".

Then he inundated me with books, letters and documents from dozens of different sources, frequently stamped STRICTLY CONFIDENTIAL, and bags of clippings going back 40 years.

There were months of unfettered early-morning interviews (Morty begins telephoning at 7 a.m., is ready to work by 7:45), months of poring over reams of words about him. It became an exhilarating mental hunt for the elusive, deceptive and many-sided critter who may be the real Morton Shulman.

When he first saw a draft of the manuscript he fell silent for three days. In the weeks that followed he begged me to take out only six items. Well, seven. Otherwise, apart from clarifying things that were unclear, and phoning and faxing no more than half-a-dozen times a day, he left me, the manuscript, and my approach to the subject matter completely alone.

He is a gallant fighter, he is outrageous, he is unique.

Several words of thanks:

To Morty.

To Jim Williamson of Warwick Publishing, who made the call. To Linda McKnight for invaluable advice. To editor Don Loney, for getting me on track, and to Nick Pitt of Warwick for keeping it all together. To my son Jamie, for chocolate bars and unflagging filial devotion.

Most especially, to my husband, Alan Ross, without whom I would never have started, and who brilliantly pulled the pieces together.

Susan Kastner

Contents

Introduction: A Brief Morty Monologue, , **ix**

Prologue: The Crunchtime Brunchtime, **xiii**

Chapter 1: Childhood, **1**

Chapter 2: Conquests, **20**

Chapter 3: An Unlikely Galahad, and the Unhumble Beginnings of Morty Millionaire, **36**

Interlude I: Transitions: Documentation from the Upward Years, **62**

Chapter 4: The Coroner Strikes Back; the Coroner Stries Out, **74**

Interlude II: Transitions: Documentation from the Upward Years, **99**

Chapter 5: From Politics to TV: the Knight of the Increasingly Uncertain Lance, **107**

Chapter 6: The Parkinson's Years: Part I, **123**

Chapter 7: The Parkinson's Years, Part II: Slide and Depression, **160**

Interlude III: To Market, To Market, or Shorting in a Limo with Luan, **194**

Chapter 8: The Parkinson's Years: Part III, **201**

Interlude IV: The Springtime After the Fall, **248**

Chapter 9: Slaying the Generics Dragon, **257**

Chapter 10: The Bestowal, **275**

Epilogue: Postscripts, **285**

A Brief
Morty Monologue

Did I ever think to myself, at any point, "Oh Christ, this time I've gone too far. They're going to find some way or another to cut me off at the knees."

Only once. When I was in the Ontario legislature and — it was a stupid thing. It was right in the middle of this Mafia thing I was going after. I was going on a holiday to Europe, and unbeknownst to me, David McDonald was at a party and he told someone, "Dr. Shulman is going to Europe to investigate the Mafia."

I knew nothing about this and the *Star* dispatched Bob Reguly to find me in Europe. The first thing I know, I get a phone call from home saying, "The *Star* is looking for you. The police are here at the house and — a certain mob connected person in the construction industry — is putting a hit out on you, and for heaven's sake, get home." And I'm sitting in San Remo, having a good time.

So I get on the next plane and I come home, and I left my camera there in the hotel room, in the Italian Riviera. When I got home I realized I had forgotten it.

Two months later, in the Legislature, there was a night session, and the Premier is sitting there, and Arthur Wishart, the Attorney-General, comes in, looks across with a big smile, waves at me, sits down beside the Premier, takes out some pictures, and is showing them to Premier Robarts.

I was worried that they were my vacation pictures.

Fergie-type pictures? Well . . . they were vacation pictures which I would not normally put in my election brochures. Let's say that they didn't have to do with the constituents' home towns in Italy.

Now I thought, *they've got my camera, they've developed the damn pictures and — I'm done.* I sent Wishart a note saying, "Please, I've never attacked you on a personal basis" and it turned out those pictures were not of me and they weren't from my camera! I pleaded for mercy, and for no reason.

He didn't have my camera! He didn't have my pictures! It was my guilty conscience. They had had Interpol looking for me in Europe. So I thought it was possible they had picked up my camera.

But the pictures they were looking at were only some pictures of Lake Moira, where I'd been raising a stink about pollution, and they were working on it. It was very funny.

That was the only time I saw my life pass in front of my eyes. As I sat there and he waved these pictures at me. I thought, "Now he's got me." I couldn't deny they were my pictures. I just said, "Show mercy."

He brought them over to me. He walked around the floor with the pictures. I didn't need to have said a word. Sure looked at me strangely, though.

John Robarts had a suite at the top of Sutton Place where he used to take girls, and nobody talked about it. He had that long time girlfriend for years and years and years. Well, it's normal. At least, it used to be normal.

I thought Ontario Premier John Robarts was an honest, God-fearing man who wanted justice done. It was a great shock to me to find he wasn't. Because finally, when I got in the newspapers, in the conflict with the attorney general when I was Chief Coroner, Robarts called me on the carpet.

That period when they were dangling the axe over my head, I was like St. George with the Dragon; and I thought I was winning.

Introduction: A Brief Morty Monologue

When I found out that they fired me, I was at a coroners' meeting. Somebody knocked on the door. I said, "I'm busy." And we heard, "You're fired!" I said to him, "You don't have the authority to fire me," and he didn't, actually.

But they fired me properly the next day: by Order-In-Council! Had tried to go through with that one time before, but then they backed off. The second time they gave me the one-two punch properly. Harold Cotnam went to John Robarts and said, "He's got to go or I'm quitting."

I think that was the point I decided, Okay, I've made a lot of money and I don't have to depend on anybody for my living or feeding my children. I am going to do what I think is right and let the chips fall where they may. I was an official, an authority. They couldn't easily get rid of me.

Ron Haggart wrote in his *Toronto Star* column one day in 1966 that "one man in Toronto is secure in his job" — meaning me — and I was fired six months later.

But I thought I was omnipotent, omniscient and invulnerable. It turned out I was wrong about all three.

Yes: it served to be the building block for the next step. It worked out all right, but it was accidental.

It knocked me for some kind of a loop when they fired me; you can believe it. In fact suddenly it was like everything was possible. And nothing was possible.

Had they not done it, had I been able to hang in — well, I was bored. I think it came as a relief. It was a shock, but there was a little relief at the back of my mind because I'd been there four years and I had pretty well cleaned the situation up, all the obvious things, and I was already reaching.

They did me a favor when they fired me. By trying to have me kicked upstairs, offering me a safe Tory backbench, they were really doing me a favor.

They solved my dilemma and they launched me on my next career. Just as Stephen Lewis solved my next dilemma.

The next career move, if I had stayed in the coronership? I was bored. I was looking around for something. I didn't know what to do and, out of the blue, this NDP thing came. I was tired of pulling the tiger's tail.

What else might I have done? I don't know. There was nothing; nothing obvious. And there was no chance that I would have stayed in that path — oh, no. A number of Tory organizations had been after me to run, as a Tory politician. I might have done that, although it would have made strange bedfellows, by that point.

Would have been that same group I'd been fighting. It turned out that there was no difference because all three groups were all the same people. That was an awful shock. That there's no difference between the parties.

Was that really a surprise to me? Yeah.

I thought a mutual fund would be fun. I'd never done one. So I put together the Guardian–Morton Shulman Precious Metals Fund in '83.

I was diagnosed with Parkinson's in '82. The symptoms were so mild at first that I didn't pay too much attention to it. But, feeling something just wasn't right.

I'd been involved in trading gold for years, and someone else had done a fund. So I was the second, I wasn't the first. The chap who did it — nobody, as far as I was concerned, nobody had ever heard of him; the company was Goldcorp — and he raised $180 million. I thought, God if — I can't even remember his name — if he can raise $180 million I should be able to raise a billion, and it looked like something that would be fun to try.

We would have made the $200 million if we hadn't been double-crossed by Nesbitt Thompson, who brought a deal out just ahead of us. They got $125 million, we got $75 million. We would have had the whole $200 if things had gone ahead straight.

$200 million was the actual figure I thought I would bring in, and I was shocked when we brought in only $75 million. But that's still a lot of money, and we got 1% a year. It wasn't bad. It paid for lunch.

The Crunchtime Brunchtime

SUNDAY NOVEMBER 22, 1992

Sunday brunch at the Sutton Place Hotel, hobnob headquarters for the Toronto arts jetset.

The front lobby is swirling with well-cut, sueded and dark-spec'd film and culture folk gathered for the Gemini Awards, the Canadian version of the Oscars. The Sanssouci, luxe and linen restaurant whose name means Carefree, is brimming with people who matter.

Not one of them flicks an eye at the gaunt and twitching little man holding shaky court at two tables against the far wall.

Not so very long ago, everyone in the place would have taken note of him.

Dr. Morton Philip Shulman.

It has been 35 years since he first slammed into the head-lines, heroic muckraking chief coroner who would rush in to hack the lid off medical scandals where none before him had even dreamed to tread. For the next two decades of his star-studded public life Morty Shulman would vault from career to career, precipice to precipice, joyously making scandals, enemies and contradictions.

There was Morty the champion of the little guy, who lived like a pasha. Morty Robin Hood and self-taught financial whiz, making a fortune in the market, blowing raspberries at experts and regulators, churning out bestsellers with audacious titles like *Anyone Can Make A Million.*

Morty the fiery dedicated GP, born in High Park — grandson of a Polish (or was it Lithuanian?) rag peddler (or was he a real estate speculator/dabbler?) — still running a medical practice in the dingy west-end office where he first began, its warping walls hung with the overflow of Morty's legendary art collection: Colville serigraphs, minor east-European masters, a semi-nude sketch of a local artist's teenaged wife.

There was Morty the free spirit, telling the press he couldn't care less what they wrote; and constantly seeking publicity. Morty the muckraking million-dollar socialist member of the legislature — hated by all political parties including his own — running simultaneously with Morty the Tory-tabloid columnist, cannonading Oxfam, Medicare and the Mafia. Morty the reviled but top-rated television talk-show host, exuberantly dicing everyone from Ontario Premier Bill Davis to the Happy Hooker.

And always, of course, there was Morty the inveterate kisser — and teller.

But the arc was slipping, the brilliant promise of the early meteor days fizzling down to parody. Though he has never been out of the news, he has become disregardable.

In all the years of thrusting his profile in everyone's face, to love him or hate him, he insisted he didn't care that every time he leaped for a new peak, more and more people swore this time he would fail. Most of them were actively praying for it.

Eleven years ago, the gods seemed to take heed.

One spring morning in 1981, he became aware of a tremor in his right leg. A year later, tremor and fatigue increasing, Morty Shulman confirmed his worst dread: he had Parkinson's disease.

By early 1987, Dopamine no longer effective, he was paralyzed, drooling and unintelligible, heaving himself around with canes and bed bars, and planning suicide. It looked like the end of the line.

Instead, by September of that year, he was launching a pharmaceuticals company. He called it Deprenyl Research Limited, flogging a Hungarian Parkinson's drug which had miraculously reversed his symptoms. He had managed to track down and buy Canadian rights to it. Against odds higher than Everest, the unsinkable Morty was walking, talking, empire-building.

The media and establishment reacted with the usual righteous indignation: Morty the manipulator is at it again, even turning his Parkinson's to profit; the swell of righteous wrath ignoring the fact that Morty the pharmaceuticals baron was also Morty the Parkinson's patient, fighting for his own life.

Shulman reborn was exultantly back to thumb his nose at all who thought (or wished) him dead. By early 1992 the Hungarian medication he blunderbussed into approval in Canada had been parlayed into a pharmaceuticals company worth $100 million.

But by October, 1992, it was almost costing him his shirt.

This Sunday in November, 1992, more than three decades after the first glory days, the Sutton Place Hotel and Morty are in similar shape: both keeping up appearances, both teetering on a shaky brink. The hotel, barely a month after the Morty brunch, will drop its veil of feigned opulence and go into receivership.

And Morty?

November has seen the nadir of a precipitous plunge in Deprenyl Research's once giddy fortunes, and all the fingers are pointing at him. He is on the verge of losing everything: his house, his art collection, the shirt off his back. And, worst of all, his control: of his company and perhaps his very life.

Before an eclectic — you could say motley — gathering of brunching people, he stands.

Morton Philip Shulman.

A skinny watery-eyed guy with crinkly grizzled hair; his illness and its medication making him flop around at the torso, white shirt crumpling out of the band of his standard nonde-script greysuit pants.

Pointy bony face, darting gray eyes bordering on the goiterous.

He's 67 years old. In spite of his frailness, he still doesn't look it.

Still a malevolent slightly mad-eyed elf; not really fully grown.

A man who has just been bailed out to the tune of $5 million in desperate last-minute loans, barely pulled back from professional and personal wipeout.

"I want to say thanks to everyone here. To everyone who supported me. You all stood by me, you helped me out you believed.

"The newspapers have heaped revilement. The *Globe* is out to get me, many of my oldest friends welched.

"I was forced out of my position as the head of the pharmaceuticals company I founded. I was made to promise not to utter another word in public. I had to agree to give up a lot of my power.

"But the people here today are the people who hung in and because of them . . . I got clear."

Eleven people in all. The last of the believers. The hard core of Morty's faithful. Among them his 13-year-old granddaughter. A bemused silver-haired banker and his wife. A female broker in a mink bomber jacket. Morty's 58-year-old secretary and her 33-year-old daughter.

Rebecca, Morty's darling granddaughter is there on behalf of her mother. Morty's first child, his brilliant lawyer daughter Dianne Saxe, virtually never comes to any function for her father.

Morty's gentle dermatologist son Geoffrey is here with his new wife, Charlene. Don Morton, Morty's newest banker is here; the earnest-faced Royal Bank officer who came up with a crucial $1 million after the Toronto–Dominion folks opted to let their once-favorite client hang flapping in the hurricane.

Next to the Mortons: Ann Worobec, Morty's faithful $2.2 million-secretary of 33 years, her finger important with an $8,000 opal and diamond ring, bought from profits Morty helped her make shorting the Canadian dollar. And blonde Debbie Worobec in her blonde full-length mink coat, a present from Morty. No-longer-little Deb, whom Morty delivered, mooned over, and subsequently employed at the pharmaceuticals-investment conglomerate that will prove to be either his final undoing, or his finest unlikeliest hour.

And, of course, there is Morty's wife, the stunning, smiling, ageless Gloria Bossin Shulman. Long-faithful in public, long-suffering in private, and possessor of a secret savings stash of $375,000 which she sacrificed to Morty's crisis, smiling as bright as ever. Morty has written their mini-palace on Russell Hill into her name.

As he talks , Morty frequently wipes at tears welling in his eyes.

Although his speech is hyper-rapid and slurred, the harsh racing voice is blaring and cutting.

He thanks them one by one, the 11 who stood fast. Stopped in its tracks — for the moment at least — the juggernaut of disaster.

"I want to say thanks again to all of you. To everyone here. If I had asked everyone who let me down I would have needed enough tables to fill the whole room."

He knows all too well what they're thinking. *For the first time in his life, has he really been shut up?*

Oh yes, he's thinking, *nobody loves me except these 11 people.*

And several thousand Parkinson's and Alzheimer's patients and their families. Unfortunately they don't have a few billions readily at hand.

But they're worth billions. All I need is a little time. Time to get back control. . . .

Will he get the time he needs? This is the unspoken question, at the fateful Sunday brunch in November.

Have they finally managed to shut Morty up?

Childhood

1930

Morty Shulman, head skewed to his desktop market monitor so that one eye is always locked on the feverish golden letters and fluttering numbers, denies that his childhood bores him.

Sometimes he can even be induced to talk about it for several minutes at a stretch, between phone calls to and from the myriad souls who swirl and nibble at the ever-subdividing Shulman amoeba, denizens of the market deeps darting at morsels of newly off-shot companies: brokers, stokers, stock-schleppers, secretaries, dream-sellers and buyers, shooters and off-shooters, before-marketers and after-marketers, and the hedgers with private lines who deal him into PetroCan and the Canadian dollar, which he has shorted to the tune of close to 10 million bucks.

A strobing mammonic cuneiform. All of Shulman's precious market nuggets set against deep, dark velvet, as the Creator of Free Enterprise dreamed they should be: in the black.

He never tires of talking of business, or repeating stories of past glories. Then the speeding voice, burred by nearly a dozen years of Parkinson's disease, belts along more pell-mell than ever, clipping superfluous corners off words and thoughts, as though only the rapidest, most truncated shorthand will do, time running out, not a half-syllable's worth to squander.

If pushed, Morty the man is willing to talk a bit about Morty the boy . . . just so long as his paling gray eye can easily swerve, like moth to flame, like snake to charmer, to the Cyclopean eye to the moneyworld on the corner of his desk.

When it comes to talk about family, the answers get short. Shorter. Shortest.

I'm not bored by my babyhood, I just don't remember much. . . .

My first memory is an Indian suit. An Indian suit with a headdress, running around the block with it, all excited. I was six then . . . five.

[The screenwatching eye locks, the memory balks, kicks back in.]

In Winnipeg. After my father was transferred there. Oh, oh, oh!

Oh, oh, oh — dollar's going down! See it losing points? We just made 51 thousand! 52, 53, 54 . . .

"You play your cards right, your son will be a millionaire. You can't ever make it, but your children will."

Thus Dave Shulman, insurance manager and fun-lover, dreamed and prophesied to his only son Morton. He thought bigger than his timorous wife, Nettie; but like her, Dave still fell short of envisioning his awkward, undersized son's true dimensions.

"Nettie Shulman having Morty," observed Ralph Messinger, married to Morty's first cousin, Doris, "was like a chicken giving birth to an ostrich."

2

Chapter 1: Childhood

Nettie Winthrope was nearly 25 — getting close to spinster-hood, in the judgment of the day — when her younger brother, Lou, introduced her to Dave Shulman. As Nettie would relate it later, Dave didn't call her. She had to call him.

She was over 26 when they married; older than he by only a year, though he never knew it. Born in 1897, she lied about her age — said she was born in 1901. She kept it secret all her life. Morty only discovered her birth certificate after her death.

Dave Shulman was tall, with crisp brown hair, a sharp dresser. He was considered to be making a great deal of money — 90 dollars a week — selling life insurance: nickel policies, door to door, the way people did in those days. It was in the depths of the Depression; that was big money.

He was a fun-loving guy, for the times. I'm told he loved ladies. He didn't drink. He gambled, though. He loved to go on holidays which my mother wouldn't go on, so he'd go by himself. We have old, old movies, 8-millimeter movies, of him on cruises in Nassau and Cuba and places like that, always posing with two or three girls around him.

My mother wouldn't go because . . . she was afraid of boats, she was afraid of trains, she was afraid. She wouldn't fly. She didn't want to leave me.

Dave Shulman's company, Metropolitan Life, promoted him from salesman to manager, first sending him to Winnipeg for a year to test him out. Back in Toronto, he wound up making $125 a week. He bought the family a square, solid duplex on Chaplin Crescent at the corner of Oriole Parkway, a respectable Toronto neighborhood in the shadow of the watchtower of Upper Canada College. But the family never shook off its worry about money.

I was close with my father, yes. But it wasn't one of those important father-son relationships. No, no, no, very Depression style. . . .

I remember, every Sunday he would take me to Tractor's on Spadina. The famous place to go for water ice, orange water ice, which is the favorite of my life, and I've never tasted orange water ice like that since. There was only one flavor and we'd sit there on Spadina Avenue and for a nickel you'd have this orange water ice and that was the greatest treat of our life. Orange water ice, and then, yeah, popsicles were wonderful. . . . Something we must talk about one day is the East General Hospital. It's never been written up and it's one of the most exciting events of my career. It was an extraordinary experience. . . .
[Pressed, he produces a brief memory of baseball with dad:]

Actually, the last ball game I went to was with my father. He took me to see the Maple Leafs play in 1942. Gloria and I hadn't been to a ball game in years and somebody gave us two tickets last year. So we went down to the stadium and it was gone! We went to look for it in the street we remembered, and it just wasn't there!

The expensive taste that later filled Morty's little palace with priceless rarities from the treasure-places of the world didn't come from fun-loving Dave or timorous Nettie.

I didn't know these beautiful things existed in the world. My parents had no knowledge of it; it was a matter of survival in those days, it was the Depression. I don't think they even looked. I don't think my mother or father ever entered a museum in their entire lives. I don't think either of them was ever in the Royal Ontario Museum throughout the whole course of their lives in Toronto.

Morty was named for his paternal grandfather, who died six months before Morty was born.

Grandpa Morton "Moishe" Shulman, who eked out a living as a peddler, managed thus to support at least four wives and 13 children by wife Number 1 — who died understandably young.

It was Grandpa Shulman's last wife who drove the last of his thirteen children out of the house — 20-year-old Dave and his elder brother, Joe. Family lore had it that the final Mrs. Shulman called the police complaining that Joe had raped her. When Dave protested she was lying, she said he had raped her too.

Most of his father's siblings stayed in Toronto. But it was with the Winthropes, his mother's family, that Morty had the closest ties.

It was a close family, a happy one. There are these public — misperceptions — of me, misperceptions of coldness.

Our whole family is very close. We've always been very emotional, and very close. Coldness I think is the wrong word, a misdescription. It's from that stupid television show, *Shulman File*. It made everybody think I was some sort of monster. Moses Znaimer paid me to play that role. And most people who saw it thought I was serious. I was just having fun and Moses paid me a lot of money to pretend I was a monster and it was like going to a party game.

Minnie and Wolf Winthrope, who were married in New York, changed the family name after they moved to Toronto just after the turn of the century. Morty's cousin Doris Messinger has her grandparents' wedding invitation, framed, on her living-room wall, along with the wedding picture: her grandmother Minnie small and neat-faced and determined; grandfather Wolf stiffly posed, handlebar mustache.

Minnie Roth
Wolf Weintraub
request your presence at the
marriage ceremony
Thursday, November 24th, 1892
at 4 o'clock p.m.
at Congress Hall, 226 Stanton St.
Supper at 6 o'clock
Dancing at 7 o'clock.

Morty believed the Winthrope name had been arbitrarily assigned by immigration officials. It's just another of those family details he tends to be shaky on.

For a year before they moved to Winnipeg, Nettie and Dave and little Morty lived with Nettie's family, in an overflowing house in High Park.

His five-years-older first cousin Doris, now 73, remembers a darling curly haired toddler with black Shirley Temple curls.

Early pictures show a tiny boy with a wary-eyed stare, deep in the leafy backyard, his hair curly as the stick-propped vines towering above him.

The house was full of people.

———

One sixty-seven High Park Avenue. The whole family — my mother's parents and everybody — lived there, all their children and their spouses and their children.

About 12 or 13 people. I remember it as idyllic.

It's a beautiful house today. It's just around the park. I'd be delighted to live there now.

———

Chapter 1: Childhood

My grandfather Wolf Winthrope was a peddler. With a horse and a cart, he'd go along the street selling rags and bones. And fruit and vegetables from the garden. My grandmother Minnie kept house. He scrimped and saved . . . built the house for $800. Today it's a half-million-dollar house. It had a huge backyard. I still remember going back and picking the fruit; nothing tasted better than the fruit you picked in your own backyard. Raspberries, he had an apple tree, and a peach tree and a cherry tree and . . . everybody did back then. There were tomatoes. Saved buying food.

There was the Winthropes' eldest daughter Rose, her husband Arthur Abiscott and their children Doris and Billy. Then Nettie and Dave Shulman and Morty. Ethel and her husband Mac Robbins and daughter Marlene. Perpetual-bachelor Uncle Lou, who became a successful though penny-hoarding dentist; and still unmarried Jenny.

It was a family of strong-minded women. Even though grandmother Minnie Winthrope dominated, she didn't dominate her girls the way she did her son Lou.

"Don't smother your kids the way I did mine," Minnie told Rose later.

Rose, the beauty of the family, had already defied her parents by marrying Arthur Abiscott, against all her mother's protests; Arthur being not only 16 years older, but divorced, with two children back in New York.

He was considered a *luftmensch* — cloud-dweller. Minnie was aghast at her son-in-law's ways, and let him know it.

He drank, gambled crazily at the track. My grandmother used to be horrified. One time he won $97 on the daily double; he was waving it around, getting ready to blow it on another bet. He had two children, sometimes there was nothing to eat. "Buy food!" my grandmother said to him. "Live!" he said. "Live!", and he laughed.

He had heart trouble. They told him he's got to give up drinking. He said he'd rather be dead. Soon after, he was.

Morty's parents were politically conventional: voted a straight Mitch Hepburn ticket; "Liberal fascist," Morty cackles. No leftish tinges such as colored many Jews in those days: no, not at all.

The worst sin was spendthriftiness. The worse-than-worst: going bust. As a 1981 *Toronto Star* piece related it:

> The worst tragedy the young Morty encountered was a family affair; the time one of his numerous uncles went broke. That, recalls Shulman, was the ultimate disgrace.

Doris Messinger, remembering the boy who would become the legend: "His drive, his guts. You couldn't see any of this when he was a boy. He was beautiful when he was a baby. But then, as a boy, as a young man, he was definitely not attractive. Skinny. Quiet, very shy.

"You want to know how Morty got all that confidence? Because his mother thought he could do no wrong. He was perfect. She was absolutely blind to anything else. With Morty or with his father. Morty's mother could see absolutely nothing wrong in anything Morty ever did, and she was the same about her husband."

It wasn't as though young Morty was spoilt or bratty. Just that his mother thought the sun shone out of his you-know-what.

"Isn't my Morty beautiful," she would say; and later when he wasn't: "Isn't he brilliant."

Though she nagged him, she never criticized him. But was afraid for him, all her life.

During Morty's years under siege, Nettie would call Doris

---

to be commiserated with: about how cruelly her darling Morty was being attacked, how terribly treated, and how fearful she was about it. Why did he do it, he didn't need the money, what did he want with the newspaper coverage, the aggravation?

Once, during the 1960s, when he was an MLA, Nettie saw Morty walking down the street holding a woman's hand. Nettie said afterwards it never occurred to her that — she never thought anything of it for a second!

(Morty swears the woman was only his longtime secretary, Ann Worobec.)

Was she putting it on? She was so innocent! That's the way she was, Doris remembers. Different from the rest of the family. Religious, timid, so innocent. And blind! None so blind as those who will not see, her sisters Rose and Ethel used to laugh.

Morty remembers a steelier core than Doris ever saw.

My father was the charming handsome one, and my mother wasn't pretty, but she was very, very sharp. Strong, aggressive. She had a lot of fears, yes — of dogs, of the Depression. Sexually she was innocent — oh sure. But she was tough. He was soft.

During his years under fire, it was Doris whom Morty would phone when he wanted someone in the family to share the glee in the goings-on, someone who got a kick out of the derring-do.

But he never paid more than lip service to asking Doris how things were with her. She knew he wasn't interested: not in her as a person, not in any person. People, she divined early, were not an interest of Morty's.

"In his way, Morty loves me, as much as he loves anybody. But if he didn't speak to me for a year, he would never notice."

Can't Somebody Shut Him Up?

Dave Shulman died suddenly of a coronary at the age of 49. It was 1947: Morty was 22, in his last year of medical school. It was ten years before Nettie Shulman remarried.

Married a lovely man. He died on her also, but not until 1984. She was with him longer than she'd been with my father. Who was Mr. Schwartz? Moe Schwartz. He was a nice man. He was a nobody. He had a little shoe store. He went bankrupt. That was his life. For the rest of his life he didn't do anything. Someone introduced them, some relative. He paid court to her and treated her nicely. He never made a mark on the world. Nobody remembers him. It's too bad. He was a nice man. My father was — more memorable. He was more romantic. I don't talk about him. My wife still throws up to me, "You get your bad tendencies from your father." I look like my father. Very, very much. [Nettie Shulman died in 1985, 87 years old, devoted and determined, terrified and prudent to the very end.]

She took care of herself. Stayed alone in her apartment on Eglinton Avenue West. She wouldn't have anybody in. She wouldn't even have a cleaning lady in. She was brought up in the Depression. She wouldn't take a taxi. Even at that age, yeah. She was very averse to spending money. She would be appalled if she looked at me now. Would give me hell for spending even then — yes, yes, to the very end. Mothers never change. She used to be admonishing me about the same things she'd been admonishing me about when I was 12. Be careful, dear. Be careful about what? Not crossing the street, not crossing the attorney general. Be careful of dogs, be careful of women, be careful of everything.

Doris has a photo of Morty, thin, his head ducked down, crooked smile, age about 11. His mother peeping out from behind him, an arm around his waist; him holding onto her hand. Nettie, not pretty, biggish-nosed. Her husband Dave beside her, looking quite unlike Morty. Fair-haired, tallish, a swaggering set to his shoulders. The father, a big deal. The mother, a mouse.

From pictures, Morty looks nothing at all like his father. He looks a good deal more like Uncle Lou, and little Nettie.

Doris' memories of her father Arthur Abiscott are of a dashing, cultured man, who ran an eclectic bookstore on Richmond St. near York, in the 1920s, called Bargain Book Store.

Also framed on her wall is a copy of a Star Weekly story from October 19, 1929, that tells of Absicott finding a rare copy of a book belonging to Prime Minister Mackenzie King, with the prime minister's initials in it: The Secret of Heroism. Arthur sent it to him; there's the letter King hand-wrote to him in thanks.

"If my family made $125, they spent $126. If Uncle Dave made $125, they saved $124," remembers Doris.

Yet there was Dave's glamorous travel, and a stylish fox stole draped around Nettie's shoulders on visits to New York.

The Abiscotts, like Doris and her husband Ralph Messinger afterwards, weren't as crazy about making a lot of money as the Shulmans. Or not, at least, about keeping it.

Like many Jewish kids growing up in 1930s and '40s Toronto, Morty Shulman found he inhabited two wildly disparate worlds. In the cocoon of the home, Jewish parents covered you in love, assured you repeatedly that you were the greatest. Step into the streets and you were a creep, a kike, the enemy.

"What nationality are you?" was code for, "Are you a Jew?" If the answer was yes, you were likely to get creamed. If you were big enough you could try to cream them back. If you weren't, you had several painful years to look forward to.

A tall good-natured non-Jew by the name of Billy Woods turned out to be an unlikely and most eloquent buddy to schoolboy Morty.

11

A *Toronto Life* magazine piece in 1972 told all about Morty's school days. Morty told the writer at the time he couldn't care less what her magazine printed about him; later, he would claim to hate the parts of the story that dredged up his awkward childhood. But there are at least three copies of the decades-old *Toronto Life* piece in the Shulmans' overflowing clippings file, along with pretty well every word ever written by or about a Shulman in the last 45 years.

Talking to the magazine interviewer, the grown-up Billy was in an irrepressibly expansive frame of mind, remembering his now-famous friend as "the young Mort Shulman. Small and fragile. So badly coordinated he had to think about it even to walk properly." His tendency was for his left arm to fling out whenever his left leg went out.

Billy, an English teacher at Seneca College, would have it that his association with Morty dated back to Oriole Park School in 1933. Wispy little Morty was getting beat up: Billy stood by him, and from then on they were the thickest of friends.

From that *Toronto Life* piece:

Getting beaten up was a part of life from the time he was six years old until he was 15. But at least from that day on there were two of them. Billy Woods, the poorest kid in the school, and Morton Shulman, the frail little kid, against the world. Oriole Park School and North Toronto Collegiate: a distinctly WASP environment, and in those days the few Jewish kids had a bad time of it. Even if they weren't skinny and shy and much too spectacularly smart in school.

"One of the finest things that ever happened to me was meeting Mort Shulman." Billy was a widow's son who was forced to seek his first job at age six, and he never had enough money to keep himself in proper school supplies, let alone spending money. But Mort, as Billy still calls him, always managed to share the wealth without ever seeming to be doling out charity. His gestures of generosity toward Billy were always carefully planned and subtly executed.

"They were always so casual, says Billy, "never overt. He'd say: Let's go for a Coke after school. And when I'd say, I'm not thirsty, meaning I didn't have the nickel for a coke . . . he'd immediately suggest going to his place instead."

What Billy remembered was the pure generosity in those Cokes, but they also form a small signpost to one of the maxims Morty will forge to equip him against the burning dread of being turned down: "Never ask anyone for anything. Only go after something if you can offer a deal." Billy had schoolyard clout, Morty had the nickels for pop. Nobody must think he was doing the skinny outcast favors. Intuiting the embarrassment of Billy's poverty, Morty offered Mortycoin in exchange for Billy's companionship, protection, the armor he offered against Morty's outsiderhood. . . .

Later, in high school, Billy grew big but never too big to stay friends with his still-little buddy:

I can remember this one girl in high school saying in a group one day, that she thought Mort Shulman might ask her to the dance. And this other guy, who was an executive in the Catholic Youth Organization, said to her: "You don't want to go out with a dirty Jew, do you?" I don't think those things were ever said directly to Mort, not in high school anyway. But he knew about them all the same.

"Morty's whole life is taking on bullies," his friend, renaissance man Charles Templeton says in the same piece.

Later, it will be found that Billy Woods does not occupy the place in Morty's memory that Morty did in his:

13

SK: Okay, now tell me about your friend at school, Billy. He
talked about you so warmly in the old *Toronto Life* —
MS: He's dead.
SK: Dead? Oh! He died young.
MS: Yes. — In my early teens I had two boys I used to pal
around with, Jewish boys, here in Toronto. They're
both alive, as far as I know, but I haven't seen either of
them in years. Billy was my friend in high school. In
high school we were very, very close. We walked to
school every day together and, of course, once I got to
university, there was no problem. His mother was a
minor official in the Liberal Party.

As for Billy's view of the battering anti-Semites, Morty says:

> "It was mostly verbal. There was the odd blow. It was
> nothing like Rodney King."

In other words, the poverty of one child, and the vulnerability of
the other may both be taken with a grain of salt.

Then there were Big Billy's vain attempts to teach Mort the
basics of social survival. He recounted them to the *Toronto Life*
interviewer:

I used to try to get Mort to go to the school dances, but he
backed off. If the first girl turns you down, you just keep going
on down the line, and eventually some girl will say yes. That
was the way I operated. If you ended up with the dog of the
class, so what? It was better than nothing. But I could never persuade Mort. Mort wanted the girl he wanted, or he didn't want
any. That was the difference between us. I WOULD go out
with the dogs. Mort wouldn't.

No, Mort wouldn't. Mort's yearnings were always, only, for the prettiest girls. When that biding time of his uncertain childhood was past, when he knew his strength, the star females, the best in his circle, would be the only ones he ever pursued.

He might even go to considerable lengths for another kick at the can with a princess who had spurned him back when he was nobody. Take one such poignant journey he made in a *Toronto Sun* column four decades later.

Forty-one years ago, I was 14 years old and I fell in love with the most beautiful girl in my class. Her name was Dorothy P. [Morty actually used her full name], and she was the most exquisite creature I had ever seen with huge, saucer eyes, long, black hair, perfect face and a slim, sylphlike figure.

For two years I stared at her in class, not quite able to believe that such a creature could really exist. My greatest desire was to ask her to go to a tea dance with me, but I never quite got the nerve — and she did not at any time ever acknowledge that I even existed.

I have not seen Dorothy for 41 years, but over the decades I have often wondered what happened to her and three years ago my curiosity got the better of me. I called North Toronto Collegiate and asked for her last phone number or address, but they could give me no information; she seemed to have just disappeared off the earth.

Three months ago I was being interviewed on TV and the interviewer asked me about my early school experiences and I mentioned my frustrating admiration of Dorothy P.

Two weeks ago a card came to the TV studio from one Dorothy A., nee P. A friend had told her about the program and she was writing to say hello. I immediately phoned to make a luncheon date and she accepted, but warned me: "You may not recognize me — I've changed." I replied that she would have no problem as I had not changed at all.

With some trepidation I set out for my luncheon date accompanied by hoots of laughter from my secretary, who predicted that the lady would be fat and quite decrepit after 41 years.

She was quite wrong. Dorothy is still beautiful, slim and a charming lady. It was like a time warp, for even though the world has changed immeasurably since 1939, she has not.

She's been happily married all this time to one man, is fiercely proud of her three children and has led a serene life bringing up her family and doing volunteer work. She appears to be a totally happy lady.

I am thoroughly delighted to find that the beautiful girl of 1939 turned out to be a beautiful and contented woman so many years later.

Who could resist tracking down the one-time ice queen who now so respectfully deferred to one's heightened status?

But in his column, the tender hues of the reunion, as so often with Morty tales, especially romantic ones, had been touched up, a detail or two airbrushed out.

The Morty-cackle crackles as he tells the story behind the story. He had picked the classy restaurant of the day, told Ann to cancel all his afternoon appointments. Then, with his secretary Ann braying and his heart beating, he set off in anticipation of a sweet afternoon of postponed, long-dreamed of delights.

The trysting site was the Three Small Rooms, an elegantly discreet romantic spot beneath the picturesque Windsor Arms Hotel. An incomparable place to meet the slim saucer-eyed Diana of a 14-year-old's dreams.

There was no remotely Diana-like being waiting to meet his eager gaze. Only, sitting shadowed at his corner table, a small elderly woman.

It was Dorothy! She had changed completely. She had
turned into a little old lady! I couldn't believe my eyes. I
couldn't wait to get out of there. I called Ann, told her to re-
book my afternoon patients, and the minute we finished eat-
ing I sent her home in a taxi.

Also unmentioned in the column was the fact that Dorothy
was that selfsame teen goddess who had given him the most
stinging rebuff of his young life when he asked her to a high
school tea dance:

I finally got up my nerve to ask a girl. She laughed in my
face and walked away — I felt so inadequate. I was small
and unathletic and over-intelligent. I was bitterly unhappy.

Yes, the one-time Diana was she who had laughed in the
poor tadpole-prince's mug.

At their grandparent-reunion in the Three Small Rooms, she
remembered nothing of it. Truth to tell, she had to admit, she
could remember Morty but vaguely.

Well, she certainly remembered him thence. Joining the rue-
ful "If anybody had ever told me" club of Morty-watchers,
Dorothy could muse:"If anybody had ever told me that 40 years
from now I'd be boasting that little Mort Shulman was once
crazy about me . . ."

A year after that brief poignant trip to and from the past, a lovely girl with long black hair approached Morty in another restaurant.
It was Dorothy's granddaughter. She was sorry to tell Morty that
her grandmother Dorothy had passed on, but it might please him to
know what a great deal their re-meeting had meant to her.

The granddaughter looked wonderful, a lot like 14-year-old Dorothy: saucer eyes, the whole bit. Morty likes to tell you he had to restrain himself from trying to rewrite history with her.

"Morty hasn't got an introspective bone in his body." Charles Templeton will be the first of many to say this over the years to come. And: "With Morty, what you see is what you get," a woman who was once in his life will repeat over and over.

But out of his childhood, two deaths will resonate deeply in years to come.

One is the death of his grandmother Minnie Winthrope in the winter of 1936, when Morty was 11 years old.

In the midst of the desperate Thirties, she was diagnosed with stomach cancer. At the very end, the family called in a famous local cancer quack by the name of Doctor Hett.

Thirty years later Morty writes in his book, *Coroner*:

Hett was a flamboyant quack who promised a cure to those afflicted with inoperable carcinomas if they would just receive his expensive weekly injections. I remember seeing Hett in late 1936 when he arrived at my grandmother's home in west Toronto. She was then dying of stomach cancer and my parents called in Hett in a last desperate attempt to save her.

I was then only 11 and I never forgot the impressive manner of that renegade doctor. Everyone we knew then was poor but he arrived in a chauffeur-driven limousine, wearing a black cloak which he swept off with a flourish to reveal a tuxedo and white tie. He only came to see Grandmother once and he offered to cure her for $2,000, but four days later, while the family was still trying to raise the money, she died.

"If I don't get better, if I stay like this, let me not come back," she said as they took her to hospital for the last time.

Her death stamps three indelible pictures.

One is the terrifying image of her dying agony.

Another is the image of wealth and plenty mantling the doctor like his swashbuckling cloak — this, in the very hungriest days of the hungry '30s. Morty will pair this image with that of a prosperous uncle, Dr. Aaron Volpe, whom he will recall many years later in a newspaper interview about career motivation: "I had an uncle who was a doctor. During the Depression years it made an impact on me when everyone was scrambling to make a living, and a doctor could make 50 cents on a house call."

And there is the picture of medical victimization of the poor, and the acquiescence of the political powers of the day. When Morty becomes chief coroner, the cancer quacks will be one of his first targets.

The death of Uncle Lou, who died a bachelor at the age of 47, resonates with an even more personal pain. Lou Winthrope, twice institutionalized for nervous breakdowns, died of stroke.

"He lingered for two years. It was the ultimate horror: trapped in his body, powerless."

Morty's eyes fill with tears as he describes the ordeal.

Trapped in his body: it was the very last thing he would ever have imagined for himself.

Chapter Two

Conquests

1948

At the age of 23, Morty is finally about to offload the unbearable heaviness of being a virgin.

Even for a medical intern in 1948 Toronto this is an only moderately delayed case of defloration.

But this is not the way Morty sees it. For him, the inability to get it on heretofore is renewed proof the whole world is enjoying that which he alone — skinny-uncoordinated-overintelligent-underathletic little son of Nettie and Dave Shulman — has been denied.

He has been burning for years, certain this is just another of the deprivations which the creator has fingered him, alone, to suffer. For everyone but him, for years and years, the woods and glades and fields have been throbbing with it. Every syllable of locker-room lascivia is taken as maddenly lubricious gospel.

Everybody was getting it, except me! I knew that and I couldn't think of anything else. When I was in high school,

---

in my last year and everybody who was getting it said —
they were all Gentiles — they all were fucking like crazy
and I couldn't understand why I wasn't! It was driving me
nuts.

By now he has dates, of course. A Jewish doctor-to-be was *ipso
facto* prime social material. And although he did not make the
rich-boy frat, he had been president of respectable Phi Delta
Epsilon.

And so, why not? He has the status. Has finished medical
school. Is interning at East General Hospital. Has fairly free use
of his late father's car: the blue '48 Nash which was the luxury
purchase of Dave Shulman's final year. With its fold-out back
seat, it is marketed as "The car with the bed in the back."

And now that it is finally happening, it is not the stuff that
dreams are made of.

In a dank dark room rich with the odors of underslept
underbathed men, Morty Shulman is finally getting rid of his
burden. The night air is thick with the aura of old socks, his
head filled with the thud of pounding, pounding, pounding.

The obliging young woman has others waiting for her to
oblige them.

The interns' free time is short, their on-call hours long.

She was a waitress who was kind to all the interns at St.
Michael's Hospital!
[Morty gives his sardonic laugh.]

Oh, I well remember it, that first experience. It was in
the intern's room and Phil somebody is pounding on the
door saying, "Will you please hurry up. We gotta use the
room next!" Oh, it was so terrible . . . so awful! It was traumatic. It almost finished me for sex forever.

Of course, it does no such thing.

There is another fitful tumble or two, though not in the car with the bed in the back.

It all goes to nurture the burgeoning Shulman credo that only the best will do. Not just any old sex, not just any old girl, never the "dogs" at the end of the line blithely picked up by his high-school buddy Billy Woods. The goal will be the peaks of pleasure: refinements, delights, blossoming horizons of sensuality.

The brief joust in the interns' room also bucks him up sufficiently to steer the blue Nash uptown to Vaughan Road Collegiate, a square old high school in a west-central working-class neighborhood; there to renew his seige of the most beautiful, most desirable girl he can think of, a girl he has continued to dream about since she froze him out nearly a year earlier. The Guinevere of the freshly-unsheathed Lancelot's dreams is a stunning 18-year-old high schooler named Gloria Bossin. . . .

It was not until 1944 that Morty, aged 19, first began to spread his social wings, and asked for his very first date.

A year earlier, in 1943, Morty had been accepted at medical school at University of Toronto, his high marks throughout high school entitling him to become part of the quota of Jewish students permitted, generally taken to be held at 20 per cent maximum.

I had a dentist model uncle whom I wanted to follow, Lou Winthrope. And they had a manual dexterity test which I couldn't pass. . . . I wasn't even dextrous — and I chose medicine as a second choice. And I liked it.

This oft-repeated story is probably apocryphal.

Yes, there is the example of Uncle Lou — not a model of stability, with his mounting history of nervous breakdowns, but

---

doing well enough financially to help carry the High Park household through the Depression years.

But there are other models for Morty's career choice, models of prosperity and esteem. His father's sister Esther is married to a distinguished Toronto physician, Dr. Aaron Volpe.

There is the memory of the flamboyant Dr. Hett, the cancer-healer, appearing at the doors of the cancer-ridden poor, tuxe-doe'd and liveried in the rawest years of the Depression.

There is Dave Shulman's vision of wealth in his children's children's future.

And there is the army: Canada has adopted the draft, and all non-medical university students are eligible. During war-time, medical school lasts four years; pre-meds have been waived.

Morty sees himself doing heroic, prosperous, highly rewarding things.

He plans to be a surgeon: a brain surgeon, for choice. He will cut a swath. He will make a pile of dough.

He will be looked up to.

He will be something big.

At medical school he has to work hard although, as usual, he gives out that it's a piece of cake.

He tells Doris he doesn't need to slug his brains out because, when you become a doctor, nobody knows how well you did in medical school. He boasts that he did not take notes, merely trusting his memory.

Classmates, though, remember Morty showing up an hour early for anatomy class: putting in a lot of extra time to make sure of being prepared.

He is obliged to join the COTC — Canadian Officers Train-ing Corps — for a twice-weekly program of reserves exercises to fulfill his military obligation. It is here he and the bagpipes grap-ple it out. At the time it seems the lesser military burden.

The first day in university, you had to enlist in something, you see; the war was on. They gave us two rifles, marched us from the St. George Armoury to the University Armouries and then back. I think to myself, This is not for me. There was a big sign out, "Volunteers wanted to join the pipe band. No experience necessary," so I volunteered. For a whole year we tried to learn to play these stupid machines. When they finally marched us out we couldn't march in time with our own music because we'd only practised sitting down. Marched us back in again, practice for another year and then the war was over and that was the end of it.

The laugh. Again and always, the laugh.

As a medical student there is instant status.

The social Morty will attain a sort of legendary status for his audacious methods of courtship, and his refusal to say die.

My friend Teddy [Morty remembers them all as his friends, now] was dating an absolutely beautiful girl, Gloria Forman. She was the most beautiful girl I'd ever seen [as are all girls beautiful in the golden glow of Morty's memory]. I tried. He succeeded, I failed. But I said to her, "I'd like one night with you. What would it take?" She said what she really wanted was a Packard; this was the status car of the day. So I went off to a second-hand car place, picked up a beat-up old Packard, paid 50 bucks, had it towed over to her house. Walked up to the door, said to her, "Okay, here's your Packard!" Unfortunately, Teddy was with her at the time. She was extremely embarrassed.

Another ex-med school co-student remembers dating a girl Morty was also dating. Eventually a crisis point approached: a major frat dance, for which the lady must choose either Morty, or his rival.

She chose his rival. Morty bowed out, Morty laughed. A few days later, the successful suitor recalls, a summons-server knocked at his parents' door, bearing what looked terrifyingly like legal papers informing the rival Morty was suing him for alienation of affections.

An obliging lawyer friend had drawn the sham process papers up. The ex-rival swears that his mother, a simple God-fearing working woman, nearly had a heart attack.

Morty laughs. That one, he says, he doesn't remember.

In any case, it was all good practice for what would be the campaign of his life: the storming, winning and, against all odds, wedding, of the fairest, most courted princess of them all.

In 1948 Morty graduates respectably, somewhere in the middle: 90th or 100th out of about 180.

Getting an internship is a scramble.

In 1940s Toronto, the major hospitals squeeze the Jewish quota hair-thin, conferring internships upon only a couple of the best, whitest Jewish medical grads.

Mount Sinai Hospital takes the next best. Morty is not among them.

He finally does his internship at East General hospital, a somewhat rough-and-ready institution serving some of the city's poorest population.

In 1948 the East General was a wild and woolly place. Unlike all the other hospitals in Toronto at that time, the GPs ran the place, and while interns at other hospitals were paid nothing, East General paid them the princely sum of $100 a month. There was no real supervision of interns; they got to do all sorts of procedures they wouldn't have done elsewhere.

In my first month I was assigned to anesthesia. The head nurse in surgery warned me that Dr. John Cameron, the head anesthetist, was a drug addict and that I should be very careful. The first patient was a 45-year old woman with a bad case of hemorrhoids. Chief resident Dr. Warren was doing the operation. In breezes Dr. Cameron. He's a handsome 45-year-old, with a perpetual smile on his face.

He asks if I would like to give the anesthetic. I told him although I'd seen anesthetics given I'd never done one myself. He says there's nothing to it, a hemorrhoidectomy only takes five or ten minutes, all you do is put the mask over her face, turn on the nitrous oxide and she goes to sleep.

Patients were routinely given 1/4 gram of morphine before surgery. Dr. Cameron injected the needle into himself instead of the patient, said, "If you need me I'll be in the doctors' room next door," and walked out.

I dutifully put the mask on the patients face, turn on the nitrous and, somewhat to my surprise, the patient went to sleep. Just like the doctors I had seen in the movies, "Go ahead," I say to Dr. Warren.

However, the hospital had just instituted a new policy for early cancer detection: every female patient who comes in for surgery must have a routine D & C. So before attacking the hemmorhoids Warren starts on her womb. After a minute he says, "Oops! Perforated her womb; I'll have to do a hysterectomy. Please put her down deep." I was scared shitless.

This charming story of Toronto hospital life ends with the patient miraculously escaping with her life, minus her womb, but with her hemmorhoids intact. The good doctors completely forgot to do it.

Then there was Morty's classmate Boris who put a cast on a

broken arm without bending the patient's elbow, using no inner padding, and causing the patient excruciating pain when the plaster had to be chipped off.

And Morty's other classmate Bob who killed his first patient in obstetrics by inadvertently flooding her with intravenous fluid.

Many years later, East General will be the target of one of Morty's last, most reverberating attacks on the medical profession — an attack that will almost cost him his license.

It will be said that this bazooka was Morty Shulman's way of getting back at them at last, for the repressions and slights of his intern days.

But for years, he denies it. Swears that his memories of East General hold nothing at all out of the ordinary.

After his internship, Morty plans on several glorious years far away. First he will go back to University of Toronto for a postgraduate medical year of pathology and anatomy, the first step in preparing himself for a career as a surgeon. Next is the University of Edinburgh, where he has been accepted to study surgery.

But first — the fateful night in the fetid interns' room behind him — he is going back to win Gloria Bossin.

Gloria today is amazingly like Gloria of nearly 45 years ago. Wings of ebony hair, skin like Snow White, dimples a man could drown in.

In 1948, she was in her last year of high school, and was about to turn 18. (She was born Dec. 24, 1930.) She had for some time been the object of a major rush by university men, discovered by Jewish health-careers-in-training when she was just 15 years old.

When 22-year-old Morty first set eyes on her, Gloria was 16: the fresh-picked high school princess of a med-school post-frat dance party, which her dentist date had crashed.

Morty was knocked out. This prize, and nothing less, this prized combination of dimples and respectability was the one that must be his. Shy, hell. Nervous, hell. He went for it.

27

I set aside my . . . normal shyness. She was very beautiful. I really wanted her. It was a guy named Bernie, who is now a dentist, who brought her to a party after the frat dance, and I offered them a lift home in my car. I dropped my date off first. Bernie was only a dental student. I was in medicine. . .

She was very conscious of her beauty. She was very happy, very bouncy, playing games, sports. Tennis. She was still in high school. She liked having fun.

Fun? How about serenades by bagpipe, that dubious art imperfectly acquired at the COTC training?

Her father couldn't stand me. I used to play the pipes under Gloria's window every night and he was ready to kill me.

But after a few months, the novelty wore off. Possibly it was the bagpipes. Or the fact that Gloria's family, scenting a world of brilliant choice for their lovely daughter, did not look on Morty's onslaught with pleasure. It appeared they believed he was none too good for their jewel — not the Lancelot they had in mind.

Gloria's father didn't like me at first sight. Her family had no money. He was a presser. In partnership with a relative they maintained a shop, a cleaning shop, on Adelaide Street. But, well, this was a very beautiful girl. And she had a lot of very potentially rich suitors. And I was not a rich suitor. I was a medical student, but a poor medical student at the time. And all these rich young men were chasing her. There was every-one in Pi Lam, a fancy non-medical fraternity.

Chapter 2: Conquests

For the princess herself, the initially overwhelming bland-
ishments of intense, ardent young Dr. Outrageous had begun to
pall.

She decided I was not — fun. Other fellows were more akin
to her idea of fun. We broke it off for nearly a year.

For all of the year after breaking with Gloria, while manfully
striving to bury his lance, her rejected knight has not stopped
thinking of her.

Now a suaver Morty renews his attack, somewhat lower key
but utterly determined.

Fun? He would show her how much fun he could be.

There was no point trying to match her jock suitors at *la vie
sportive* Gloria so healthily adored. He forced himself to take her
horseback riding — once. At least here a fellow could imagine
Freudian undertones.

But this, he knew, was not the terrain from which to mount
his winning skirmish. He might be a bundle of left arms and feet
on the tennis courts. But what 18-year-old princess could resist a
seige of pure poetry? Not tennis, but Tennyson. No big dumb
handsome jock could match that.

On, Tennyson! On, Cyrano! On, Napoleon!

And so was born the fable of the siege of poems and flowers, a
fable enshrined and imprinted for decades in stories decorated by
Gloria's smile, the smile of a beautiful woman who beautifully
retold, each of the many times she was asked, that she decided to
plump for ardent little Sir Morty over the other knights because:

"I knew I would be well-loved. And I have been."

Toronto Life magazine in 1972 would embellish the fable in a
lyrical description of Morty's hidden self: the side that Dr.
Morty the Outrageous, now a millionaire NDP MLA, kept most
guarded from the world:

Morty Shulman the husband, father, close friend. A man who showwith with with s himself to no one but the people he loves. Warm, sentimental, wildly generous. Moved to tears by the breakup of a friend's marriage. Face contorting despite himself, even now, when he speaks of the death of a childhood friend in Hurricane Hazel. Author of 180 love poems, 40 lines each, that arrived special delivery at Gloria Bossin's front door, one a day for six months, until she finally capitulated and agreed to be "pinned". Incurable romantic, a man who has just written the outline for his first novel, a love story.

———

Yes, it was quite a campaign — flowers every day. Flowers and a poem. A poem written by Sid Halpern, flowers taken from funerals. Patients would die, I'd take the flowers.

Oh sure: Sid Halpern wrote the poetry. I could never write a poem. I tried. Never was able to write poetry. Can't make things rhyme. At what point did I tell her it was his poetry? Oh, I think she knew all along. He certainly told her. He was my roommate. We roomed together at medical school. Had to live in for several weeks at a time. He used to write poems all the time and I said, "Would you write one for me?" So he said, "Sure." I did some work for him on a dissertation that had to be done or some . . . homework and he'd write the poem. *Quid pro quo.* Does Gloria still have them? Long gone! [Laughs] Why should she save Sid's poems?

———

Was this the behavior of a man wracked with inferiority? Morty will admit that for a shy wonk, it was quite a courtship.

———

I sneaked back on the scene and I finally seduced her. In the poetic sense of the word, of course. Finally swept her off her feet.

30

I just wanted to hurry and tie her down. As soon as I
could, I put a ring on her finger.

———————

It was not the knockout stone that might have been prof-
fered by one of the bigger-league medical knights. It was a pretty diamond, a respectable size, but it had a flaw.

It was his mother Nettie's engagement ring.

Morty thought it was romantic. He felt Gloria was not completely thrilled.

After a heroic courtship of his own — there were times
when he walked all the way from his hometown of Havelock to
spend an evening with Nettie — Dave Shulman had presented it
proudly enough to his bride-to-be. For a beginner insurance
salesman in the Depression, it was the best he could do.

Morty had a matching wedding band designed for Gloria,
studded with diamonds, to set off the heirloom ring. But soon
after they married she took off the marred gem and put it away.

There would be jewels to outshine it, plenty of them.

The family remembered a beautiful, sunny, sparky young
girl — very young. Gloria was still 16 when Morty first brought
her home. Her tendency to flare up was remarked upon by
Morty's adoring aunts. Cousin Doris' mother, Morty's Aunt
Rose, used to call Gloria's tizzies "tempests in a teapot."

The jewels, the rich house, the travel, the rich life of the
senses would go some way towards offsetting the fact that the
circles in which they travelled might not have been exactly what
a young princess dreamed of.

The Shulmans would always be outside society's in-groups.
Morty's determined nose-thumbing, his quickening boredom
with the familiar, would always keep them outside the gates of
the refined establishment, an establishment with which Morty
professed groaning ennui.

But in the twilight years to come there would be reckonings.
Gloria, pining after the more acceptable Lancelots she had

———————

ditched would rage comically: "No more Ukrainians!" Morty would yell back that his friends — bridge dreamers, journalists, promoters — might have a whiff of raffishness, yes; but her upstanding earthbound bunch bored him silly.

Those jagged days are still decades in the future.

Here is a picture of Morty and Gloria at Muskoka Lodge, the best resort in southern Ontario lake country, the summer before their marriage. The sun is shining. They are on a beach towel on the grass: Morty sitting awkwardly on backward-bent knees, Gloria stretched out, beautiful and lush in a strapless bathing suit, leaning back in his lap, against his narrow bare chest. A lock of her dark hair trails softly on his shoulder; her left hand is spread to show her engagement ring, a sparkling serene smile lights her face. Morty's head, characteristically ducked, wears a look of sly wolverine triumph.

Despite the soft aura of sunshiney intimacy, cousin Doris says she is sure they hadn't slept together before the ring was bestowed. It is, she says, exactly what Morty would say.

Years later Doris decided to invoke the privilege of censorious elder cousin, say to Morty what was on her mind: not only, "How can you play around?" but, "How can you play around so openly?" She herself, Doris said, though no angel, had never been with another man since her marriage.

"You're old fashioned," Morty snapped disdainfully (meaning both about playing and flaunting).

To him flaunting was always a key to enjoyment: sticking it up the world's nose. Private pleasure would be no pleasure at all.

Morty and Gloria married when she was nineteen-and-a-half, he 25.

The respectably large wedding, May 30th, 1950 at Beth Sholom synagogue, was chronicled by Gloria with loving care: smiling pictures punctuated by carefully arranged souvenirs.

The albums today are stacked willy-nilly on overflowing closet shelves in the suite of rooms that now constitute Morty's roaming ground through his restless nights. Supplies of medication and water glasses on tables mark out his fitful nocturnal trail.

From the shelves spill wedding albums, honeymoon albums, sweet fading scraps of innocence from Scaroon Manor on beautiful Schroon Lake, N.Y., a popular Catskill Mountains honeymoon haven. Matchboxes, stubs from the nightclub. The menu from the newlywed's first breakfast, the resort's rosebud-rimmed logo: Hearts are Happier at Scaroon Manor.

From other shelves sift big glossy pictures of the party days a decade thence. A court of pretty Forest Hill socialites, Gloria front and centre, all in full Louis XIV rig: crinolines, powdered wigs, beauty marks, necklines low, bosoms high, and Morty, the leering spindle-shanked Sun King. There are flashes of other pictures, quickly whisked away, hinting at expanses of sun-tanned flesh and no crinolines at all.

Later that summer, after their marriage, the young couple was to sail to Edinburgh where Morty would plunge into surgical training, fulfilling that long-time dream which Gloria enthusiastically shared.

But in April, his postgraduate year of pathology and anatomy done, Morty found himself with three months to kill before the Edinburgh residency began, and a lucrative locum opening in the office of a Bloor St. GP named Dr. Addison Taylor.

He found he liked the hurly-burly of general practice. And the one-time $20-a-month intern was delighted to find himself making real money for the first time in his life — and not only as a doctor.

A shining new window swung open, only months before his marriage. A relative of a relative of Gloria's introduced Morty to the stock market.

On his first shot he lost $350. On his second, he emerged $14,000 richer.

Shaky-handed surgeon versus potential market sure-shot? Surely there was no contest. Going into general practice, finding his feet in the stock market, felt like a lot more fun.

Seemingly on the spur of the moment, Morty announced he was ditching the surgical residency. He made the decision, on his own, four days before their wedding.

Needless to say, Gloria was not thrilled with that either.

On a cold beleaguered spring day 44 years after the springtime of their courtship, his voice tired and slurred after a week of desolate battle with his mutinous Deprenyl family, Morty is thinking about the early years, the years when there was no battle that seemed not his for the winning.

Secretary Ann Worobec's daughter Debbie, his favorite office assistant, has given him a present: a new T-shirt that tickles out a memory of his battle to win Gloria from her disapproving family.

It seems one question in the Bossin family's mind about their daughter's unlovable suitor had to do with Morty's father, the handsome, fun-loving Dave.

Gloria said when she met me — of course I think, I suspect, but I'd never heard this before — she said her parents warned her that she should stay away from me because my father was a woman-chaser and I'd be the same way. I don't know where they got that from. I don't know if it was true; I never knew anything about that, I still don't know if it was true.
[His glittering eyes, as usual, bely his words. He rushes on, savoring it.]
The only thing was that once my father was charged with being in a bawdy house! But he swore to me up and down that he was there collecting premiums.
[He gives the laugh.]
And it may be true! I don't know . . . I never heard it other than from Gloria. She's repeated it over the years. He

----

liked to look at pretty women, but I don't think he would do anything more than look at them, s'far as I know.

The laugh. Again, the laugh, always the laugh that says You can't shaft me or shame me, because I'll always get there before you!

And grinning manically he is holding up the T-shirt from his beloved Deb, a T-shirt with the logo of a friend's heavy metal group.

Ludwig Band, it says on the front, with a cartoon head of Beethoven; and on the back: "I'd rather be fucking."

An Unlikely Galahad, and the Unhumble Beginnings of Morty Millionare

"If a man has been his mother's undisputed darling
he retains throughout life the triumphant feeling,
the confidence in success, which not seldom
brings actual success with it."
—Sigmund Freud,
A Childhood Memory of Goethe's

1950

The worst was the bowling.

At least once a month, bowling was the sport *de choix* of the circle of young doctors Morty and Gloria moved in, a group who were nice enough, sure, but . . .

Then there were the 16-hour days.

In June of 1950, Morty set up practice, not far from the neighborhood where he was born. He used part of his $5,000 inheritance from his father to make a downpayment on a plain square brick house at 378 Roncesvalles Avenue: plenty of space for a medical office on the first floor, a two-story apartment above, but not the house he really wanted.

That one would require cash from his mother, but Nettie wouldn't go for it. The first big chasm yawned between Mama and her offspring. Nettie prevented Morty from leaping. It was the last time she would be able to do so.

I wanted to buy a house at the corner of Dundas and Prince Edward Drive, a big house on a huge lot, five acres of land. It's now all huge office buildings. The owner was asking $35,000, and my mother said, "What, you're going into the real estate business?" So, we bought this place for $12,000. And I often think if I had bought that five acres of land at Dundas and Prince Edward Drive, well, for one thing I would have been very rich, very quick, because of the whole corner turning into a factory development.

If my mother had gone for that I can't even begin to fathom where we would be today. It was a major turning point which I didn't realize at the time. It's like so many things, indirectly, which might have turned your life into something completely different. Who knows? All because of my mother's caution. She said, "A $10,000 mortgage you can handle. How are you going to manage a $30,000 mortgage?" She made the same comment when I bought the Russell Hill house in 1959. At that point I didn't ask her. I just bought it and she said, "My God, Morty, how will you ever make the payments on the mortgage?" I paid it off the first year.

Those regrets over the Prince Edward palace do not run deep. There was a flutter of regret over the missed economic opportunity, but not over the choice of a venue for his future life.

In a corner of his heart, where he keeps his secret picture of his place in the universe, Morty's view is not really different from Nettie's.

It turned out that Roncesvalles was an easier place to set up a practice because, instead of looking up, I was looking down.

If I had lived on Prince Edward Drive I would have thought I was serving my betters. Here I was serving poor English, poor white, poor immigrant. I thought I was serving people I was . . . equal to.

Working-class Eastern European immigrant patients, a social circle of young doctors and their wives who seem already to have slipped into suburban middle age. . . .

Young Doctor Morty began his grown-up life serving and living amongst no one he needed look up to. His equals.

Among them but not exactly like them. Although his friends soon became aware of his fortune, few of them knew the extent of it, even in those early days.

And you couldn't tell it from the pace he set for himself at his practice.

Well, I was determined I was going to be a success, and the only way you can get patients is by going out in the middle of the night when nobody else wanted to go. So I went, and I didn't care where or when. I went over to the Island for four dollars. I made a house call to Toronto Island for four dollars.

By 1952 I was earning $22,000. That was a lot in those days. It was a hell of a way to live, though. I was out every night until two, three in the morning. No social life. It was terrible.

And, of course, this is pre-Medicare. Sometimes you collected and sometimes you didn't. The ratio of non-collections I'd say was about two-thirds.

38

You'd have strangers, and most of them didn't have any money, or a lot of them didn't have any money. You get married and you're struggling and hustling and you get stiffed, what are you going to do? You can't sue 'em.

I built up a good practice. People are grateful when you come in the middle of the night.

"Mrs. Lambie, how did you happen to come to me first, as a doctor?"

In the old Roncesvalles office, early one morning 42 autumns later, Morty raises his voice to get the attention of a tiny white-haired woman who has been quietly sitting in his waiting room reading a paperback called *When Prayers Are Answered*, since Wheel-Trans dropped her off three-quarters of an hour earlier.

"Are you talking to me? Well, Jim had come home and had a bad throat, and the hospital wanted to keep him and I phoned the police for a doctor and you came on the Emergency."

"What hour of the day was it?"

"What hour of the day? Noon hour, I believe."

The police would phone the Academy of Medicine and the Academy of Medicine had a roster. They had my name in East Toronto and West Toronto. They tried to do it geographically, but there just weren't enough doctors for them to do it. . . .

"How long ago was that? Did you hear that, Mrs. Lambie?How long ago was it?"

"Oh, that was a long time ago."

"It's got to be 30 years anyway."

"Dr. Mmmff was practicing then," the woman mumbles.

"Well, he died in '55."

"Well, it was way before then. When he died, we came over here and that was, oh, I think in the '40s."

"You were one of my first patients."

"You mean today?"

"Never mind, Mrs. Lambie'"'

Eight a.m. to 9 p.m.: I worked by appointment to try to train the patients to come at specific times. My last appointment was 8:45 at night.

Living above the office, it was perfect, from my point of view. You're always right at hand. That was the idea. I wanted to go into practice. I wanted to make money. I was very ambitious.

Once, I thought I'd be a great surgeon. Thought I would be a brain surgeon, but I would have been a terrible surgeon. While I was in training I did some surgery and I found out I was very bad. I was very inept; it took me an hour to take out an appendix, and it took someone who was good five minutes.

Sure, in my practice I delivered lots and lots of babies, but I wasn't the greatest obstetrician in the world.

I wanted to be big. I wanted to be important. I wanted to do something worthwhile.

I wanted to do something important.

Although the practice is burgeoning, Morty finds the hospital world the same nightmare he remembers from his own training days.

It was a wild and woolly experience. You saw deaths from morphine, from improper administration of anesthetic. No

---

supervision of junior staff. When I was an intern, residents used to boast about putting in an intravenous, they would race to see who could jab it in quickest. Look how fast I can get it in. Once a patient threatened to lay a complaint, it came to nothing. It was a big mess and nobody could do anything, everything was hushed up.

Still, the new GP can't get privileges in any of the hospitals.

Not because of the quota. No, I was just rejected. I couldn't get into a hospital. . . . I applied to every hospital in the city — eight. I was rejected by every hospital in the city.

Well, Toronto was very tough in the '50s for young Jewish doctors. I was rejected by Mount Sinai because I hadn't interned there and they said, "If we weren't good enough for you to intern here, why should we take you in?"

I told you what happened to me at St. Joseph's. I didn't apply to get on the staff there, but I was applying for Catholics who came in and were pregnant and, if you booked them seven months ahead, they'd give you the bed. And this went on for about a year, and then the Sister Superior called me in and said, "Everyone bringing patients here should be on staff. Would you mind making an application to be on staff?"

And I said, "I'd be delighted, Sister." So I filled it all out and they rejected me. They said I could no longer deliver babies there. Then, 30 years later — I couldn't believe it — they had their fund drive and asked me to head it. I turned them down and sent them $500. Wrote the story of why I wasn't heading it in my column in the *Sun.*

They never did respond to that, but what could they say? It didn't help their campaign any.

To deliver my babies I had to go to St. Mary's, which

was just a house. Oh, it was terrible. And there was also the Burnside, but it was even worse.

I went five years in practice before I could get on hospital staff, and by then I'd been a coroner for three years. It would take me that long, and then I only got a staff appointment because I did them a favor.

One night in 1950, providence drew for him a house call to a local Tory wardheeler by the name of Jack Barnet.

I made the house call to Jack Barnet, not specifically because I knew he was a big man in local politics. It was the Academy; I got a phone call at 3 a.m. I didn't know him from Adam.

He appreciated my coming and I became his family doctor. When his wife became pregnant, he asked me to book her into Toronto General. And I said, "I can't book her into the General, there's not a chance in hell." He says, "Why not?" So I told him and he says, "I'll fix them. I'll make you a coroner."

He didn't get it for me, but he had put the bug in my ear.

Jack Barnet, 38, was a slum boy turned slumlord, the king of the backroom boys in St. Patrick's, the riding which housed Morty's practice. Barnet's *Turf Club Hotel*, with its busy beer parlor on the ground floor, was a favorite boozing and canoodling spot for several local politicians, who in turn aided Barnet in his rise as a wardheeler.

Morty and the Barnets became part of one another's social lives. Barnet enrolled Morty in the Progressive Conservative party, and the newly hatched GP was soon rubbing shoulders with some of the boozecan-owner's influential friends: MP Roland Michener, later Canada's governor general, and a couple of local MPPs.

With just two exceptions, only true-blue-and-orange WASPS had ever been picked for coronerships. Dr. O'Hara, a Roman Catholic, and a single Jew, Dr. Lou Breslin, had gotten appointments as a sop to minority voters, but neither was ever sent on a single call.

Still, Morty and Barnet lobbied gamely, the Shulmans faithfully showing up at a boring round of Tory riding functions. But in the end Barnet didn't manage to make good on the coronership he pledged after the fateful night when Morty came out to heal his flu. A combination of uppers, downers and drink took their toll, and only a year after this promising friendship began, Barnet kicked off.

Morty was not going to let that stop him. He presented himself, his ambition and his patients as constituents to another ambitious but fallen Tory insider, one W.J. Stewart. Bill Stewart had been mayor of Toronto in the '30s, was subsequently elected MPP for West Toronto and appointed Speaker of the House, then forced from his post by Premier George Drew, who apparently loathed him.

In 1950, Stewart lost his seat to the CCF candidate, and he was now burning to get it back from the upstart socialist.

"I had a large practice in Mr. Stewart's riding of Parkdale and I took time to visit each of my patients to solicit support for Bill Stewart. In early 1952 he won the seat by an overwhelming majority. Two months later I received my appointment as a city coroner," Morty wrote in *Coroner*.

With all of that, it would still be three years before a hospital opened up to him. Or, rather, before Morty had the means to kick in the door.

In 1955 I went down to Toronto Western hospital on a coroner's call; the nurse hadn't put the sides up on the bed and the

---

43

patient had fallen out and died from a broken neck. I entered it as an accident. Two weeks later I applied for a staff position staff and got on. Finally got on staff at Western, in 1955.
[A coronership! Political entrée! Hospital privileges! And $10 for each and every call!]

The Tory Association was very happy to have me out there. I was active and young and vigorous and they were delighted at my energy because they'd been beaten here so often and they saw a chance for victory.There are no spoils if you don't win.

I was obviously plugged into a big ethnic constituency with my practice.

I had total support of the MPP, Bill Stewart.

Yeah, life certainly started humming. I would go to all these meetings with Gloria and to Tory events. That didn't excite me very much.

Teas, rallies and meetings. With the executive of the local Conservative Association, who were small business-men, and their wives. It was hard work.

How did Gloria take it? She was fine. Seemed to enjoy the whole thing. There was power in the air.

The power centered around a huge hard-drinking football hero named Dr. Smirle Lawson.

The sight of his new true-blue Tory Jew appointee to the coroner's office filled Lawson with irrepressible glee. He dragged Morty from office to office to show him off. An unforgettable tableau, it was: six-foot-plus Lawson, immensely bald, and hung over as usual, dragging dark wiry little Morty at his side. "Look at my new coroner," Lawson would roar, laughing like crazy. "He's a Jew!"

Lawson helped make Canadian football history by scoring a touchdown and kicking two singles in the very first Grey Cup game: Varsity Blues 26, Parkdale 6. Better loved as a jock than as a meds achiever, Smirle boasted he got 100 in surgery because his professor of surgery bet Smirle he wouldn't make three touchdowns in Varsity's semi-final game against Ottawa.

Smirle was a juggernaut of instant death on the field, and known for bucking himself up for mid-game brawls with a full glass of rye in the locker room beforehand. He was the quintessential lovable Toronto Old Boy. They made the affable Lawson Ontario's chief coroner in 1937, and he would rule the inquest roost, protecting the political and medical establishment for an unprecedented 25 years before being dragged from office in 1962.

When Morty breached the WASP inner sanctum that was the coroner's office, Smirle had things working quietly and smoothly. The day-to-day operations, the apportioning of those valuable coroners' calls, Smirle left to chief clerk Eddy Armour, who doled out calls for a kickback of 50 cents apiece. Morty quickly learned to fit right in.

"When he found I caused no difficulty I soon went up to my average of fifty cases a month, which represented a very substantial part of my income."

Despite the outward flash of impetuousness, Morty was not an imprudent hero. Although he loves to talk as though he takes great blind leaps, Morty does not precisely fly by the seat of his pants.

Oh, I do, but I'm a realist, basically. Before the seat takes off, I think about it. . . .

By '55, when I got on staff at the Western, I had also made the first stock break, but hadn't made any waves as coroner at that point.

Nothing major. There had been no press attention although periodically I would get written up for some of my cases. Jocko Thomas wrote about me. The very first time, I think, was the death of a kid on a ride at the Ex [Canadian National Exhibition]. He wrote, "The young coroner is going

---

to try to take on the police; and that was the first time anyone ever looked at me. "He's crazy. Get rid of him." The
word went out and . . .

There was a big evolution of a certain sort until I was in
the position which was what I strived for; that is, a position
of strength. In the beginning, kept buttoned up until I was
solid enough. No choice. Well, I recognized the situation
and if I had tried to do these things early on when I had no
base of support . . .

The first big press attention, over this death at the Ex,
around 1954, didn't help my position in the establishment;
they started to get testy.

Then there were a number of cases that hit the papers.
The thing is that I realized the value of publicity, clearly, but
at the very beginning, it was a two-edged sword. I had to be
very careful.

And by this time I've joined the Conservative Association here in Parkdale and I'm the president.

The publicity, as I say, was palpably a two-edged sword.
Because, if you got them pissed off, all Smirle had to do was
phone down and say, "Take him off the list." Ed Breslin was
a coroner for 30 years and never got called on a case. So I
had to toady up to Smirle.

As far as which cases were to get publicity, cases to get
publicity, Eddy Armour was getting the feedback. Not only
was he the clerk in charge, but he was a close friend of
Smirle's, and he would let you know what to touch and
what to leave alone. He'd say, "Don't say anything about
this." That served as a guide in the cases that Smirle did not
want to get publicized.

The ones that did make the paper, you were aware that
you'd check it with Eddy. So you had a clearing system so
that there were no delicate ones.

Chapter 3: An Unlikely Galahad

There was many a delicate one. There were all those falls out of hospital beds to be entered as accidents. There were other deaths that would be embarrassments, like the suicide in a particularly prominent Toronto family. At first, Smirle would step in and handle the touchy ones himself, but more and more, he learned he could leave them to Morty.

The key to it all was learning how to handle Smirle.

He was a lovely guy, but he was a terrible lush. And it was getting more and more out of hand.

Bill Stewart had told me, "Smirle' a monster man." Smirle was a big man in every way. He was big and he was scary and he personified a certain kind of scary rottenness.

He was very racist. He had said, "No Jew will ever serve in this department," and I was very nervous. I mean he was big. If you could have seen the picture hanging in the Coroner's Office, he's charging across the football field, across the goal line, with six men attached to him and he's going to cross. And they're all holding on and he's not even stopping.

He was a brute and he was intellectually ,— zilch. And he had no sensitivity. When he met me, he looked at me in amazement. He towered over me like ... God, I was terrified. He dragged me out of the Crown Attorney's Office and he yelled at the top of his voice, "Everybody look at this! This is the new coroner! He's a Jew! How'd you get an appointment? Who'd you pay off?"

But he was really crazy; he was crazy as a hoot-owl. And doing very funny things. At the Queen's Plate, the Queen was there — and Smirle unzipped his fly and peed. He would walk around with his shoe laces undone. He was pretty far gone, he was getting more and more impossible.

Smirle had enjoyed his potentate status for an unprecedented two comfortable decades, but he was becoming an embarrassment. However, Smirle did not want to go. The rumblings grew louder; several of his coroners issued a statement protesting too much power was concentrated in his hands.

Smirle kept promising to resign, backing off. Morty stood by him, and for a while his loyalty offset the effect of the publicity that had slipped by Eddie Armour.

When Smirle was being attacked by *The Globe*, and I wrote a letter defending him and they published it, I became his little fair-haired boy.

Harold Greer wrote a series of columns attacking the coroner system and specifically attacking Smirle Lawson, in the late '50s. I wrote a letter to the editor defending Smirle, saying everything was hunky-dory, no matter how bad he was. I made a great defense of the system. He took note. He made me acting chief coroner. Then I smelt it. I knew I was close.

For nearly three years, Smirle held off the resignation they were clamoring for, by threatening to blow the lid off all the scandals he had covered up through the years.

One September night in 1961, Smirle finally wrote his resignation at a party. He was deeply in his cups, and the next morning he tried to take it all back. In the process the grand old specimen of Toronto establishment flailed out to try to knock Morty off his precarious new perch. He accused Morty of forging his signature on the resignation. In fact, Morty was the instrument of getting Smirle to resign.

Attorney General Kelso Roberts nailed down June, 1962, as the irrevocable resignation date.

But Smirle's departure did not automatically lead to Morty's anointing. The establishment was not quite ready for a Jewish

---

chief coroner, much less one who had already pushed himself into the limelight.

They were pushing him and pushing him to retire, and finally the Attorney General, Kelso Roberts, asked if I could get a signature on a resignation, and afterwards Lawson denied signing it!

I got the signature and he promptly accused, first Eddy Armour, and then somebody else, and then finally me.

But someone, thank God, who'd seen us at the party together, signed an affidavit saying Smirle had signed it himself.

When they finally got him out. . . . they let the job sit for nearly a year. It should have been me but I finally realized — anybody but me.

For nearly nine months the post stood vacant. There were three other candidates for the chief's job; all upstanding young members of the WASP establishment.

Then, under newly elected PC leader John Robarts, Kelso Roberts announced that old-boy medico Dr. Harold Beatty Cotnam would now act as supervising coroner of Ontario. The key post of chief coroner of Metro Toronto would not be filled.

Morty burned, but he did not idle. Mobilizing his Parkdale patient-constituents, he presented himself as the overwhelming choice for Tory candidate in High Park. That terrifying spectacle seemed to do the trick.

In exchange for throwing his support behind the favored candidate — one Casimir Bielksi, a young lawyer who would ostensibly draw the Polish vote, without making unseemly waves — Morty was appointed chief coroner of Metropolitan Toronto by the new attorney general, Fred Cass, in March, 1963.

Bielski was clobbered by his Liberal opponent.

And so the PCs ensconced Morton Shulman, the first Jew ever to become the city's chief coroner, the dead-ambitious little mover they prayed would be a "safe" Jew; a climber grateful for his years of political patronage who could be counted on to move into lockstep papering over messes, as they had for years.

The funny thing is, in the meanwhile, Morty is worth $200,000 in stocks and bonds.

The seeds planted during Morty's engagement to Gloria put down the roots of his whole future life; planted him deeply in the stock market, forever, at the age of 24.

This is how it happened. With Gloria's fair self irrevocably pledged to her ardent piper-poet, a tip filtered down through the family to the struggling 24-year-old medico, a hot inside stock tip from a very dear, close relative.

Ostensibly it was a sign of acceptance — it might have appeared, later, to be a convoluted backstab, except that the favor would boomerang on all of them except Morty.

For upward-yearning bourgeoisie, gambling on horses and dice was regarded as a pastime for bums, but the stock market was a place of bankable golden dreams. So that autumn of 1949, when the Bossins got the solid-for-sure hotter-than-hot goods from their dear, dear rich stock-promoter cousin of an in-law of a cousin Sam Ciglin, about a penny mining stock guaranteed to quintuple, they all jumped in.

The stock was called Duvay Mines. It was trading at 17 cents in late summer of 1949, but by Christmas it would hit a buck — Christmas, absolute latest if not before . . . a buck minimum if not well who knew how much? Sammy assured all close friends, relations and passersby.

Issie Bossin threw in a good chunk of the modest take from his Nine Minute Press Shop on Adelaide Street West; Morty chucked in his total small fortune: $400 in savings.

By Christmas Duvay was literally worth two cents.

"He should have called it *Oy Vay*," said Issie Bossin, the

only quip of his father-in-law's Morty ever bothered to repeat.

Morty sold out in time to recoup $50. Shook his head to think what a bath poor Sammy Ciglin must have taken: broke, busted, covered in shame, on his way to the poorhouse.

But, no. Just a few weeks later a lush and leafy Forest Hill street was throbbing with the rich hum of construction. Ciglin was building himself a mansion.

"It finally dawned on me that I'd helped pay for it. That's when I decided to learn everything I could about the stock market."

The Duvay slicedown had two major consequences.

First of all, although Sam Ciglin gained a mansion, he lost himself a set of dear, dear cousins of in-laws of cousins. Gloria now describes him, in the curtest possible tones, as an extremely, extremely distant relation, whose wife's relatives may have come, a hundred years ago, from the same village in Europe as the Bossins.

The second consequence was that Morty Shulman resolved on the spot he would learn everything Sam Ciglin knew, and then some. He would become master of the market.

At the point when I first started getting interested in stocks, I was making a lot of money in my practice. But if the stock thing hadn't happened, I would have done something else. I wasn't going to remain a G.P. I was too ambitious. I didn't know what I wanted to do, but I knew I wanted to do something.

Seventeen years later Morty the marketmaster will write a bestseller that selectively shares his secrets with *hoi polloi*, and the Ciglin lesson will be re-tooled and tidied to fit the blurb, typically eliminating the fuss, muss and 12-year span between the first pratfall and the final windfall: *Anyone Can Make A Million: How one man parlayed $400 into $1 million.*

Through the '50s, after his kindergarten market lesson with ex-relative Sammy, Morty continued to study for higher grades, having, as he put it later, "dimly begun to perceive that there was more to investing than bad tips." An important part was the question of where you were in relation to the tip: on which side of it, and how early you made its acquaintance.

He began honing the ineffable and indispensable market art of tip-sifting: all about trends, openings, opportunities, and how to spot them. He finds he has what may amount to genius for combining disparate flakes of information to produce a solid-gold nugget. He studies the business press home and abroad, pumps broker friends for information, puts together a picture that is uniquely Morty marketwise.

Burning to learn from the wipeout on Sam Ciglin's manipulated tip, so it'll never happen again, he learns. He makes his first bundle acquiring low (with borrowed money), and reselling high, mining stock.

The Morty "Midas Touch" is born.

Mining promoter M.J. Boylen had acquired a gleaming aura for discoveries and stock promotions through the '40s, and when Morty read in the papers that Boylen was offering mining shares directly to the public, he got right on the phone.

What happens next establishes further the pattern of Morty-life: the event, the memory of the event, and the retelling suitable to the moment. In *Coroner*, this was how he described the first post-Ciglin breakthrough, barely six months after his initial pratfall:

By the spring of 1950 I had painfully built my bank account back up to $300, and was anxious to try again.

One day there was a front-page story in the *Toronto Star* relating a huge new copper discovery down in the Maritimes and the article concluded, "Mr. J. Boylen, discoverer of the new mine, has named his company Brunswick Mining

---

and is issuing stock to the public at $16 per share. Brokers on the street indicate that it may begin trading at much higher figures." I phoned Mr. Boylen and told him that I would like to buy one hundred shares of his stock. He said that would be fine and did I want to send a cheque or would I prefer that he deliver the stock to my broker against payment. I quickly suggested that the latter idea would be fine (not having the $1,600, I had very little choice).

I now phoned Cliff Lowe, my next-door neighbor and a stockbroker with Doherty Roadhouse and Company, and explained my problem to him. Cliff laughed and said, "Not to worry — that stock is already $20 bid. I'll sell it for you and we will send you the $400 profit after we get delivery."

I had never dreamt that money could be made so easily and I quickly phoned Boylen back intending to order another hundred shares. No such luck, for he was allowing only one hundred shares to each applicant, so I became very busy phoning all my friends and relatives asking each of them to order one hundred shares of Brunswick Mining from Mr. Boylen and promising each one $100 for his phone call. Before the day was out I had made $8,000, had a stake to work with and had picked up a million dollars' worth of knowledge in the form of the secret of "free riding," or the purchase and sale of stock without the use of money.

By 1984, in Alexander Ross' lively market study *The Traders*, the story had altered and opened thus:

Shulman read in the papers that M.J. Boylen, a well-known mining promoter, was so fed up with paying commissions to underwriters that he was selling stock in his company, an established mining firm called Brunswick Copper, directly to the public for $12 per share, with a maximum of 100 shares per person. Then

Shulman discovered something remarkable: The same shares that Boylen was selling for $12 were trading on the Toronto Stock Exchange for $15!

"By the end of the day I had all my friends and relatives phoning Boylen, each buying 100 shares; I promised them half the profits when I resold. By the end of the day I'd made $14,000. I couldn't believe it! Here was I, a 24-year-old kid, working as an intern for $20 a month. And in one day I'd made myself $14,000. That's when I said to myself: 'This is a very interesting business.'"

As with every other step in his life, including the most towering, Morty tries to make it seem easy, seamless. As *Coroner* would have it:

My next venture was in the field of government bonds. At that time interest rates were falling, which meant that new bond issues rose in price before payment date arrived. Using my $8,000, I purchased eight new government bonds and resold them the next day at a small profit. No one asked for payment for the bonds and so I began trading larger and larger amounts. Within three months I was doing blocks of bonds as large as a quarter of a million dollars at a time, and within a year I had made close to a quarter of a million dollars in this way. I never looked back.

And *Traders*:

Shulman's next coup came when he discovered that it was possible to buy an almost unlimited number of Canadian bonds, for delivery in six weeks, without putting up any money. He also had a hunch that interest rates would continue to fall, which would force up the price of the bonds. He gambled on his hunch and signed up to buy ludicrous amounts of bonds: $25 million, $50 million.

His gamble paid off. Interest rates fell. When he resold the bonds after taking delivery of them six weeks later, his profit was $200,000. He was 25 years old.

The year of the coronership brought another cause for celebration. Dianne, their first child, was born in 1952: a striking bright-eyed child with some of the look and all of the spunk of her grown-up father.

In *Coroner*, the children will get the only family dedication in any of Morty's books: "My years as chief coroner gave me many satisfactions, but they cost me too much time away from my dear ones. This book is written so that Dianne andGeoffrey, born in 1954, will know what I was doing during those busy years."

The combination of stock success and medical status was making a major difference in the Shulmans' social life. They had already begun to begun to occupy a special niche in their circle of doctors and local Tories, and Morty was coming into his own.

The great turning point when I realized it was all in my own hands to be as self-confident and sexy and all of that as I wanted. It happened when I was here on Roncesvalles, living here. Here I'd become a doctor, of mediocre standing, wasn't bad, had these dreams of becoming a surgeon, then thought, oh hell, I'll try to become a general practitioner. Practice and make some money and I was running like crazy, and then I met Jack Barnet and that wound up leading to the coronership in 1952. And women who had always ignored me, started paying attention to me. They started to be attracted. Wonderful things were available in this world. . . .

By 1954, the year sweetly smiling Geoffrey arrived, the money from all that brilliantly unorthodox bond trading was arriving in buckets.

That year he walked into the elegant Bloor St. gallery of première Toronto art dealer Blair Laing, his investment earnings burning a hole in his bankbook, to make the first of his really big up-your-nose gestures.

"Show me some old masters," I said. The fellow looked pretty dubious.

Brought me out a Dufy, a Utrillo and a Rouault. "Wrap 'em up," I said. Wrote him a cheque for $12,000. Blair couldn't believe it. Never seen me before in his life. Read it, it's all in his book. I wanted to take them with me, but he had them delivered. Probably wanted to make sure my cheque wouldn't bounce.

Today Morty admits he downplayed the cost of the artworks, presumably so as not to overwhelm his proletarian readers. The Dufy, a Nice scene, cost $7,500, the Utrillo street scene $4,000 and the Rouault head $3,500.

Within a couple of years he would fork over $16,000 for Renoir's Head of a Girl, describing the art spree later as the time he was "spending money like crazy." Not completely crazy, however.

Blair Laing got him $10,000 for the Rouault. The Utrillo would auction for $50,000, the Dufy for $125,000, and a Japanese dealer would take the Renoir off Morty's hands for $85,000.

Which not only supported a lifestyle like a pasha's, including the purchase of a $72,000 house like a castle barely five years later; but provided a valuable and saleable lesson in art as investment. Morty would generously pass it on to Joe Blow in years to come, in a book he would title *Anyone Can Make Big Money Buying Art*.

Chapter 3: An Unlikely Galahad

The Shulmans already had a live-in-maid-and-caretaker couple on the third floor of the Roncesvalles building. And the year of the Old Masters was also the year the fun-loving young Shulmans threw the first of their gala parties, setting a tone for years to come.

The first party we threw, we rented a place that's now gone, it was up from the old Tivoli Theatre, on the north side of Richmond, a nice house, and we had a Chinese party. We had great fun, so we invited everyone we knew and we had a Louis XVI party. We also had the Roaring Twenties, in 1955.

I had all this money and I didn't know what to do with it, I made it in 1954, and I was going crazy.

A hundred people at that first big party. I don't remember what it cost me. Then we had a Louis XVI party, all dressed up with these great gowns. That was at a hotel on Jarvis Street, which has also gone bust and disappeared.

We had a Tamburlaine the Great party. That was the first one we had at our new house on Russell Hill, where all the women had to come as dancing girls. And when I was chief coroner, in '63, we had one where everyone had to come as some disease, and one fellow came in a hearse and parked in front! Mel Glass came as a corpse, and he was carried in from the hearse.

We had a lot of parties. It was a great house for parties and, at first, we didn't have the inside pool but we soon recognized the possibilities. Put the inside pool in, '62, '63. We were having such a great time in the outside pool, but it was only for four months of the year. And I had read about Hugh Hefner's house and the wonderful parties in his indoor pool, all the possibilities. . . .

I always had this fantasy: women in fur coats and naked underneath. A couple of years ago they took this picture of

---

the staff, two women and two men with their arms around them. And then, afterwards, I had the photo shop across the street take off the women's bodies and put on naked ladies, so it looked like these two men had their arms around these two naked women.

How did my mother take to the whole thing? "Morty, please be careful. You're going to get into trouble." But I managed to get away with it, always.

The party themes, Gloria and I would talk about and plan. It was mutual. She never felt swamped by the idea of the whole new life and its scope. She liked it.

She was the one who was pushing me out of Roncesvalles. I was happy here. I would be here forever.

I'd still be here, except for two things. We were getting a little cramped, with the two children, so I asked the city for permission to extend the house forward to the sidewalk line so I could have more room. I went to all the neighbors and got their permission, had it all signed, took it down to City Hall. Then the neighbors thought about it and all of them came down, changed their minds and voted against it. So it was turned down and then, two weeks later, a Detective Tong was shot by a crook, two blocks from here, and Gloria said, "Well, I'm not bringing the children up in this neighborhood. We've got to move." So I said, "Well, okay," and I'd let her go look and whatever she finds, I'll just say I don't like it because I'm fairly happy here.

And she came back the first day and she said, "I've found a house. It's not for us, but you've got to see the way other people live." So I went with her that evening after office hours, and saw this place, and it looked so fantastic, I couldn't believe it. Built by members of the Eaton family.

So, from this seemingly modest doctor-based existence in this house, I went into that house and a completely different style and it seemed completely natural. Everything was just happening so fast, but I guess it did seem completely natural. I remember Geoffrey walked in and we showed him his room with the domed ceiling and he said to me, "We must be very rich." He was six.

And then there were the trips.

By 1956, Morty was doing so well that his cousin Doris and her new husband Ralph Messinger were taking their turn at living-in at the young Shulmans' beautifully decorated apartment above the Roncesvalles Ave. medical office, babysitting Dianne and Geoffrey while their parents went to Europe on the Queen Elizabeth II for five enviable weeks, making a delicious side-trip to a nudist colony on the continent.

The magical trips continue, every year. The Soviet Union in 1957. China in '58. Galapagos and Peru, 1959.

Then a new world of delights opened: group vacations with a stunning young sailing couple who crewed fantasy cruises for four or more through the southern seas.

The Shulmans and several friends at Toronto's Island Yacht Club put up the money to buy the beautiful sailing duo a yacht down south, to crew parties for the partners on command.

It broke everyone's heart when the two sailors decided to divorce.

Gloria loved to sail. I joined the Island Yacht Club, but I would never go. One day Gloria said, You've got to come look at this girl; she's the most beautiful thing you've ever seen. So I went, and I was knocked out. Jenny, she was the wife of the sailing instructor, Joel. They were both gorgeous.

So seven of us bought a yacht for them, they became charter boat sailors. And they opened up a whole new world of...wonderful things, haha! They would take us, parties of four, for a cruise in Antigua for a week...a cruise of delights. The rest of the year they would rent it out for regular charters.

In the end the Jenny and Joel went their way. We're still friends.

They're still down south somewhere, in Antigua, in English Harbour.

But Joel and Jenny divorced, and Joel married Judy, and Jenny married John, and the four of them live in one big house together.

It was very traumatic for the rest of us.

It all lasted from '59 or '60 to 1968. A rotten, happy sail.

Meanwhile Morty is turning into a market child-prodigy. Or is it just that the market is made for the likes of Morty?

But still, he will give out that it is because he relied for his bread on the coroner's stipend, that had to keep quiet about everything he swept under the carpet.

Why the schizoid life: immigrant patients, bowling parties, $200,000 market killings? Why hustle so hard, when he is so rich?

"Because I didn't think it would last," Morty says. "I didn't believe I could go on making that kind of money."

Nettie-cautious; Dave-dreaming.

And there is a bigger reason to keep working for $30,000 a year, including the coronership: as he will keep going later, spending all of his salary of $18,000 as an MLA and more out of his own pocket, on extra staff, equipment, special investigations.

Because Morty wanted to be a hero.

He has always wanted that, as much as anything he has ever wanted in his life: the pleasure of money, of women, of power.

To be the whole thing. Rich and heroic.

In the next decade he will became one of the first in Canada to deal in the ever-mysterious world of puts and calls, to work up an expertise awesome enough that his explanation of trips, strips and straps, straddles and spreads goes completely over the head of an Ontario Supreme Court judge who is hearing a $2-million suit for damages against the Toronto Stock Exchange by Morty's financial partner.

He will not, still, feel six feet tall, however.

Doris Messinger's beloved Ralph, whom she married in 1952, was tall, handsome, imposing, but by no means as successful as the much younger Morty. A few months earlier, Doris and Ralph had managed a brief theater weekend in New York.

After the theater they strolled into Sardi's, without a reservation. When the maitre d' regretted, said the storied hangout was full, the Messingers turned to leave, only to hear the flunky, evidently impressed by Ralph's distinguished appearance, suddenly discovering he had a table — a very good table.

When Morty heard the story, he gave his cackle. "If it had been me they would've put me behind a pillar."

Transitions:
Documentation from
the Upward
Years

1957

The fragile sheet of blue onionskin copy paper bears a black
Government of Canada coat of arms and the letterhead of The
Secretary of State for External Affairs, Canada, Lester B. Pearson.

Ottawa, April 16, 1957

D.M. Johnson, Esquire,
Canadian Ambassador to Russia,
23 Starokonyushenny Pereulok,
MOSCOW, Russia.

Dear Mr. Johnson:

Colonel John Hunter, M.P., Toronto Parkdale, has mentioned to me that a very good friend of his is planning a visit to
Europe, Poland and Russia this summer. He is Dr. Morton P.
Shulman, 378 Roncesvalles Avenue, Toronto 3. Dr. Shulman is
a practicing physician and he is interested in seeing what Russian doctors are doing. He is also a collector of paintings and is

anxious to see the art gallery in Moscow and similar exhibitions in Warsaw.

Dr. Shulman is planning to arrive in Warsaw on July 7 and will remain there until the 11th. He will then fly on to Moscow and spend from July 12 to July 18 there.

I have told Dr. Shulman that I will be glad to let you know about his visit and have assured him of the kind co-operation of yourself and the staff. Any courtesies that may be extended to Dr. Shulman will be greatly appreciated.

Yours sincerely,
L.B. Pearson

Toronto Star, Sept. 2, 1958

CHINA UNDER RED RULE LAND OF WIDE CONTRASTS
by Gloria Shulman

(Dr. Morton Shulman and his wife, Gloria, have a habit of taking off every summer for a month in a foreign country. Last year it was Russia and Denmark. This year it was Red China. Mrs. Shulman keeps a day-by-day account of their trip. This is the first of three articles by her.)

The Chinese government is preparing its people for war with the West. This is the most important fact that strikes the visitor to China. In every city, in every village there are banners and posters inciting the people to hate....

[Gloria goes on to supply many colorful details, with a flair and sense of positioning that rings familiar:]

One of the major interests in my recent visit to China was medicine. Because my husband is a general practitioner and coroner in Toronto, we wanted to see what would be the position of his equivalent in China. We very soon found there just was no equivalent — inquiries about coroners

63

were quite useless for there just are no such animals — the
Chinese blandly insisted that as there were no murders, or
insurance problems at death, there was no need of the coroner system...

In fact, Morty wrote the pieces, but decided to offer them
under Gloria's name.

———————

In '57 we were in Russia. When we were in Moscow, very
few travellers in Russia at that time, we met the Chinese
ambassador. I said, I would love to go China but nobody's
giving a visa. He said, — I will see that you get a visa. So
here we were in China and the only foreigners left in there
were the missionaries who were being shoved out, expelled,
and under ransom, and here we were travelling like big dig-
nitaries.

A month. In June. It was very hot. I, got arrested the first
day.

Well, I'm wandering around with a camera. So the first
thing I did was take pictures of bands of raggedy soldiers
marching — there were 50 soldiers — BANG! They arrested
me! Next thing I know I'm in the jail and Gloria's back at
the hotel wondering what's happened to me. And finally
someone came who spoke English and I said, "I'm a guest
here." And there was much consultation, they gave me a
picture book of Peking and sent me back to the hotel.

It started in Canton. Went to Cheongchow. And then up
to Shanghai and Peking. It was quite an adventure.

I sent postcards to Americans I hated: Hello comrade!

I didn't think it was good publicity for me so I wrote the
story and I put Gloria's name on it.

She didn't write it, she can't write. But I think she's pret-
tier than me. Made it look much more spectacular.

She had no ambitions in that direction. Nor abilities.

———————

Interlude I: Transitions

I came back warning about the yellow peril...Haha! I
thought it was a nation of ants. They all behaved like ants.
all heading in one direction. It was pretty scary. Said China
is preparing for war. They were.

Toronto Star, October 24, 1958

RED CHINA WANTS TO FIGHT — SHULMAN
Burma, Indonesia, Malaya and other Far East countries will
"realize the cause is lost and go Communist too" the day the
West recognizes Red China, Dr. Morton Shulman predicted
last night. "We were looked on as spies and treated as enemies," he said...Dr. Shulman said he was "at a loss to explain
the propaganda going on in the editorials of one big Toronto
newspaper"...whose publisher recently visited the country,
for recognition of Red China.

He disagreed "most violently with those who favor recognizing the country "acknowledged as our enemy."

We went back in '76. As guests of the government, with 12
people! Some people never learn!

The way it came up: China and Canada recognized
each other and to celebrate the event, at the Ex, the Chinese
government rented the Home Beautiful Building and put in
this huge exhibit of machinery and jade.

Chap by the name of Larry Rice, former Head of American Motors, somehow got the concession and he bought the
jade for next to nothing. And I went down the first day
with Gloria and I said, I approached him and I asked if I
could buy a piece, and he said, "No." He said, "It's the
biggest coup of my life. I've sold it all to Neimann Marcus,

---

the fancy department store family. I'm sorry, I can't do anything, but you might approach them and they might be able to sell a piece to you."

So I said, "Forget it." and I got a phone call the day the Ex was closing. The representative of Neimann Marcus came up here to close the deal, stepped off the airplane, he had a heart attack and died. Which means he can't sign the deal. I have to come up with the money within 24 hours.

When I met him at first he boasted he was selling this for a million bucks, he'd paid $80 thousand dollars for it. So I said, "Well I'll give you $80 thousand bucks for it." He said, "Oh, don't be ridiculous!" The next day he phoned back and he needed cash. We had this huge mountain of Chinese ware, gave a lot to the ROM.

Well the next thing that happened, some years passed by and I get a phone call from Mr. Soo Chow who said, "I'm running an exhibit of Chinese goods similar to what you bought at our last exhibit four years ago and I'm showing it at the Sutton Place and none of it is selling. It would be very bad for me if I were to take everything back to China. Can you help me?"

So I set up a syndicate, we bought the whole collection, donated it to the Chinese Cultural Centre out in Vancouver, got our money back in a tax deduction and the Chinese government extended me an invitation to lead a tour, as their guest ... a tour of 14 people to China ... as a guest of the Peking Arts and Crafts. And what a trip that was!

They opened all the warehouses to us. We went in eight cars and Gloria and I sat in the front car which was a Packard. I took the whole family.

I also took Sam and Esther Sarick — that was when we became friends. My brother-in-law, Shier Bossin, who was also my accountant, said, "I have this client who's very wealthy. He's a lovely guy. I'd love you to meet him. I've wanted you to meet him for some time and he would love to come".

Interlude I: Transitions

I phoned Sam up and he sounded great. We met, he's a
lovely man. Sam bought three whole containers of Chinese
stuff. You should go and visit his house. It's really wonderful. He's in real estate. Made a fortune...very wealthy.
And, there were my friends the Fines and my brother-in-law
and sister-in-law...Ten days, and we spent the whole time
going to warehouses of seized art goods. We brought back
so much stuff, a container full. We could go in the warehouses, take anything we want no matter how old. And
brought magnificent things back.Beautiful. Beautiful old
watches and cutlery...for next to nothing.

Toronto Star, December 18, 1960

OPTION BID BY CORONER

The mystery man behind the baffling offer to shareholders of
Canadian Chemical Co. this week has been revealed as Dr.
Morton Shulman, assistant coroner for Toronto.

Dr. Shulman, through a nominee, offered stockholders
80 cents per share for the right to buy their holdings for
$5.75 per share at any time during the ensuing six months
and 10 days.

The nominee was postal clerk M.R. Worobec, husband
of Dr. Shulman's niece. [*Sic* — Russ Worobec is none other
than the hubby of Morty's secretary Ann.]

Asked to confirm reports he was the offerer, Dr. Shulman
replied, "One of them." He refused to divulge his associate
or associates, nor did he give his motive for the offer.

Canadian Chemical is about 80 per cent owned by
Celanese Corp. of America.

Can't Somebody Shut Him Up?

Toronto Telegram, June 10, 1960

CORONERS HIT LAWSON 'DOUBLE JOB'

Peel County's eight coroners yesterday criticized Dr. Smirle Lawson's double duties as Toronto's chief coroner as well as supervising coroner of Ontario. [The Toronto title had been added three years earlier.]

They told a three-man inquiry into the coroners' system that the supervising coroner should be independent of any one municipality and available for guidance to all.

Their brief to the attorney general's committee also said that, although the law does not require it, coroners customarily investigate deaths in hospitals within 24 hours of admission.

Dr. David Gemmell, a member of the committee and chief of the Ontario Medical Association's coroners' section, said coroners in some areas can make a good living out of hospital investigations alone. "I think it is very wrong, but it is apparently being done," he said.

The Peel brief said such investigations were needed only if the patient had been unattended before admission, if he died on the operating table, or if circumstances seemed suspicious.

Dr. W.J. Copman of Burks Falls suggested that Ontario has too many coroners and the job could be done more efficiently if there were fewer but better-trained men. Other representations argued that district coroners should be replaced by provincial ones with jurisdictions outside their own counties or districts.

Toronto Star, February 4, 1961

DR. SHULMAN PLANS GOLD BAR OPTIONS

A put and call option specialist who normally concentrates on options on stocks, now plans to apply the option technique to gold. He is Dr. Morton P. Shulman, a 35-year-old physician who has been a major factor in supplying buy and sell options on shares for some years.

Now, with broker-dealer W.D. Latimer Ltd. acting as agent, he plans to make available six-month-10-day call options on gold bars at $40 per oz. for $235 per 100 oz. One-year options will cost $325. With the option price nearly $5 (Can.) above the official U.S. price of $35, the option deals are obviously beamed at investors who think the gold price is going to be raised, and fairly soon.

Moreover, it's designed to attract U.S. speculators . . . barred by law from holding gold anywhere. The option device would enable them to speculate in gold without actually owning it.

. . . New U.S. President John F. Kennedy announced in this week's State of the Union address that he would take no action to increase the dollar price of gold. . . . But Dr. Shulman is betting that many investors believe a continuing deficit in the U.S. balance of payments and further loss of gold by the U.S. will result in devaluation of the U.S. dollar soon — meaning a rise in the official gold price. . . .

The option venture is one of several undertaken by the young Toronto doctor. Last time he made news was late last year when, through a nominee, he offered to buy options on publicly-held shares of the big $80-million Canadian Chemical Co. . . . His options on about 62,000 shares were accepted . . . at a profit of 45 cents a share. Dr. Shulman was working as a member of a private U.S.-Canadian investment group. He has a silent partner in the gold deal. . . . He jumped into the put and call business in 1957, when it was just getting started in Canada. When he began selling in Toronto he was the only one. Now the business has grown and he has 10 competitors, he says.

The put and call business is his main financial activity now, but he also manages a private investment fund.

Can't Somebody Shut Him Up?

Toronto Star, September 15, 1961

DR. LAWSON RESIGNS AS CHIEF CORONER

Dr. Smirle Lawson, 72, chief coroner of Toronto and Ontario since 1937, has submitted his resignation. It will be effective in May.

Dr. Morton Shulman, 36, a provincial coroner for eight years, is mentioned in some quarters to succeed Dr. Lawson as chief coroner. He said today he had no knowledge of Dr. Lawson's decision to resign. "I would miss him. He has in many ways been like a father to me, kind and helpful," Dr. Shulman said.

Dr. Lawson, the original "Big Train" of Canadian football, was a husky halfback who led the University of Toronto to victory in the first Grey Cup game in 1909. He entered Toronto General Hospital today for a serious operation next Monday. He has been chief coroner longer than any of his three predecessors. Dr. Lawson is one of Toronto's best-known surgeons. His career outside medicine included racing horses and a run in 1926 as Liberal candidate for Parliament in Toronto East Centre, now Rosedale. It was one of the few times he ever lost. . . .

He was known originally as one of Canada's hardest-hitting athletes. Before one game, Ottawa University quarterback Jimmy Dean warned teammates, "When Lawson has the ball, tackle him from the side and try and run him down when his back is turned, but under no circumstances imagine you are martyrs and grab him when he is facing you. If you do, the ambulance will be working overtime."

As a coroner, Dr. Lawson has never backed away from a tilt. One of his concerns was the number of men who died of heart attacks because while aging or out of condition, they tackled physical jobs such as snow shovelling.

Under him, there was 100 per cent identification of victims of the SS Noronic fire in 1949, the first time in the history of mass disasters that this was accomplished.

Interlude I: Transitions

Toronto Telegram, Jan. 30, 1962

MORE CHOICES AS TORONTO'S MOST BEAUTIFUL.
Mrs. Gloria Shulman, nominated by Irwin Burns...

Toronto Star, April 28, 1962

TOWERED HOME ON THE RAVINE IS FILLED WITH
COLLECTOR'S ITEMS

Dr. and Mrs. Morton Shulman are young — much traveled — collectors of art and curios from around the world. Taking the tip from their parents' collections of carved jade and Shanghai ivory and antique timepieces, the children have started collecting too. Guppies.

[In the photographs, Gloria poses elegantly, bosomy and bee-hive-haired, with a silver tea set on the gleaming oak table:]

Dining with a view over the ravine at the rear of their house is always a pleasure for the Morton Shulmans. The high-back chairs and long oak table are from a St. Catharines estate.

[Young and lean and ebony-haired, Morty leans down to tickle one of his famous antique watches:]

Dr. Morton Shulman doesn't waste time. He keeps his collection of timepieces under glass and enjoys setting off the mechanisms that bring tiny figures to life.

[Mischievous little daughter and son, dressed in Sunday-best for the photographer, peep from behind the hallway arches.]

Underneath the arches is a good place to play hide-and-seek

---

for Dianne, 9, and Jeffrey, 7, but they really prefer the tree house and the fort in the backyard.

The Shulman's home is baronially towered and set into the side of the Nordheimer ravine with a bird's eye view out over the tree tops. "We bought the house on an impulse last year," said Gloria Shulman. "We had been living over my husband's office for many years and just decided to change."

Dr. Shulman, a coroner for Toronto, says he just seems to get caught up in things — but he didn't say if luck or good planning played the most part.

His collection of pre-revolutionary automatic French watches is one of the best in North America. He has 26 of the 400 that are distributed throughout the world. One is from deposed King Farouk's collection — one is from the Russian Imperial Court. These tiny bejewelled watches have little men with hammers to bang the hours, waterfalls seem to flow, stately ladies parade, and all in timepieces under two inches in size. Dr. Shulman showed me one of his favorites — a musical box with a half-inch songbird inside that pops up and flaps its wings and turns on a pedestal while it opens its beak and sings.

That artifact may have been a favorite of Morty's because, like him, it could do so many different things at the same time.

The reporter goes on to ooh-ahh over the wide golden oak floors, "all fitted and pegged," the stone patio, balconies, circular wrought iron outside staircase, the pool, the original stained glass windows. Morty's antique gun collection, which "occupies a wall downstairs and more upstairs." The skin of the tiger Morty ran over in his car, on a trip to India. And, of course, Dianne and Geoff's custom-built treehouse.

She was not treated to a peek inside the locked cupboard in the anteroom off the master bedroom, with its Hefner-shaped bed. In the closet, only brought out for special guests, are the antique watches with naughty men and ladies. And the wonderful exotic images from Henry Miller's collection of porn photos, books and original drawings.

A female university acquaintance of Morty's — one of those who did not succumb — wound up a close companion of the wizened American sex-scribe.

When Miller needed cash, she had him pawn some of his porn pearls to Morty at close to fire sale prices.

Later she will write to "Dear Morton and charming Gloria", brokering "a marvellous Fagonard" on behalf of an impoverished Contessa acquaintance; "a large bargain" at $45,000.

"The reason that I thought it might interest you is because (a) it is a fine work of art, and (b) it is very pornographic. I thought it might be able to join the books and the watches. To be specific, it depicts a satyr in the woods (very distinctly) performing an act of cunnilingus on a young maiden who appears to be enjoying it imensely. It is really worth a trip," she urges.

What are friends for?

Chapter Four

The Coroner Strikes Back; the Coroner Strikes Out

It is only six months into Morty's new posting as Chief Coroner of Toronto, and his masters and all their masters would give anything to dump him.

The Attorney-General has suddenly announced the government definitely believes Metro Toronto doesn't really need a chief coroner of its own, after all. They will abolish the post, leave it all to Ontario's chief supervising coroner.

But Morty Shulman is too big. He has already begun to take on mythic proportion, with the people and the press.

Gloria Shulman, as usual, is putting on the smiling unified public front but at home, as usual, is letting Morty know she thinks he's blown it.

Morty's mother, as usual, is terrified.

Morty, as usual, is showing it to no one, but is pretty damned scared himself.

March, 1963

The public aura of luxuriant quietude in the richening Shulman life, which masked that behind-the-scenes frenzy of political maneuvering over Smirle Lawson's job, had come to an end, at last, nine months after Smirle was finally shoved out the door.

The new Tory government under Premier John Robarts, faced with the prospect of a Morty viper in the bosom of the backbenches, finally bit down hard, and did the deed.

When Attorney General Fred Cass made it public on March 8, 1963, he cited — and was markedly brief about it - Morty's distinction in "a number of major inquests, including one into the deaths of two men working on the Metro east-west subway. The inquest, which heard 100 witnesses, was the longest in provincial history. The new coroner will be paid $9,000 a year. It is an important position."

Morty's face, ascetic, intense, and intensely photogenic, gazes piercingly from the news pictures. His eyes do not veil their triumph. On his lips is a small smile.

Poised for action, champing at the bit, Morty snapped into it on several fronts, hitting all three papers.

Toronto Telegram, March 9, 1963

CORONER WANTS NEW EQUIPMENT

Equipment in the Metro coroner's office is 25 years out of date, according to Dr. Morton Shulman, who became Metro's chief coroner yesterday. "For example," he said, "post-mortems at the coroner's office are done with equipment set up 25 years ago. There isn't even an X-ray machine for finding bullets."

He also called for establishment of a central coroner's office for all Metro, which would operate around the clock. "Under the present system the city health department takes over the phones after 4 p.m. and on weekends and will not accept a call from outside the city limits. A person reporting a death in, say, Forest Hill at those times is forced to look around for a coroner on his own."

The *Toronto Star* announced that Morty "characteristically, immediately planned to make the 'Toronto coroner's office the best in the country. The coroner's office has two functions, of preventing accidental deaths and detecting concealed homicides. In both cases there is room for improvements,' the new chief coroner said."

The *Globe & Mail* hailed "an outspoken and aggressive young man who enters the post with 11 years' experience and the conviction that the coroner's department needs to be thoroughly shaken up. . . . an improvement in the system of reporting deaths, an increase in the staff of the coroner's office, a revision in the system of authorizing cremations.

"During his 11 years as a Toronto coroner Dr. Shulman became known as a fighter who was not willing to sit idly by while recommendations arising out of inquests were ignored. He admits freely to using the press to publicize his findings. 'Through the years I found that public pressure was the only way to get any good results out of an inquest. The best way to exert this pressure is through the press.'

"As an example, Dr. Shulman cited a recent Federal Department of Transport ruling requiring a lifejacket or life-saving cushion to be carried for each passenger on any boat. The regulation, a direct result of an inquest last summer, will make boating safer this year, Dr. Shulman said."

The next few months are a breathtaking heroic whirlwind.

The city of Toronto learns to expect a new revelation, at the rate of one a month.

It was a thrilling, intense time, clear and bright and indelible in the memory.

In no time at all, straight out of the gate, he was taking them one, jab-pow; one-two, one-two, out!

I learned my lesson early. After that long and horrible dance, when I was finally appointed chief coroner for Metro, after having for 11 years studied Smirle Lawson, I stepped in like Godzilla!

I recognized what was going on and for all those years I acceded to it. Every important case I'd call him and say, "What should I do, sir?" I licked his ass. And still did it all wrong, everything I did was wrong at first. Someone fell out of bed at St. Michael's Hospital and they told me I should get the hell back down to that hospital and cancel the autopsy and apologize to the nuns and, "Yes, sir," I did. And then some relative of John Bassett's died, suicide, and they didn't want an inquest, and I had ordered one, and Lawson told me to get back out there and have the inquest cancelled. And I cancelled it. And I learned, some day I'm going to be in charge here and I'm going to cut their throats. And I did.

Where did I get the nerve to go in like Godzilla? Well, I had learned, when I was meek and mild, in the early days, I couldn't get anybody a hospital bed, I couldn't deliver a baby. So I said, "Do this, do that," and by God, they all started doing it, and I suddenly realized power was what you assume. And if people assume you have power, they jump. And if you ask them, put it nicely, "Would you mind . . . ," they think about it. So you say, "Do this," and somehow I had the whole goddamn police department jumping to my tune, and an investigative staff and the press following me around and, by God, I was learning fast.

Out of the gate he bursts, hitting everything from budget-padding to cremations.

The deep, aggrieved sound that filled the air was the bellowing of personal oxes being gored, and the lowing of sacred cows hustled out to pasture.

He will save the city $20,000 a year. He will install a central switchboard at the morgue; he will dump such questionable and

expensive practices as calling coroners to the hospital to pronounce dead-on-arrival patients dead at $10 a call — a tradition-
al source of stipend for Smirle's inner circle of half a dozen
favorites, they who drew 80 per cent of all the calls.

Now, calls would be dished out in rotation, further dashing
the hopes and slashing the take for those half-dozen favored
ones.

And cremations would be checked "to eliminate the possibility of a homicide going undiscovered!"

The first time he hit print, he can still remember the feeling.

Yeah. I felt: "I'm doing good. I'm getting praised." It helped
my social life. Suddenly being very popular, you're invited
everywhere. I was the sort of person who had never been
noticed in his whole life and, suddenly, people were paying
attention to me, and in a nice way — praising me.

And at the same time, I had the city highway commis-
sioner saying he did me such a great favor he came out and
said, "It's good to have the new chief coroner. He says such
crazy things." He taught me something very interesting, that
officials often don't think before they defend, they automatically defend what they've done.

I got invited places I never was invited to before. By
people like Pierre Berton, John Bassett. . . . I could get anybody to come to my parties, too!

Going back over Morty's forays is like plunging backwards
in a time machine. In today's (betimes illusory) ambience of
openness and accountability, it is hard to recreate that quasi-
medieval atmosphere of vested interests operating in secret protected covens; a huge leap of imagination to recreate even a
measure of the atmosphere in which he sallied forth, the closely
buttoned universe Morty was intent on ripping open.

The ground Morty was carving out seems as though it has always been a given: the basic principle of coronership. But, in fact, it was the fiercest battleground of all.

Morty took his definition from the traditional British one: "The main, sometimes the sole purpose of inquests is to present recommendations which will prevent similar deaths in the future." But the old guard maintained that the inquest's function was to determine, in its strictest narrowest terms, the cause of death.

The first test of the strength of Morty's precept comes four weeks later.

Today, an inquiry into a death like Louis Pisceny's would proceed along a clear well-worn path. A thirty-year old man falls out of motorboat in Lake Ontario and drowns. Pisceny has no lifejacket; there's none in the boat. His friend at the tiller has never run an outboard motor in his life.

To Morty, this is where the coroner's office shines; where the inquest does its true work. This is the time to make a point about the necessity for lifejackets and recognized outboard motor savvy.

Especially as, in response to protests from camping and canoe-racing organizations, the federal government has just announced it is revoking regulations that required lifejackets in all small boats. At the inquest Morty tries to get expert witnesses to testify to the need to keep those regulations.

But they won't, and the government backs them up.

So, when a Department of Transport small-boats officer refuses adamantly to venture an opinion on boat safety regulations, Morty adjourns the inquest and goes as high above the small-boatsman's head as he can; he subpoenas as an expert witness one Captain Keith Angus, head of the nautical safety department in Ottawa.

As Morty related it in *Coroner*,

The roof now quickly proceeded to fall in. The deputy minister of Transport in Ottawa called his friend Dr.

Christie, the assistant deputy minister of Justice in Ottawa, to stop that pesky coroner in Toronto from embarrassing the department. Christie then called Bill Common, the deputy attorney general of Ontario, and Common in turn called Dr. Beatty Cotnam, the supervising coroner of Ontario. Dr. Cotnam wrote me to tell me that "there has been considerable discussion from various government departments in Ottawa concerning the conduct of the above inquest.

Captain Angus shows up at the inquest with a Crown counsel for protection. The Crown refuses to allow the good captain to give any opinion on boating regulations — on the instructions, he says, of the deputy attorney general of Ontario.

Morty calls in his eagerly waiting buddies at the papers.

"Coroner stops Crown silencing witness" the headlines applaud, whilst "Anarchy on the water," the editorialists warn.

Morty managed to get his expert condemnation of the boating regulatory scene at last, from the superintendent of the Toronto Harbour Police.

The inquest jury brought in two muscular recommendations: that powerboat operators pass written and operating tests, and that all small-boat passengers be required to wear approved lifejackets.

Thanks to Morty's tempest, the rescinding of regulations is rescinded.

It's only the first week in May.

Reading through the now-yellowed newspaper articles, all neatly clipped by Gloria with pinking shears, is like reliving an ancient time when one lone, crazy gladiator is doomed to face an endless succession of lions. When one of them finally succumbs to his short-armed flailing blade, they whisk out the corpse and wheel in a new fresh-fanged contender.

Morty now takes a shot at a construction industry that has routinely claimed the lives of half-a-dozen workers a year. Here he is astutely picking up on a punchy series about slipshod construction safety by *Toronto Telegram* reporter Frank Drea (later, a Tory labour minister for Ontario).

On May 17, Morty's inquest jury calls for charges which were laid against a major construction firm in the death of a worker on a jobsite.

This is part of the special talent Morty hones on his own, the sort of thing for which seasoned politicos retain a full staff of aides and advisers: to alert them to budding actionable trends, what's hot, what's not.

Now, Morty galloped out to exorcise at last the memory of his grandmother's exploitation at the hands of the caped cancer crusader, Dr. Hett.

"Inquest Grills Doctor" is a *Globe* headline from September 4, 1963.

Cancer quacks. The phrase sounds like a joke, but barely a generation ago these pariahs-to-be were licensed to practice their idiosyncratic and sometimes fatal brand of "medicine," with not a soul to say them nay. There were simply too many backs being mutually scratched, and let the hapless patient take the hindmost.

Investigations would take place, the meritricious medico would pull strings, the whole thing would be ignored.

The vampire-cloaked Dr. Hett, who tried to charge $2,000 to dabble in grandmother Minnie Winthrope's final agony in 1936, enjoyed many more years of unimpeded, lucrative practice. As Morty described it:

The year after my grandmother's death, the College of Physicians and Surgeons investigated Hett's activities. They discovered that his magic injections were a mixture of liver and opium, which undoubtedly make their recipients feel better temporarily, but of course would not affect the course of their disease.

The College held a hearing and ordered Hett's medical licence revoked. They never carried out their order because then-Ontario Premier Mitchell Hepburn was an admirer and friend of Hett's and he threatened the college that if they did not change their decision the government would revoke their licensing powers. Hepburn was at that time all-powerful in Ontario, and the College did not dare defy him, so Hett kept his licence and continued to prey on the sick and the gullible until his death several years later.

Because of their fright at Hepburn's threats, for the next 26 years the College of Physicians apparently made no further attempts to control any of Ontario's cancer quacks, and when I was appointed Chief Coroner in 1963 I found that these men were still flourishing in Toronto. I determined to drive them out, but soon found that my activities in that field brought me into direct conflict with the authorities at Queen's Park.

This was Ontario in 1963, the landscape on which Morty Shulman chose to carve a mark.

Here now, in the old news clippings, is Thomas J. Glover, a bald mad-looking chap, improbable possessor of a medical degree. In the aging pictures he stares with a bizarre, absent smile, an unrepentant cheery 80 year old, who for 44 years has been squirting his homegrown horse serum into cancer patients, while the medical authorities maintained a discreet silence.

One Mrs. Elizabeth George, 66, had developed a cancer in her breast several years earlier and her family doctor made an early diagnosis and recommended surgery. But she had heard of Dr. Glover and sought his opinion. He advised that instead of surgery she should receive regular injections of his serum. She followed his advice for four years until 1962, when her condition had so deteriorated that she now agreed to receive proper medical treatment. It was far too late, however, and the cancer spread through her body until she died.

82

Listen to the vacantly beaming Dr. Glover's testimony, wrung at Morty's bitterly achieved inquest into the death of Mrs. George:

Toronto Telegram, September 4, 1963

Under persistent probing by chief metro coroner, Dr. Morton Shulman, the bald, elderly "cancer research doctor" several times contradicted his own testimony.

Dr. Joseph C. Dawson, registrar of the College of Physicians and Surgeons, then read from a thick file dating back to 1921 telling how the medical profession has tried time and again to check Dr. Glover's theories without success.

Dr. Glover injected his serum into Mrs. George of Genhorn Ave. for three years before her death last month.

He said he has discovered a bacteria in cancer and arthritis patients but which no bateriologist he has met can classify. He said he grows it in a fluid containing "sunflower seeds, Irish moss and Icelandic moss." He said they are "pre-amorophic" organisms that go through various cycles and appear differently at various times when seen through a microscope.

He filters the fluid and injects the bacteria into horses.

"I have only three horses now up at Shanty Bay. I'm no authority on horses, but they are healthy horses," he said.

He tests the horses' blood regularly and when he judges the time is right he bleeds the horses and uses the blood for the serum he injects into his patients. Asked whether he had conducted autopsies, he said he didn't because "I didn't have much time."

[Dr. Dawson] said that in 1948 the registrar of the College of Physicians and Surgeons suggested that Dr. Glover's practices be investigated. Other physicians wrote letters complaining of Dr. Glover's treatment methods, Dr. Dawson said. . . . Its executive tried but failed to find sufficient evidence for charges against Dr. Glover after he refused to appear before the executive in 1954.

Dr. Glover's lawyer gets the inquest quashed.

From then on it just didn't stop. From the coroner's office, where for time immemorial had reigned the silence of the old-boy tomb, there was just no shutting the revelations down. And to be sure, there was a growing flotilla of folk trying.

In September, Morty shared the front pages with U.S. president John F. Kennedy, who was going after the Alabamans who had massed to stop black children from attending white schools.

And Morty was going after cancer quacks, construction companies, even the federal minister of transport. And for his masters, it had all become too much.

As Morty recorded in *Coroner*, "After only six months in office the government decided they had to get rid of me.

"October 1, 1963: Deputy Attorney General William Common announces the post of chief coroner is to be abolished and my duties would be taken over by Supervising Coroner Beatty Cotnam. The change would be made in an amendment to the Ontario Coroner's Act."

Dr. Cotnam openly approves: "I concur in this decision. I have never seen eye to eye with Dr. Shulman. This fellow has a remarkable ability to distort the truth. He has constantly refused to accept advice or instructions. If all 420 coroners thought that way there would be chaos. He's been smearing the reputation of 6,500 doctors in Ontario and this of course includes all his own coroners. I don't think an inquest should be used as an instrument of persecution. He pictures himself as a Sir Galahad on a white horse trying to clean up all corruption at once. I can't accept that."

As the clippings show, there was growing concurrence with this view, although the powers that be would have to wait a bit longer before striking their first blow against the mighty Morty.

A golden opportunity presented itself a few short months later.

Dr. Earle Shouldice ran an internationally famous hernia clinic in downtown Toronto. Patients travelled from far and wide for treatment, and Dr. Shouldice was connected at the highest political levels.

In July, 1963, a patient died following a hernia operation at the Shouldice Clinic. Morty had had the temerity to call an inquest. Dr. Shouldice mustered all his forces to have the inquest findings, and even the fact of the inquest itself, wiped off the record.

Toronto Star, December 13, 1963

QUASHES INQUEST, REBUKES CORONER

Mr. Justice E.A. Richardson today quashed an inquest into the death of a patient at a private hospital last July. The case brought before the court by Dr. Earle E. Shouldice sought a court order quashing the inquest on the grounds that two coroners had presided and the law provided for only one.

Dr. Morton Shulman, Metro's chief coroner and Dr. Elie Cass, city coroner, presided over the inquest last September into the death of Horace Leslie Burnett, 71, of Scarborough, who died following a hernia operation at the Shouldice Surgery.

The inquest recommended a major overhaul of operating practice at the hospital.

Justice Richardson said: "The public is aware of the tremendous work Dr. Shouldice has done. The inquest should never have been brought before a jury. I don't agree that any mistake was made (at the hospital), but if one was, it should have been taken up by the College of Physicians and Surgeons." Mr. Justice Richardson noted that Dr. Cass had been appointed to handle the inquest. "I can't for the life of me see why Dr. Shulman was at the inquest," he said. "He had no business to be there and he should know it. It was quite irregular. The chief coroner could have conducted the inquest himself instead of appointing someone else, but apparently the coroner appointed was not equipped and he [Dr. Shulman] had to assist him."

Toronto Telegram, December 14, 1963

CORONER BACKS UP INQUESTS

Metro Toronto's chief coroner Morton P. Shulman said yesterday he won't be pressured into treating the medical profession like a sacred cow. He was replying to criticism levelled by Mr. Justice Edward A. Richardson in quashing the inquest yesterday on a man who died July 10 after an operation in the private Shouldice Hospital on Church St.

The Ontario Supreme Court Judge said Dr. Shulman should stop calling uneccessary inquests and read up on the Coroner's Act. It is the second inquest the Supreme Court has quashed on Dr. Shulman since October.

Dr. Shulman said he will continue to investigate and hold inquests into hospital deaths where negligence or inadequate facilities might be a factor. He will appeal the ruling.

Dr. Shulman said there has been continuous pressure to keep such deaths from the public. He blasted in particular the Ontario Medical Association. "The OMA doesn't want doctors being investigated by anyone. Needless to say I don't agree with this position. I believe that medical mistakes should be investigated. The medical profession is not a sacred cow.

"I greatly regret that I was not notified of the date of the hearing before the Supreme Court as I would have liked to have presented all of the facts to the learned judge before he made his decision."

In quashing the inquest Mr. Justice Richardson said hospital deaths requiring investigation should be handled by the Ontario College of Physicians and Surgeons. The College works *in camera.*

It evokes a chill, a deep thrill, reading through, reliving those urgent, embattled times.

This is a period of pure, heady and, in retrospect, almost incredibly heroic derring-do.

It will prove to be the purest, most heroic period of his life and, especially later, the most closely scrutinized.

Nobody before him had ever taken on the great big red-brick combined establishment, the solidly interlocking edifices of medicine and the judiciary, big and square and as impenetrable as the thick-walled buildings they constructed to club in, shutting behind them thick oak doors as solid as prison gates.

Morty remembers, "I was terrified. The times I would go home and think: Jesus Christ. What the hell am I going to do now?"

By December, Morty and Beatty Cotnam were open, public enemies. The establishments could not believe their eyes: where had this viper in their midst grown so muscular?

Geoffrey Stevens of the *Globe* caught the atmosphere (and began a years-long career of Morty-watching) in a perceptive piece on December 16, 1963:

WILL THE OUTSPOKEN CORONER LOSE HIS JOB?
A judge of the Supreme Court of Ontario last Friday censured Metropolitan Toronto's chief coroner, touching off speculation that Dr. Morton P. Shulman's position may be in jeopardy.

Mr. Justice F. A. Richardson told Dr. Shulman that his time would be better spent reading the Ontario Coroner's Act than pursuing investigations into hospital deaths. In effect, he was advising the chief coroner to keep his activities within the traditional jurisdiction of the coroner's office and stop rocking the boat of established practice.

Dr. Shulman immediately returned the fire. He announced he had no intention of submitting to presure from medical groups. He advised the judge he intended to appeal his ruling quashing an inquest into the death of a patient in a private hospital.

The exchange was typical of Metro's aggressive young chief coroner and indicative of the opposition that has grown up against him in little more than nine months. This opposition could cost him his job.

The chief coroner has met substantial opposition in his attempt to change the direction and philosophy of his department. He said in a recent interview that the coroner's office had been regarded for too many years by persons in the medical, legal and government fields as a convenient rug under which embarrassing cases could be swept, safely hidden from public scrutiny.

"It is no longer possible to bury things in the coroner's office," he said. "A complete investigation is undertaken and where there is any possibility of negligence or of a third party involved, an inquest is immediately ordered." He said he is determined to keep the system free from pressure. "The coroner's office should be a branch of the public. I think we are more responsible to the public than to any branch or level of government or of the medical profession."

Dr. Shulman admits now he rushed too quickly into a field where few coroners had dared to tread. Doctors, he says, have washed their dirty linen in private for too many years for them to accept public airing of abuses. Most doctors prefer to deal with such matters behind the closed doors of the College of Physicians and Surgeons, he says.

Stevens goes on to tabulate the Shulman accomplishments, things taken for granted, today :

He insists it is in the public interest to deal with all questionable deaths at an inquest, even if they involve doubtful medical practices or possible negligence or inadequate facilities in hospitals.

He feels inquests are particularly valuable in cases involving quackery because they warn the public and bring the matters to the attention of the authorities.

As chief coroner, Dr. Shulman suffers from the nature of the Ontario coroners' system. Coroners in Metropolitan Toronto are serving two chiefs, Dr. Shulman and Dr. Cotnam.

. . . Their disagreement touched off a shouting match at a recent inquest at which Dr. Shulman was presiding. Dr. Shulman says there is no love lost between them. . . .

"The pressure from medical groups is getting worse every week, but I'm not quitting — they'll have to carry me out first."

Geoff Stevens made note of the "joint opposition of medical profession and hospitals" to the troublesome coroner.

He also noted: "Dr. Shulman has a successful practice on Roncesvalles Ave. and is independently wealthy."

* * *

Who the hell was this supposedly safe coroner?

And what the hell was he smoking?

Morty is taking it directly to The People. When he calls a press conference there's nobody who doesn't show. As the battle is joined, there is nothing he shirks from saying.

Toronto Telegram, December 16, 1963

REFUSES TO WHITEWASH DEATHS

Three influential groups have attempted to have coroners ignore or whitewash some cases of death, according to Metro's chief coroner.

89

. . . Government officials, the medical profession and industry have all applied pressure, said Dr. Morton Shulman.

In one case, an effort was made by an official of the attorney general's department to hand-pick an inquest jury, by-passing the normal selection system.

One of the proposed jurors was connected with a company involved in the death under investigation, said Dr. Shulman.

Toronto Telegram, December 19, 1963

PUBLIC BACKS ME, SAYS CORONER

Dr. Morton Shulman says he has received an "amazing" vote of confidence from Metro citizens. . . . "More than 100 letters have come in and most of them are from people I don't know. One woman even volunteered her services as a stenographer." On Monday Dr. Shulman charged that influential groups have attempted to have coroners ignore or whitewash some cases of death. Government officials and the medical profession and industry were named. . . . "Needless to say, I have not received a phone call from any of the organizations I named," Dr. Shulman said.

The editorials give qualified endorsement: "So long as a coroner exercises balanced judgment and does not pry for the sake of prying, such assiduity and independence as Dr. Shulman displays are a reassuring public service."

A more prudent, seasoned fighter would never believe, or delude himself, that this sheer, unadulterated appeal to The People would be allowed, in the long run, to triumph over old-boy teamplay.

It is this very point that is addressed over and over by Morty's frustrated fellows.

Ontario Premier Bill Davis will level this charge again, when he reviews Morty's peformance as a politician, many years later.

Morty, Davis charges, was not a team player. Davis shoots this volley as his sternest cannonade.

Greater sin hath no man than this: that he end-ran The Team.

Why did Morty keep on? Rather ask: why did he start?

For, having started, Morty must either accept a velvet hand-shake, or cement overshoes . . . or go for broke.

I don't think it's quite that bad now.

Because there's no one individual now that has the power that those men had in those days. They controlled the newspapers. They controlled the legislature. Who would speak against them? And I stepped into a vacuum, because there was no way of getting rid of me!

There I am, bursting on the scene — in the early '60s well, I thought they wanted me to clean up the mess. They thought I would know enough to keep it under the rug.

Everybody was staring in amazement for the first little while and finally I got into a great crisis there with (Attorney General) Fred Cass. He said, "I'm not going to fire him, I'm going to have a talk with him."

I was afraid to get a lawyer, I was afraid to go alone; so I took Ann as a witness. They thought she had a tape because she carried a purse. They said, "Are you carrying a tape recorder?" "No." "Would you mind emptying your purse?" "Yes, I do mind." He said, "We have to look inside." She said, "No." "Ann, open your damn purse." So she turns it upside down on the desk and all these Tampax come rolling out.

So everybody burst out laughing and Fred says, "Go home. Don't bother us any more."

That was that. For the time being.

There will be three more years of hanging on by his fingernails, creating breathtaking and boundless waves, surviving one more attempt to dump him, before the final truncheon falls at last.

People are marching in impassioned support; letters are pouring in from desperate people, begging him to investigate the wrongs done to them and theirs.

In February, 1964, he will present his most famous scandal: the case of Patricia Morgan, who died with forceps sewn inside, after a bizarre surgical opera that involved no fewer than six different doctors in the operating room.

He will take on drunk driving, dangerous highways, too-hasty cremations.

Amazingly, the establishment openly battles each of Morty's inquest jury recommendations. Don't waste doctors' time counting instruments before you complete surgery.

Don't bother with breathalizers. Why reinforce guardrails? No need to monitor cremations.

Morty takes the further audacious step of bringing out annual reports; four of them, longer and more damning of his superiors each year.

There are more and bigger headlines as Morty goes hurtling towards what everyone but him sees as the inevitable crisis where his masters scramble and storm to unseat him.

He thwarts their second attempt to fire him in 1965. And so, by the end of 1966, he knows it's just a matter of time.

His fourth Metropolitan Toronto Coroner's Office Statistical Report is the one that does it for him. On the cover is a tortured mash of stoved-in metal, a car with hood sheared back and windshield impaled by one of the deadly highway guardrails. The car looked in about the same condition as Morty Shulman, in the early days of 1967.

Morty's report begins with the hope that the work of his office will be continued "in future years."

He inserts a quote from an eminent British coroner, which is the credo Morty has adopted for himself:

> The coroner is an entirely independent functionary who is answerable to no one save the public and represents no other interest.
>
> — Gavin Thurston,
> Chief Coroner of London, England

He then goes on to stir up as much controversy as possible in what even he senses is likely to be his very last official document:

> The reason for the independence of the coroner is that his efforts are directed towards improving unsafe conditions whether they be in industry or in the fields of the muncipal, provincial or federal government. The government of this province has rejected this view and have insisted that the coroner must give his first loyalty to the provincial government with the public interest coming second.
>
> . . . There has been a vacancy in North Toronto due to the retirement of two doctors which it has not been possible to fill. A highly qualified physician with a background in research applied for this post but it was the position of the attorney general's department that they would prefer to leave the area unserviced rather than appoint a coroner of ethnic birth. . .

The Benefits of the Coroner's Work

1. To prevent deaths through change of dangerous conditions and through change of law where necessary.
2. To prevent deaths by warning the public of dangerous situations and through public education.
3. To prevent or disclose concealed homicides.
4. To prevent death or disease through collaboration with other groups in the field of research.

The report details a raft of important recommendations that stand today as beacons for the protection of the public:

- Higher fines for breach of the Construction Safety Act; the employment of safety inspectors and improved safety inspection systems by the provincial Department of Labour; the laying of automatic charges where two stop-work orders have been issued; and the placing of overall responsibility for job safety squarely on the shoulders of the prime contractor.
- Compulsory seatbelts in cars; construction of median guardrails on the Gardiner Expressway.

That does it.

The Ontario government sets up the Parker Commission: a full governmental commission whose mandate is ostensibly to investigate the allegations in Morty's reports.

In actuality, it is arrayed against a single enemy: the unbearable Morton P. Shulman.

He shows up each day for weeks of hearings on his own, lawyerless.

Aggravating, slight, scrappy, burningly heroic.

He keeps a bulging brief of notes under his arm from which commission counsel Charles Dubin never allows him to read.

He finally hires a lawyer; Dubin refuses a remand to allow the lawyer, Walter Williston, time to prepare. Williston drops out.

The NDP scent an opening, the chance to snag a profile-getter.

Ontario NDP leader Stephen Lewis calls in his socialist-legend lawyer father, David Lewis, to step in for a brief dazzling show as the hero's firebreathing counsel.

It is all for naught, coronership-wise. The commission finds soundly against all Morty's charges, roundly condemns him for the unforgivable sin of unbridled individualism.

* * *

Looking back, Toronto's then-chief coroner reflects on what made the establishment that had hedged its bets on a "safe Jew", start running so scared.

My independence. They couldn't depend on me. If there was a political death or one that had politically awkward implications, they couldn't depend on me to do the "right" thing.

It seems as if there's a greater sophistication in the craft of politics today: I mean, you see it happening a lot. but they know how to take things . . .

In other words, if that situation occurred today, they would promote me to chief of some obscure department with a big raise in salary, but they didn't have the finesse.

We used to have an ombudsman once, Arthur Maloney. He had a huge staff, lots of money. Why don't we hear from an ombudsman anymore?

Because you get bogged down, because an ombudsman is a pain in the ass. It was a stupid idea in the first place when the government decided it, and they couldn't fire her, or him and, while Maloney was there, he had too high a profile to attack and they waited until Maloney left. They put in a nonentity as the ombudsman, and the ombudsman disappeared, so they could save five bucks here, 10 bucks there.

The ombudsman used to do things. Now they write letters, back and forth, and cases go on for years. You never hear from the ombudsman any more.

These days, they have much more sophisticated ways of shutting you up. In those days, they'd call some sort of show commission.

They called the Parker Commission on me.

The Parker Commission brings out a lengthy report, finding there is no basis to any of Morty Shulman's allegations about

---

interference or bigotry, absolutely no cause for any investigation. In short, it finds absolutely no shortfall in the coroners' operation, nor a shred of substantiation for Morty's dark charges of official obstructionism.

They fire the maddening Morty by an Order-in-Council.

In the end, they abolished the post of chief coroner of Toronto, and it stayed abolished.

And what of the man who found Morty's self-styled Galahadism so "unacceptable"? The good Dr. Harold Beatty Cotnam hung in as Ontario chief coroner for 20 years, retiring every bit as reluctantly as Smirle had; protesting strenuously that mandatory retirement should be scrapped.

Looking back on the years that followed Morty's de-horsing Harold Cotnam was pleased to consider himself to have been quite the hellion, in his own dignified way.

In the kindly newspaper profile on the occasion of his unavoidable retirement in 1983, he takes credit for a great many measures that Morty Shulman pressed for.

But in 1978, an amazing correspondence took place between the valiant chief coroner, and the Ontario College of Physicians and Surgeons.

They are preserved in a file that has, somehow, fallen into Morty's hands; although it is clearly stamped:

"SECRET AND CONFIDENTIAL. This Document or any relative photographic or other material may not be published or any information contained therein released in whole or part without the written consent of the Chief Coroner for Ontario."

The correspondence sheds a pinpoint of blinding light on the backstage workings of Ontario's medical establishment, and its relationship with the province's chief coroner.

The college is rapping Cotnam for a newspaper piece in which they feel he has shot his mouth off; and he is rapping back:

With regard to the quote that "doctors often don't tell next-of-kin everthing concerning causes of death and have falsified statements and changed medical records to cover themselves", I may say this quote is not quite accurate or complete, because I also stated that on occasion certain records disappeared conveniently from medical records, and in fact, appeared to be stolen.

I will give you examples that I can recall quite readily, because I conducted the inquests. . . .

After four astonishing pages of such examples, the fearless chief coroner further notes:

These are but three outstanding examples of medical records being altered, or stolen deliberately, or disappearing in some manner. Through my sixteen (16) years here as Chief Coroner, reviewing countless medical records I can recall seeing myself, or being informed by my staff or other Coroners, of numerous instances where records had been altered by detecting different brand-writing or colour of ink, or where erasures had been made, etc. Some of these may be quite legitimate, but at least any changes should be intialled by the person doing it. Some of these alterations were of no significance, but some were; however, we were unable to determine who made them, although we had our suspicions. I am sure you have encountered many of these alterations in reviewing medical records during your many years with the College.

Not a single word about these routinely-occurring "alterations" ever reached the public eye, but Harold Beatty Cotnam quotes ringingly from the revamped Coroners Act, which was based largely on changes instututed by the detestable Morty Shulman.

And Dr. Cotnam is also pleased, now, to use a feisty term to describe himself, a term which invariably made him see red, in the bad old days when Morty insisted on using it about himself:

> As a matter of fact, during our discussions with the Law Reform comission, the term "watchdog" was used with respect to the Coroner's concern about medical deaths, and although it does not appear in the Report, I have used this term frequently in my lectures over many years...

The file closes with a letter sent in 1982, three months before the mandatory retirement Dr. Cotnam felt was so untimely imposed, to the Honourable William G. Davis, Q.C., Premier; pleading for his retirement to be delayed for at least a year.

This touching appeal, with its poignant invocation of heroics, fell on cordial but deaf ears.

As the redoubtable and tenacious Smirle Lawson discovered before him, even the most faithful of coroner servants must, gracefully or otherwise, one day loose their hold on the bone.

When a watchdog's day is done, it is done.

* * *

And so, in 1967, the chief coroner's door has been slammed in Morty Shulman's face.

Stunned and scared and enraged, he kicks it in in their faces. He announces he will run for parliament.

The Office Wife, and Morty in the Money

It had all ended in quite a blaze, the last packed year of Morty the Crusading Coroner.

In February 1966, such was his glory that the CBC modelled one of their best drama series ever on his dazzling career. *Wojeck* featured the exploits of an embattled anti-establishment coroner. It drew openly on Morty's freely supplied files, and was the model for the long-running U.S. television drama *Quincy*.

That very month Morty was cutting a deal that would enshrine him as a populist millionaire, and make him a million as well.

Ron Hume, an enterprising trade-book manager at McGraw Hill, presented himself to Morty to suggest the time was perfect for a tome that would share his down-home money secrets with everyman — a venture perfectly in keeping with Morty's double-sided persona.

They decided to call it *Anyone Can Make A Million*. Morty whisked it out in four weeks, secretary Ann Worobec sturdily agreeing to type it for a share of the profits. Morty sets up a company to handle what he reckoned would be a modest side-venture, with Ann and Gloria, and Gloria's accountant-brother Shier, as partners.

The homespun how-to-profit manual hit *The New York Times* bestseller list and stayed there for 30 weeks.

The millionaire coroner appeared on all the major U.S. talk shows, from Johnny Carson to Merv Griffin. The venture brought revenue pouring in for years — Ann's initial take was $26,000 — and launched Morty as a get-rich maven in a series of follow-up works that expanded on the easy-as-pie theme: *How To Profit From Inflation; How To Make Big Money Buying Art*; and the updated *Anyone Can Still Make A Million*.

The 1960s also brought an indispensable into his life: the perfect office wife. It takes a special personality to walk into a hearing with the attorney-general, spill tampons all over his desk, and walk out giggling.

In the very first year of the decade Ann Worobec, merry, sturdy, unflappabale, and possibly one of the world's worst spellers, walked into Morty's office very, very pregnant.

———————

It goes back 33 years with Ann. She came in as a patient. I delivered her baby and then two weeks later —- I'd hired a secretary who was useless. I ran an ad. Eighty-nine girls applied. I picked the prettiest one. It turned out she couldn't type. I couldn't think who to hire. In desperation the next morning I phoned Ann. I liked her. She's perky. I said, "I need a secretary desperately." She said, "I'm not a secretary." I said, "I know, but come in and fill in for two weeks until I can find someone. Get your mother to take care of the children." She never left.

She was very innocent and naive and she was of a Ukrainian peasant family and she lived on Garden Avenue and her parents were born in the Ukraine and she had a lot of peasant common sense.

———————

Ann has heard the story many, many times. Today, at the age of 58, she can recite it all, and often does, louder than the master himself.

* * *

A   He said, Ann would you fill in for a couple of weeks until I get a proper secretary — I had worked as a secretary before but I wasn't working at the time because I had 2 children that were like 2 and 5; so I said: So what do I do with the kids? and he said, Just come and help me out for a couple of weeks! — Doesn't your mother live on Grenadier Road? wouldn't she look after them? — Never thought of that; okay! couple of week's be okay, so — couple a weeks! Thirty three years later! — The poor old lady's dead & gone, the kids 'r grown up and have their own kids and —

M.   And you live in a mansion!

A.   Pardon??

M.   You live in a mansion.

A.   I live in a mansion. You're right. — And (SINGSONG) it's all because of you cause you're a wonderful person and that never stops doing things for me and that's what I want printed.

* * *

She is a woman who understands the delicate position of an office wife.

* * *

Y'know what, Gloria and I get along VERY well. And, yes -- I get upset sometimes at the way she treats Morty but I get upset at anybody that doesn't treat Morty nice, cause I'm the only one that's allowed t'yell at him. Far as I'm concerned she probably feels she's the only one that's allowed to yell at him. No, no Gloria and I get along very well.

* * *

101

And it all has paid off. Big.

My first book made me a million dollars, and that was just the beginning because everything went into the company I set up. All the extra monies, from there on in, went into this limited company, and Ann had 10% of it.

The column and everything other than medicine. The short on the Petro-Can was through the company.

And she still has 10% of that company, yes. And she still comes into work every day.

What's she going to do, stay at home and fight with her husband?

She bought her house for $46,000. Right after she came to work for me. She bought just at the right time, in the early '60s, before inflation had taken hold.

Today it's worth hundreds of thousands.

Almost as nice as mine.

1963

Meanwhile, back in the moneypits, the battling chief coroner and self-taught financial prodigy has not been wasting the hours of his day outside those dedicated to his coronerhsip. There are lots of folks who couldn't care less; don't see him as a coroner at all, but as a ticket to pot of gold. Some of them are asking him to write books about how he does it.

Toronto Star, May 17, 1963

JUST DABBLING MADE $100,000

A business that was started as a hobby to dabble in the market made a net profit of $103,761 in less than a year for a

---

Toronto doctor and his three partners, an Ontario Supreme Court was told yesterday. . . .

Dr. Morton Shulman, who is now chief coroner for Toronto, said Lido investments, in which he held a 50 per cent interest, made a profit of $27,725 in its first year of operation ended May 31, 1959.

Then it lost $33,693 the following year. And it went out of business in May, 1961, the year it made $103,761, when Wilfred Posluns — one of the four principals — was fired as a director, shareholder and employee of R.A. Daly and Co., a member of the Toronto Stock Exchange.

Dr. Shulman was the first witness called in the suit brought by Posluns against the TSE and George Gardiner, who was TSE vice-chairman in 1961, now chairman.

Posluns charges the defendants conspired to have him fired by Daly, that he was denied natural justice, and that his name and reputation suffered. He seeks damages of $2,100,000. Posluns and his brothers Irving and Jack each had a one-sixth interest in Lido.

In its final year, Lido was not active "for several months," said Dr. Shulman.

Dr. Shulman, who was in the witness box for five hours, said he believed he was the first in Canada to deal in puts and calls — the buying and selling options on stocks at specified prices for specified periods of time. He said he had no formal training in the "very fascinating" business.

For three years he kept no books, counting only on his memory. He began bookkeeping in 1960 because his new financial partners, the Posluns, insisted on it, he said.

Dr. Shulman explained a put and call dealer could make, for example, a profit of $7,500 on a $1,000 investment in a "call" on a stock. But the same $1,000 invested in the stock itself with the market behaving the same way would yield a profit of only $1,700.

"One can also lose," he added. He also explained

strips, straps and spreads — variations of put and call dealings in which only sophisticated traders engage, he said. You need a lot of money to deal in puts and calls, the witness continued.

"For every $100 you take in options, you must be prepared to put up $1,000 in capital." In Lido, said Dr. Shulman, "I was to look after the day-to-day business and Wilfred Posluns was to look after the financing."

Walter Williston, plaintiff's counsel, asked: "When Mr. Posluns went to Daly and Co. (in January, 1960) did he have anything to do with the buying or selling of options?"

Dr. Shulman: "Nothing whatsoever." Witness said he ran Lido from the building on Roncesvalles Ave. where he had his doctor's office. His office was connected to Lido by an intercom system.

Posluns came to the office once a week, at first. . . .

In 1961, only Lido, John Lynch, a Peterborough druggist, and Watson, a TSE member firm — these three, were dealing as principals in puts and calls, said Dr. Shulman. He said that he showed Lido's books to an accountant, Sam Orenstein, in mid-1969, "a month before Gardiner Watson went into the put and call business." Was he your accountant?" "No." "You showed him your books?" "Yes, he took the books." "When did Lido cease the put and call business?" "Immediately after Mr. Posluns was discharged from R.A. Daly. Brokers called the next day and said they didn't want to deal with Mr. Posluns."

From August 1959 to January 1960, Lido entered into about 700 put and call transactions, suggested defence counsel A.S. Patillo. "We began slowly, then began to increase from month to month," replied the witness.

When court adjourned last night until Tuesday morning, plaintiff's counsel and the court packed up a stiff assignment of weekend homework.

Mr. Williston was given a stack of work sheets compiled

by the TSE audit staff. The sheets will be argued by defence counsel for admission as evidence next week.

And Mr. Justice G.A. Gale, who has frequently interrupted counsel and the first witness for explanations, was given a book *Understanding Puts and Calls* by author Herbert Filer.

Toronto Star, June 21, 1963

THE CORONER WAS AN EXPERT ON STOCKS
by Alastair Dow

NEW YORK — A trader for one of New York's two biggest put and call stock option firms yesterday testified to the trading skill of Dr. Morton Shulman, chief coroner for Metropolitan Toronto. Stanley Kleinberg, an employee of Thomas Haab and Botts, told a commission hearing that he thought Wilfred Posluns was Dr. Shulman's "assistant" in Lido Investments.

Posluns, a partner of Dr. Shulman's at Lido, is suing the TSE and one of its officers, George Gardiner, for damages arising from his dismissal from TSE member firm R.A. Daly & Co.

Mr. Justice G.A. Gale of the Ontario Supreme Court conducted the hearing yesterday and Wednesday at the Waldorf Astoria hotel. Court reconvened for the 16th day of the trial in Toronto today. Kleinberg told the hearing of a list of stock options circulated from time to time by Thomas Haab and Botts, showing the price the firm was willing to pay for each of these options. As a seller of put and call options, Dr. Shulman was "mostly" able to negotiate a better price from the firm, Kleinberg said. He estimated Dr. Shulman, or Lido, was his biggest individual customer and accounted for roughly 1 per cent of the business of THB in 1960. Kleineberg told of how he would phone Dr. Shulman to solicit options on certain stocks.

. . . "What kind of investor usually sells strips, straddles or straps?" Mr. Williston asked. "A fairly sharp investor," Kleinberg replied. "It's not a thing an amateur should get involved in."

The final year of his coronership was also the year that Morty tried LSD, ostensibly to learn first-hand about the weird substance that was behind drug-induced suicides that had been increasing in number since 1965.

That acid trip would be fodder for his foes for years to come.

Chapter Five

From Politics to TV: The Knight of the Increasingly Uncertain Lance

June, 1968

A habitually dozy question period in the lazy, hazy days of the Ontario legislature's summer session.

There are generally no more than a dozen members on the government benches putting in official time, easing the pain by getting comfy, putting their feet up and weary heads back, and catching 40, 60, or 120 winks.

Suddenly the sweetly sleeping parliamentarians are violently awakened by a cacaphony of indignation.

Dr. Morton Shulman, new NDP member for High Park, has breached the decorum of the ages by whipping out a camera and snapping pictures of two of the loudest snorers, Tory backbenchers Ellis Morningstar and Norris Whitney.

The Speaker roars his disapproval. The sergeant-at-arms, ordered to seize the camera, claps his hand to his ceremonial sword, prepared to take whatever measures necessary. Morty loses the camera but tosses the film to the nearest NDPer.

When the film is developed, the pictures don't come out. The story does, though, in newspapers across the land.

June, 1975

Another habitually dozy question period in the lazy, hazy days of the Ontario legislature's summer session.

Shocked to full alert by a cacaphony of pure panic.

Dr. Morton Shulman, the NDP member for High Park, has flipped open his jacket, pulled out a semi-automatic rifle, and is waving it at the government benches.

Several Tories dive under their desks. A few Liberals follow suit.

The NDPers hold their heads and moan softly.

The sergeant-at-arms claps hand to sword prepared to defend the menaced house by force, if duty demands.

Morty tells them all to calm down. He is only making a point about the laxity of Canada's gun laws.

He is also bored out of his gourd.

* * *

Morty has already moved on to a different place in history. He has already taken another step — having determined that he will return to fight them where they dread him most: in their own arena.

The conventional political waters did not part to admit his parade, however.

Only one party had the vision to see his potential — or figured it had nothing to lose.

The NDP comes to convince him of their brotherhood under the skin.

This was why they sent David Lewis in Morty's darkest Parker Commission hour: to seal their troth.

This perverse pairing, not at all what he had originally conceived, provides Morty in the end with a bitter delight.

In his dreams, he never saw himself as a backbencher for the opposition least likely to see the light of power in Tory-locked Ontario. But, on the other hand, they are so respectful, so deferential.

And so, the Lewises — David and heir-apparent son Stephen — along with Ontario leader Donald MacDonald, take Morty's hand and all dance down the aisle, together.

Morty, the Renoir Robin Hood, and the tiny party of the people are one. An important alliance is forged from mutual necessity.

Morty wins by an avalanche over the Tory incumbent. He lofts Gloria's hand high; his children cluster in the background.

Smile, darling, we're NDP.

Gloria gives out that the whole thing couldn't be more perfect.

"I'll be a politician's wife and that will be lovely. Lovely to have more of Morty."

The Russell Hill firebrand's maiden speech set records for both tone and length: Three days. In it he hits out at all his old enemies, from the supervising coroner to the attorney general, and in so doing makes several new ones.

And so the NDP years slip away.

Morty waving a semi-automatic rifle or snapping sleeping legislators in the granite-walled Ontario Parliament building.

Morty fingering drunks in the Tory cabinet, and Trotskyites in the NDP.

Morty chasing heroin on the tourist boats at Niagara Falls, and fulminating against the exorbitant cost of fine wine at the government-run liquor stores.

Morty sneaking past a security guard to show how easy it was to infiltrate a nuclear power station, and infiltrating a coal mine to expose the danger of underground fumes.

Morty flogging copies of Xaviera Hollander's *The Happy Hooker* in the halls of the Ontario legislature, to make a point about censorship and pornography.

Morty packing a gun, watched over by a bodyguard, saying he has been warned that a Mafia-linked Toronto developer has put a contract out on him.

Morty locked in rhyming couplets of mutual detestation with the government benches:

Health Minister Tom Wells: "You have a closed mind."
Shulman: "You have no mind."
Wells: "You practice the big smear and the big lie."
NDP Leader Stephen Lewis: "You're a cynical and impossible guy."

The legislative years, eight of them, are like that: a blur of headlines and happenings, the worthwhile mixed in with the nonsensical. They lack the clarity, the pure feeling of dragon-slaying that characterized the coronership.

In 1969 he hits one big one. He takes on the Mafia, and acquires a private eye, and a gun permit, for life.

An anonymous tip on OPP stationery instructs him he can receive valuable information from the Justice Department by putting an ad in the *Star*'s personal column: "Mary come home, all is forgiven."

This leads to a hush-hush recounting of a tale of undercover officers framing a police informant, and a cloak-and-dagger series of meetings that lead to a heavy-duty Ontario industrialist by the name of George Clinton Duke, and a broth of associations with the OPP, certain Italian developers, and mobster Johnny Papalia.

There were gifts to the OPP, cancelled speeding tickets: a fascination foofera that led to a full-scale commission to investigate organized crime.

The OPP tell Morty there is a $50,000 contract on his head.

But largely, as a backbencher in a throwaway opposition party, Morty is markedly without the clout, the control, the access to inside information he possessed as coroner.

And as a politician, Morty is no longer press-proof. Politicians, unlike coroners, are presumed to be skulduggerous, automatically suspect, relentlessly ridiculed.

Imperceptibly, inexorably, the solitary shooter was becoming a target.

The *Toronto Star*, maintaining a tone of tolerantly amused sympathy, calls him "The Knight of the Occasionally Uncertain Lance."

He is skating on a layer of thinnest civility with the NDP brass. For Morty, the give-and-take required in caucus is a frustrating bore, so he refuses to attend caucus meetings.

His relationship with his leadership is further strained when he backs moderate Walter Pitman to succeed Donald MacDonald as Ontario chief in 1970, instead of Stephen Lewis. Morty's explanation for his opposition to Lewis at the time was that a party led by the "brilliant and hawklike" — i.e., too far left — Lewis could never be elected.

In his later, unmellowing years he chooses to jot some juicier notes on the whole matter. For Morty, it is never too late to rewrite the past, especially if he can make it a better story.

My relationship with Stephen Lewis was an uneasy one and I thought that I would improve them by inviting him and his wife Michele [social issues columnist Michele Landsberg] for dinner at our home. The other four guests were two provincial judges and their wives.

After dinner Gloria and I and Stephen and Michele were sitting talking in the living room . . . when to my horror the two judges' wives came up from the pool wearing only towels, whipped them off and advanced on Stephen, saying, "We want you!" He bolted out the front door closely followed by Michele.

The final rupture took place a year later when he decided he would replace Donald MacDonald as leader of the NDP. Stephen sent Gerald Caplan to seek my support. In response I stupidly blurted a rather cutting remark about Michele Landsberg. Caplan wasted no time in repeating the story and I had made two enemies for life."

111

Can't Somebody Shut Him Up?

By his second term, another landslide election, the Renoir Robin Hood knows this session as a socialist will be his last.

When he is approached by the Tory tabloid *Toronto Sun*, a paper that stands for everything his party loves to hate, to write a column, he snaps at it like a happy pike.

He may have to live with the pinkoes for another four years, but that doesn't mean he has to pretend to love them.

Toronto Sun, January 3, 1972

All my life I have had the ambition to be a columnist, visualizing myself as a cross between Pierre Berton and Gary Lautens; i.e., the fearless expose done to the tune of the belly laugh. . . .

So here I am.

I have two conflicts of interest. My first problem is that I own one of those other papers. When the *Toronto Star* went public a year ago I bought 75 shares. . . .

My second conflict is whether it is proper for an MPP to be writing a political column. . . . I have decided that that is not a real conflict because I have confidential information that the member from High Park is not going to seek re-election.

So I am going to try — I will be here every week. The Sun has given me column freedom and I will attempt to keep you informed about the foibles of government as I see it from Queen's Park.

So here he is.

One of his favorite column targets is union corruption, which he is pleased to find everywhere from the giant Seafarer's Union to the minuscule Toronto Musicians' Association.

In the legislature he borrows from U.S. consumer-crusader Ralph Nader and rallies a volunteer band of youthful zealots he dubs "Shulman's Raiders" to check for asbestos pollution on construction sites and crusade against shady bail bondsmen.

In the *Sun* he chronicles his trip to Detroit, paid for by the Ontario Provincial Police, to admire and chronicle the efficient anti-crime activity and swift administration of justice practiced by the Detroit police department.

In the legislature he speaks out eloquently for disabled workers, rails against the draconian review measures of the Workmen's Compensation Board.

The *Sun* columns frequently glitter with accounts of exotic travels from the lush resorts of South America to the sex retreats of southern California, as Morty remembers fondly today:

Alex Comfort had written *The Joy of Sex* and in his book there's a Chapter on Sandstone. I went twice, actually. I was on the Merv Griffin Show twice plugging my books, and each time I went down I had an extra day, so I went up to Sandstone. It was — educational. It was a mutual benefit society.

It was owned by John Williams and his wife and basically — this was before AIDS, herpes and all the horrible things, when you used to be able to enjoy sex and nobody ever heard of condoms — this was a place for strangers to go and meet each other and — talk. Couples only. You could go there either for parties, which they had there on the weekends, or for a course. I went through a course on "Increasing Sensual Awareness" and then I went to a party.

Actually, it was pretty funny. The chairman asked me to start off. You take your clothes off and you wash each other's feet and that's the initial ice-breaker. As it goes along, they build up to the evening where everyone's fantasy gets fulfilled, whatever your fantasy is, and it was quite disastrous because he said, "What's your fantasy?" and I said, "Well, I grew up before *Playboy* or *Penthouse* and the

---

only magazine I had was *Esquire* and, every month there would be a picture of a little fat man with a turban sitting on two pillows, and dancing girls in front of him."

He said, "That's very common." I said, "It is?" And I turned to Gloria I said, "What's your fantasy?" She said, "I don't have fantasies." I sensed — negative vibrations. It was funny — a funny business.

Did they bring out the dancing girls? They fulfilled everybody's fantasies. Mine was dull, compared to some of the others. You feel naive. We went down there a second time, for a weekend.

The whole experience was supposedly to try to better humanity. If people could get the barriers down, get their clothes off and in bed together, war would end and everyone would be happy.

But war didn't end. In fact, it didn't work out at all because they found, to their horror, that husbands were persuading their wives to go there and the wives were enjoying it and the husbands were getting jealous and there were big fight scenes.

Gloria takes up bellydancing, poses for newspaper pictures doing a decorous version of the new entertainment she has been offering guests at those legendary Russell Hill mansion parties.

The fascination grows with the anomaly: the millionaire crusader, the rich-man Robin Hood. And the utter openness of his affluence, and his enjoyment of it. The collections of vintage wines, paintings, tapestries, antiquities; and those long hours put in every week by the dedicated politician-medico, continuing to treat his humble hordes of devoted patient-voters. "Of course, I was unbeatable in High Park. No one ever votes against their doctor."

In the early '70s, an anti-developers reform group on Toronto city council tries to tempt him to run for mayor. But Morty means his second term on the political fringe to be his last.

He is, by now, a well-established money guru. In 1975 Ron Hume's *The MoneyLetter* teams moneystars like nouveau-millionaires Morty and the astounding self-made stocketeer Andy Sarlos, as well as old-moneymen Fred McCutcheon and Trevor Eyton.

Morty is a must on the money-lecture circuit. His investment tips in *The MoneyLetter* attract such a following that sometimes Hume has to ask him to lay off certain vulnerable stock areas to prevent the market from tipping over completely. Hume has to put a guard on the garbage bins outside his office, to fend off investors pawing through discarded proofsheets for an advance look at Morty's tips.

And when the doors of the legislature close behind Morty forever in 1975, another savvy media maven is waiting with semi-open arms

Moses Znaimer, the brilliant creator of Toronto's tabloid-television station City TV, offers Morty a slash-skewer-and-strip the guest show all for himself.

The Shulman File is syndicated across Canada, spices the airwaves for nearly a decade.

The CityTV show didn't deal with the kind of things that the column did.

The TV show, I hadn't the slightest clue what it was going to be. They'd hand me a file and I'd go out and make people feel foolish. It was a joke.

The column was serious. Or it was meant to be serious.

But the TV show was entertainment. The idea was to bring in every fraud in the world — people selling diets and sexual perverts — a sexual pervert is someone who does things I don't do — and it was just pure entertainment. It was great fun. I loved it.

My relationship with Moses — well, every year we negotiated for my salary. I mean we'd just storm, rant and

---

rage at each other and walk away and then he'd say, "That's it. You're fired." And I'd say, "I'm never going to work for you again." And then the next day someone would phone and we'd sign.

I turned down his last offer and never got a phone call the next day.

Everybody thought I was making a million bucks from him. It was some kind of a joke. It actually wasn't a hell of a lot.

I hadn't seen him before and I haven't seen him since. Don't have any personal or social contact, never had any real contact with him at all.

The only contact I had with his girlfriend Marilyn Lightstone was when he'd pass an order down and every show on the station had to do a review of that stupid movie, *In Praise of Older Women*, that she was the star of, and I refused.

He ordered me to do it, so when she came for the interview my first question was, "What is your relationship with Moses Znaimer? Why is he ordering every show to carry an interview with you?"

The show was live and suddenly I hear a rumpus behind the camera and he's glaring at me. I thought I was finished! But I finished the program and he didn't say a word and I just went on the next day.

I had Barbara Amiel as a guest, several times. She was my editor at the Sun for a while, after Peter Worthington was fired.

Peter never touched my columns. She often did. I hated it. I'd read the column and the whole point would be lost.

Finally I phoned up and said, "I quit" *Sun* publisher Doug Creighton gave her shit, and she phoned back the next day and said, "No, we won't touch your columns from now on" and I kept writing and that was the end of that.

March 28, 1981

Barbara Amiel, dishy and devastating new *Toronto Sun* editor-in-chief who will later go on to happily wedded wealth with mega-mogul Conrad Black, shoots a smoky chuckle at the scrappy little TV host who has invited her to be a guest commentator on his show.

The theme of the show is *Take A Shot At Shulman*.

"Honestly," Barbara vamps in her English whisper to the scissor-tongued star of the top-rated nationally-syndicated *Shulman File*, "Morty is the only person I know who is even *nahstier* than I am.

"Morty is wonderfully irritating. Makes even me look pleasant," she adds.

The NDP's up and coming Bob Rae describes the millionaire gadfly host this way: "Morty makes Judas look like a team player. Judas took his payment in silver, Morty takes his payment only in gold."

Morty is nominated half a dozen times for an ACTRA award as best host.

Although he never wins, and although he sees the TV show as make believe and the column as serious, the column is not widely perceived that way.

But it does ring up one or two echoes of the old firebrand days.

In 1978, Morty gets a telephone tip that a cancer patient at Toronto's East General Hospital was given three pints of the wrong blood.

The hospital insists the mistake had no ill effect on the woman, who died of cancer five months later. But Morty lays a complaint, against the hospital and several doctors, with the Ontario College of Physicians and Surgeons.

Between his columns on the bad blood scene, and news coverage of the whole thing in the rest of the media, Mortymania enjoys a brief bright resurgence. For a short shining time it's like the old days.

His columns, with titles like "Blood-letting at the East General", have Torontonians from all walks of life avoiding the hospital like the plague.

The College dismisses Morty's complaint, and finds him guilty of medical misconduct: for breaching patient confidentiality by publicizing the case in his column.

They summon him for a reprimand.

He refuses to attend.

He appeals the reprimand. He loses.

He rejects it anyway. Never does show up for a hearing at the College.

Years later, perhaps it is the illness wearing him down that makes him forget at first just how much of a splash he made that time.

The East General Hospital thing — it's never been written up and it's one of the most exciting events of my career.

It was an extraordinary experience. My last big hurrah before Deprenyl.

It started with an anonymous tip from a nurse, saying that a patient was given the wrong blood and had died.

Everybody, every sort of media in town covered it.

I started out with a normal investigation, as a columnist, and it turned out that the story was true but I couldn't get anyone to do anything about it.

I called the doctors, and the family. I didn't have researchers; Ann was working for me, I guess.

I laid charges of malpractice against the doctor who gave the wrong blood and, in return, they charged malpractice against me for revealing the information. They were dismissed. I was convicted!

I started it in my column in the *Sun* and, finally, it became so big that the *Globe* picked it up and then it got out of hand and the government finally was forced to step in.

It was such a scandal, such a cover-up. The coroner covered up and the hospital covered up and the doctors covered up and the College of Physicians tried to cover up. And, finally, they made their big mistake in convicting me of malpractice. For breaching patient confidentiality by writing about the case. But I wasn't writing as a doctor, I was writing as a columnist.

That was the most amazing experience of my career. Because I had no official standing, no legitimate way to look at the information. I wasn't an MPP any more. I wasn't the coroner. I was a columnist for the *Toronto Sun*, which is not read by, or claimed not to be read by the powerful of this city, but it's amazing how that column ate away at them, ate away at them.

I wrote column after column, coming out with more and more information. At first they responded by denying it, which was dumb. If they had just told the truth at the beginning, none of what followed would have happened.

But at first, they laughed at me. Then, they stopped laughing and decided to take me seriously and then the whole house of cards came tumbling down.

I wrote several more columns and I came to an impasse, and, finally, in order to get the thing going again, made the mistake of asking the College of Physicians and Surgeons to investigate. They investigated and, next thing I knew, they had laid a charge against me. For breaching patient confidentiality — it wasn't even my patient!

I took it as a great joke. I wrote another couple of columns and there was a College disciplinary hearing and I was found guilty and then it stopped being a joke because I was found guilty and charged with malpractice and I was ordered to be reprimanded.

We took it to the Court of Appeal and they upheld the finding. I was in shock. They said the College was within their rights and they upheld the finding —

And — oh, oh, oh, oh, good, good, good, good! — We just made $50 grand, $51 grand, $52 grand, $53 grand. . .

Anyway, on the East General thing — well, then, of course, it became a scandal and I refused to appear and the College didn't know what to do next because they were afraid to carry it any further. They didn't want to disbar me. It was a total travesty. So, they backed off and the newspapers then took up the cudgel. The *Globe* ran an editorial. The *Sun* ran an editorial and, suddenly, the government 'stepped in and took over the hospital. The doctors involved were all kicked off the staff.

But the discipline finding against me — it's still on the record that I was disciplined and I'm guilty of malpractice — but nobody wants to talk about it because it's too embarrassing.

Nobody else was found guilty of anything. The only person that was punished was me!

The College today — it varies from year to year. It depends on who gets elected. The registrar is pretty well without power. It's the Health Disciplines Board that decides.

The College is hepped on sex. For years you could chop the odd leg off and they wouldn't care but, if you laid a hand on a nipple, you were in deep trouble.

Today you'll hear of malpractice suits now and again. But for years, in 1950 after I graduated, until about ten years ago, the only cases that ever came up were when someone was brought up on a sex charge. You would get the worst cases of malpractice and nothing would happened, as long as you kept your fly buttoned up.

Now it's gone so far the other way that they persecute doctors for no reason whatsoever, or for little reason. They're so frightened of the public that every letter that comes in, no matter how absurd, they investigate. At the present time, in this province, 60% of all the doctors have been investigated.

I've had three investigations. For nothing. Letters from ex-patients saying, in one case I gave the wrong pills, they said, so they wound up losing weight. And they investigated that. But nothing really has come of it. It's just a waste of time.

Sexual harassment is the popular thing to hit today and everyone is afraid. True or false, some woman can get up and say I pinched her bottom. Or looked at her while she was undressing. Lasciviously. And, whether I did or I didn't, then there's a hearing.

Only I'm old and have Parkinson's. I may not be seen as able to move fast enough to catch them and give a pinch.

I made a speech to the Entrepreneurs' Club — I was joking about sexual harassment and Jacqueline Le Saux, our Deprenyl lawyer who has absolutely no sense of humor, came in while I was going over it beforehand and said, "You can't say that." But I did. I said, "I'm sexually harassed because the girls line up each morning and they insist on kissing me good morning." I thought it was rather funny. But Jacqueline was so offended she actually refused to attend.

The East General stir-up will be one of the last memorable flare-ups; truly, Morty's last big moment for some time to come.

The OSC stayed pretty quiet after my registration battle. But it all came back at me 11 years later.

In 1983 I floated my first public stock issue: Guardian-Morton Shulman Precious Metals.

Norman Short of Guardian Capital, Fred McCutcheon, who was the wealthiest man in Canada, Phil Holtby, president of Midland Doherty and I went accross Canada and Europe giving dog and pony shows extolling the virtue of our new issue. Disaster struck in Winnipeg. In my speech I said that I intended to invest my own money in the company and I would do my best to maintain a good after-market. I didn't know it but these two promises were crimes and against the rules of the OSC.

When I returned to Toronto I got a notice to appear for an OSC hearing and give reason why I and my partners should not be compelled to return the $75 million we had raised. As I went up the OSC elevator with Bob Hamilton, our lawyer from Tory Tory, Hamilton whispered, "Tell them you didn't do it, and promise you won't do it again!"

In the hearing I showed more humility in ten minutes than I had in my whole previous life. I did everything but shine their shoes. Hamilton didn't think it looked good, but the next day we got permission to go ahead with the issue.

The assistant to the director of the OSC was my old friend Harry Malcolmson.

The OSC never left me alone for good though. They've hounded me for years and years and years.

———————

In 1983, he and Moses have their final falling out. The yearly dance of the salary-scuffle is finally over. And the high-flying uncaring Morty years are over.

This decade will throw Morty Shulman's life into a new tailspin, and bring him nearer than he has ever been to crashing, forever.

Chapter Six

The Parkinson's Years: Part I

Desperation, Deprenyl and the
Day-to-Day Life of an Unlikely Drug Lord

Stages of Idiopathic Parkinson's Disease

Stage 1: Unilateral symptoms. Resting tremor and/or akinesia
(paucity of movement) and/or rigidity.
Stage 2: Bilateral symptoms or signs, no gait abnormality.
Stage 3: Bilateral symptoms with gait abnormality.
Stage 4: Spontaneous falls.
Stage 5: Wheelchair or bed restricted.

Ultimately, the victim becomes incapable of movement,
although mental powers often remain intact . . . leaving the individual with the unfortunate fate of being fully aware but
trapped within an immobile body.

Mortality in IPD patients usually results from unrelated
causes such as myocardial infarction, pneumonia, or pulmonary
or gastrointestinal carcinoma.

* * *

It was in September, 1992, after pretending for a year that his growing malaise was only a minor controllable affliction, that Morty was for the first time confronted with the uncontrollable. He learned that his growing tremor, fatigue and stiffness were unquestionably symptoms of Parkinson's disease.

Six years later, in 1988, he would set part of the story down, in a document intended to be at once a chronicle of his miracle, and a selling piece for his miracle cure.

It began in the summer of 1981. I was running a part-time practice and had a weekly confrontation TV show. I was healthy, happy and comfortable, but one day while sitting at my desk I noticed a slight but persistent tremor in my left leg.

I found I could stop it by concentrating on it, but as my attention drifted away to other things it would gradually return. I did not pay too much attention, but it worsened over the next few weeks and then I noticed I was developing a slight shuffle in my walk.

I dug out the medical books and decided I was either developing the early symptoms of Parkinson's disease or I had a so-called essential tremor, a shakiness which can affect men and women in their productive years and which responds beautifully to a drug called Inderal.

I tried the Inderal but it had no effect whatsoever, and I felt some slight depression for Parkinson's is a miserable disease.

The disease had already made inroads; by the time the symptoms of Parkinsonism manifest, 85 per cent of the midbrain has already been damaged.

But you couldn't have told it by looking at Morty. He was still raking them across the coals in his *Toronto Sun* column; his rasping staccato attack-pup mien was still a familiar sight across the land on his nationally syndicated *The Shulman File.*

His symptoms were still barely visible, the heightened erratic movement merely an exaggeration of the discoordination he had had since childhood. Only his family, the closest inner circle, knew the truth.

In 1817 [Morty wrote later], in his famous *Essay on Shaking Palsy,* James Parkinson, a London doctor, first described the three characteristic symptoms of the disease: tremor, rigidity and poverty of movement. The tremor is present at rest and disappears with activity; the rigidity makes it difficult to initiate voluntary movements; and the poverty of movement shows itself by the striking absence of normal motion including swinging of the arms when walking, varying facial expressions and the normal fidgety actions all of us have.

The disease is intractable and gradually gets worse as the years pass and ends with the patient being almost totally immobile and dying of pneumonia or other complications of immobility. There is a very high suicide rate among Parkinson's patients due to the depression that accompanies it.

In September, 1982, Morty's internist, Dr. Leslie Goldenburg, confirmed his worst fear: the diagnosis was Parkinson's. Dr. Tony Lang, a neurologist and a leading Parkinson's authority at Toronto Western Hospital, started Morty on the standard therapy: levadopa and bromocriptine.

Within a few days my symptoms settled down and I returned to apparent good health. "Apparent" is the operative word, for while levadopa masks the symptoms of Parkinson's, the disease progresses inexorably even when the patient is feeling well.

---

* * *

In 1983, Morty had thrown himself into the launching of his very first mutual fund: the Guardian–Morton Shulman Precious Metals Fund, scrambling around playing bluff and counter-bluff with underwriters, finally winning the respect of Guardian Capital's eminent Norman Short.

The fund wound up breaking almost even for the investors, and leaving Morty with a quarter of a million dollars in legal fees. It petered out into White Knight Acquisitions, with Al Friedberg as partner. The venture lacked Morty's usual Midas touch.

That year he also quit *The Shulman File*. The official story was that after seven years the still-popular show had run its course; that Moses Znaimer, owner of City TV, had dug in his heels against raising his star's fee.

But Morty's friends were noticing something was wrong: the increasing stoop, the shuffle, the frailty and most of all, the growing listlessness. Morty too tired to finish a hand of bridge? What was going on?

He and Gloria doggedly kept up the pace of social life, but when they gave dinner parties Morty would eat early, by himself: the growing tremor was too evident. Or they would carefully map a menu that didn't include certain things. Never soup: his hand shook too much to get the spoon safely to his lips.

There was the early success, then the inevitable failure of the standard levadopa medication. By 1986 Morty was giving himself 10 times the normal dose but it had simply ceased to work. His body was shutting down.

The disease came back with a vengeance. It was worse than it was before. I was treating myself, trying all the minor drugs.

In the spring of 1987 I began to shake again, and over a period of a few weeks developed rigidity, sudden freezing of

---

126

motion and an inability to initiate voluntary movements that manifested itself most severely in bed. By the beginning of June I could not get out of bed without assistance. I had to use a cane around the house.

I had trouble walking, I couldn't get out of bed, couldn't turn over in bed. I had bars built outside the bed so I could reach up and pull myself up.

My wife had bars installed on the sides of the bed and the bath tub so I could pull myself out. My handwriting became difficult and I developed the unpleasant symptom of drooling.

It was a nightmare. My hands were curled back, like this. I just shuffled.

With l-dopa you have to layer more and more but eventually no matter how much you take it doesn't affect it. I went from 100 milligrams a day to 1,000, and I was getting no result.

Five years after his diagnosis, he is immobilized. Everyone believes it is, at last, game over for the unsinkable Morty.

By June of 1987, the man who once proclaimed he could never see suicide as an option for anyone of sound mind, is seriously contemplating his own.

It is at this point that Dr. Tony Lang tells him about a relatively long shot: a Hungarian medication called Eldepryl — better known by its generic name, deprenyl — that has had a long period of respectably successful use in Europe. If Morty could lay hands on some. . . .

His long-time buddy, travelling companion and investing partner, developer Sam Sarick, is in Europe on a wine tour. Morty phones him. The same day, Sarick manages to wangle 100 Eldepryl tablets from a chemist in London, saying he forgot to bring his prescription from Canada.

Three mornings later, Morty is taking his first dose of Eldepryl.

What happens next has varied from telling to telling. Sometimes it happens in an hour, sometimes half a day, sometimes two days.

Eldepryl's dose is five milligrams, taken with breakfast for the first few days and then taken twice daily with breakfast and lunch. I took my first tablet the morning after I received them.

It was like a miracle. By noon [Morty had said in an earlier interview it had taken 12 hours] my tremor had gone as had all the other symptoms and I felt a rush of energy as thought 10 years had been added to my life. By the end of the day my secretary Ann said to me, "You are working me too hard — I liked you better the other way!"

I have remained well ever since and basically returned to the state of health I had before I developed my first symptoms of Parkinson's!

But not only does Eldepryl turns his symptoms around. Not only can Morty miraculously rise from his coffin of rigidity and walk. Talk. Eat normally. With Eldepryl he can not only do everything as he had before, but one thing even better.

I am not sure how to put it delicately, but my interest in libidinous activity increased enormously, as did my ability to carry out my desires.

My wife was quite amazed and what had been a twice-weekly activity became and has remained a daily delight!

A Morty Shulman does not merely come back from the dead. He rises from the ashes better than ever. As Supermorty.

---

* * *

And so begins Morty's Deprenyl caper. It starts out as terrific fun, almost enough fun to make Parkinson's seem jolly.

This time, I even surprised myself. In my wildest dreams I never thought of running a company, any kind of company. Who the hell thought I'd be running a drug company? A drug company that ends up with 50 employees, another 20 on the road, all these responsibilities. What do I know about drugs?

I took all my staff away with me, the whole damn company, to Barbados last November. I find it very hard to act like a boss! I find it hard to treat them the way a boss is supposed to treat his employees. Maybe this is the way a boss is supposed to and I'm just a century ahead of my time. I have seven girls working in this company and they all love me, and it's just wonderful, I love coming to the office.

"Why have Parkinson's if you can't make a buck from it?" he cracks to one of his many new associates, the controlled outrageous quip as usual reflecting exactly what everyone expects him to say, the image exactly the one he wants you to see: it's the self-same old-time youbetcha cocksure maddening up-your-nose old Morty!

Never the drooling, stiffening Stage 4 Parkinson's casualty, atrophying powerlessly in the cage of his ruined body. Against all the odds Morty is flowering, when by rights he should be spinning his shroud. Turning The End into The Beginning-over. Going from fatality, to pharmaceuticals pasha.

This is Morton Shulman hurling himself off the highest precipice, slamming himself against the biggest door of all. In the outraged mesmerized contemplation of that, the world could forget, and Morty could push deep into a dark corner, the reality of the fate he was holding an arm's length away.

It's said those who make the most effective stock market players come from outside — the street, or at least not from business school, which decreases risk-taking nerve. The real geniuses have dealing in their blood. The best are those who do it as though they have nothing to lose.

Who else but such a one would have jumped into the pharmaceuticals game this way? And gotten so far, so fast?

My feelings of elation rapidly turned to anger as I thought of the thousands of people in this country who also could be helped if the drug were only available. I sent off a nasty letter to Federal Health Minister Jake Epp asking, "Why is Eldepryl not allowed to be sold in this country? Does one have to be either rich or influential to receive proper treatment for Parkinson's disease?"

My angry letter received a gentle answer from the minister, who said that he would be delighted if Eldepryl was available in Canada, but no one had applied for permission to sell it.

Quite amazed, I phoned Eldepryl's manufacturer, Chinoin Pharmaceuticals and Chemical Works in Budapest, and asked who held the Canadian rights. I was informed North American rights were held by Somerset Pharmaceuticals of New York.

It takes six weeks to track down Somerset in Denville, New Jersey and tickle their interest in a share purchase over the phone. Less than a week later, Morty is flying and limo-ing to Somerset, 40 miles north of Newark, with his faithful accountant brother-in-law Shier Bossin and two fellow bridge players: broker Harold Unrot, who thinks his firm might go for an underwriting; and, for a second opinion, Alex Rudnick, another GP. The date is August 14, 1987.

We were greeted by the Somerset president, Taylor Maxwell and the chairman, Don Buyske, who had acquired the rights to Eldepryl and several other drugs from Chinoin.

Chinoin is a huge 100-year-old drug company with 6,000 employees and 700 people working full time on research. Its products have never had a market in North America and the officials of the company were delighted to give Johnson's Wax, in the person of Buyske, the right to market its drugs.

Somerset, dirt-poor after nearly eight years of clinical trials and attempts to get the FDA nod for Eldepryl, is trying to raise cash by offering to sell 15 per cent of its shares. The German pharmaceuticals giant, DeGussa, is the favored contender, but Morty is invited to make his pitch to a Somerset board meeting two weeks later.

On August 18, back he flies, this time on his own.

Morty offers U.S. $1.4 million against DeGussa's $1 million, but he senses that Kurt Johnson, son of the company's eccentric founder Sam Johnson, and Art DelVesco, Johnson's moneyman, do not like the cut of Morty's jib. They tell him they intend to offer DeGussa first refusal at Morty's price — a charming method of having it both ways. They may, however, be open to offering Morty Canadian rights to Eldepryl.

I flew back to Toronto very depressed. The following Tuesday, September 1st, Maxwell phoned me to say, "Congratulations. DeGussa asked for a week's extension so their board could meet but we had given our word and you have bought all the stock."

A few days later Taylor Maxwell, his lawyer Nan Mantell and director Peter Howsam flew to Toronto to collect my cheque for U.S. $1.4 million, in payment for 1,562 shares of Somerset.

Morty jubilantly sets up Deprenyl Research Limited. For another $1 million plus 600,000 shares of Deprenyl Research and warrants for another 300,000 shares, Morty also buys the 20-year rights to distribute Eldepryl in Canada — to humans.

(Later still, he will experience a middle-of-the-night brainwave about Eldepryl and animals that will waken Gloria with a jolt, not to mention the investment communities in two countries. But that is still a year away.)

Morty's lawyer for the Somerset negotiations late in 1987 is Jacqueline Le Saux of McCarthy Tetrault. Le Saux was the assistant to the lawyer who set up White Knight Acquisitions Inc. which Morty, with the fine insouciant madness of a freshly besotted lover ditching an old flame, now describes as "a failure and a debacle."

And so, on this September day in 1987, within three months of first taking his miracle drug, Morty has set up his very own pharmaceuticals company.

The board of directors is to be Morty as chairman, son Geoffrey as president, reliable son-in-law Stewart Saxe as secretary-treasurer. His underwriter Wood Gundy will be represented by David Kassie and John Plaxton, and there will be three Somerset directors: Don Buyske, Peter Howsam and Joe Castelli.

First, of course, he must come up with that U.S. $1.4 million.

In the 10 days since Maxwell's call telling me the good news I had been working like mad to raise the money.

I incorporated a new company, Shulman Diversified, and sold 30 units at $50,000 U.S. each, with each unit rep-

resenting two shares of stock. The purchasers ranged all the
way from my secretary Ann Worobec, who bought one unit,
to Andy Sarlos who bought four. Investors included people
like Fred McCutcheon whom I phoned, and people like
Howie Beck to whom I told the tale casually at a party.

I was amazed at the people that turned me down and
declined subscriptions including my son Geoff and long-
time broker and cousin Bill Abiscott.

With the $1.5 million U.S. that I raised, I paid Somerset
for its shares. In six months each unit purchased for $50,000
U.S. turned into 48,000 shares of Deprenyl Research worth
$600,000. One year later, it was worth $2,000.000.

With huge blocks of shares disbursed amongst family, friends
and friendly brokers, Morty begins lobbying furiously on all
fronts to clear the way for Canadian distribution. The first step
is to get approval from the federal health ministry to provide
Eldepryl on a compassionate basis.

This permits physicians to prescribe a medication which has
not gone through the formal clinical trials and health approvals
process in Canada; to patients for whom it may be considered a
last resort — for whom other drugs are not, or have ceased to
be, effective. Hence the official name of government program
that permits this — the Emergency Drug Plan.

Meanwhile, Morty files an application starting the process of
gaining federal Health Protection Branch approval, allowing doctors to prescribe Eldepryl as a recognized Parkinson's treatment.

Morty also begins the process of having the drug included
in the Ontario Drug Benefit Formulary, which would allow pro-
vision of Eldepryl free to pensioners and people on welfare.

He hires health lobbyist Ivan Fleischmann and gives him
10,000 warrants to buy stock at $3. Against all odds, the compas-
sionate approval which can take years to acquire, is bestowed
on Eldepryl by the HPB in February, 1988.

In the next year, pushing for full approval, Morty will fire off enough letters to health officialdom at the federal and provincial levels, to make the post office and the paper industry profitable for years.

One notable exchange in November, 1988 is with Ontario's deputy minister of health, who has had the undeflectable Morty fobbed off on him by beleaguered health minister Elinor Caplan. The deputy minister who is assigned to smooth Morty's bristling hackles is a brilliant newcomer to the civil service named Dr. Martin Barkin.

If anybody had told Martin Barkin that in barely two and a half years Morty would be his boss, he would have sent the witless forecaster packing.

His symptoms almost masked, Morty is once again in control of the face he presents to the world, so successfully that everyone concentrates on rage or wonder, and not on the link between the Deprenyl stock push and Morty's fight for his own life — which is the last thing Morty wants them to see, unless it somehow helps sell stocks.

* * *

The drug that Morty says will change the world was smuggled into England, fought for in the U.S., and was at the end of a long, arduous haul into North America when Morty pitched onto the scene.

It was the product of the unlikeliest confluences, the wildest combination of searchers and scientists. Among them was an ex-German army doctor who may have been SS; a concentration camp survivor; Israeli and Palestinian biochemists; the hoarders and the trackers of the Hungarian crown jewels; an eccentric heir to a floor-wax fortune; not to mention Dr. Morty.

These were only a handful out of the starting gate. Before the deprenyl loaf has finished rising, who knows who else will have carved a slice?

The deprenyl story, which Morty calls "a romance," started 30 years ago in Budapest.

Deprenyl was first synthesized as an anti-depressant by a Hungarian team headed by an ambitious young world-beater and concentration-camp survivor named Joseph Knoll.

Deprenyl proceeds through an exotic growing up: it was first used, without a great deal of success, in Soviet psychiatric wards before its potential to combat Parkinson's is stumbled upon simultaneously by doctors at opposite ends of the world.

The shortcomings of the 1970 anti-Parkinson's breakthrough drug levadopa had become evident. L-dopa ceases to work after a period of time: sometimes months, sometimes years. Users counter by upping the dose. But high doses or prolonged use commonly produce a nightmare gallery of side effects: severe nausea, confusion that can mount to psychiatric proportion, and involuntary writhing that intensifies the hurdy-gurdy of twitchings caused by the disease itself.

In 1977, Walter Birkmayer, an eminent Vienna neurologist with a World War II German army past, reports a healthy delay in the onset of symptoms, in patients treated with both Eldepryl and l-dopa.

In 1982, William Langston, a physician in California's drug-dazed Silicon Valley, finds a slew of drug-takers in their early 20s turning up with the symptoms of advanced Parkinson's. All are discovered to be taking a synthesized heroin containing an agent which is converted in the body to a brain cell killing poison — attacking the same area of the brain murdered by Parkinson's.

This prompts Langston to set up a small clinical trial with Parkinson's patients, using deprenyl to inhibit the MAO that produces that brain-destroying poison. At the same time, Birkmayer is discovering that patients on deprenyl plus l-dopa are actually living a year longer than those on l-dopa alone.

The results on both sides of the globe prompt a dazzling possibility; maybe deprenyl could actually block the progress of Parkinson's disease.

Turn the clock back to the late 1960s and '70s when Don Buyske, a tall rambunctious and enterprising U.S. pharmaceuticals researcher, then with Warner Lambert, is doing what a great many of his hip capitalist confreres are doing: trolling through the Iron Curtain countries, looking for new drugs that can be snapped up for a song from the Reds.

Buyske has met Hungarian chemist Joseph Knoll, tried to cop U.S. rights to market deprenyl for depression, but is meeting distressing resistance from the Chinoin, which is Hungarian state-run. But then the tireless Buyske manages to win himself special status by helping the Hungarians get back their crown jewels which were spirited out of Budapest at the end of World War II by free-enterprise-loving U.S. soldiers eager to keep them out of the hands of their allies, the too-swiftly-advancing Soviets.

Buyske lends his support to a Hungarian lobby in the U.S. that persuades his government to return the royal stash, secreted at Fort Knox since World War II, and comprising such priceless twinklies as the 1,000-year-old crown of St. Stephen. This act of goodwill earns Buyske and his new employer, Johnson's Wax, the North American rights to deprenyl.

Johnson's spins off Somerset Pharmaceuticals to handle the Chinoin drug rights. But what to do with them?

In 1986, after the initial Birkmayer-Langston findings, there is enough interest in the drug as a Parkinson's treatment to fund a formal 54-patient trial by Langston, as well as an enormous 800-patient study at a cost of $10 million, in 28 different centres, called DATATOP, funded by the U.S. Government.

These results will not be published until 1989. But in the meantime there is another intoxicating buzz about versatile little deprenyl.

Joseph Knoll, now approaching 60 and pharmacology chief at Semmelweis University in Budapest, suggests you don't have to be sick or dying to benefit from deprenyl. Healthy seniors can add a glow to their declining years by taking daily doses of the stuff. He does so himself. And he produces extensive lab studies that show a significant increase in the lifespan and sexual abilities of rats.

Major U.S. researchers are admitting they are impressed with Knoll's data on rats. Buyske is off and flying. The Parkinson's market is nice, but not enormous. But the market for de-aging and potency . . .

All this is percolating away when Morty arrives serendipitously on the scene, in the summer of 1987.

* * *

It is February, 1988.

With permission to sell Eldepryl on a compassionate basis, Morty sets up shop in his basement, hiring a friendly broker's girlfriend to help out.

After a protracted legal set-to and the heated exchange of another forest's worth of paper with the Ontario Securities Commission — whom he accuses of "acting like we had applied for a licence to sell cocaine instead of a treatment for Parkinson's disease" — the SEC has at last approved the Deprenyl Research Ltd. prospectus. The stock begins trading on the Toronto Stock Exchange and on NASDAQ, the American over-the-counter exchange.

Only now does Morty go public with the story of his affliction, to coincide with the issue of the stock. The painful details appear as a backdrop, a springboard for promoting the wondrousness of the drug behind the stock. The last thing he wishes to be seen as is a victim.

He sallies forth to sell his miracle to the media.

Deprenyl seems to reverse the degenerative Parkinson's process! Retards it. In my case my wife is convinced it's caused regression of the disease. It's certainly caused my symptoms to disappear. Before I took it I had to go to bed at 4 o'clock every day.

I'm better now than I was a year ago. It's cumulative. It's affected my energy level, my ability to travel, go out, make love. It's quite amazing!

If I had taken it when my Parkinson's started five years ago, I'd be a hell of a lot healthier than I am today. A hell of a lot younger than I am today. I got it late.

You know that a study of 10,000 U.S. Parkinson's sufferers taking deprenyl over five years shows three died, all of them by drowning. What's happened is they've just felt so good — they just went out and did things that they normally wouldn't have.

The first sympathetic story breaks in the business section of the normally hardboiled *Globe & Mail*. It strikes exactly the notes Morty would wish: the right semitones of sympathy, courage, sobriety, derring-do and a well-rounded profile of the drug product's properties:

MORTY TURNS ADVERSITY INTO A NEW ENTERPRISE
Philosophically, it would be incorrect to say Morton Shulman is a victim of Parkinson's disease, although that is the correct medical diagnosis.

Indeed, he has suffered on and off with the disease over the past six years and last spring he appeared seriously ill. But, since then, he has turned the tables on his illness, making it the springboard for yet another addition to his long list of enterprises. . . .

The newspaper goes on to lay the cornerstone for another chunk of the deprenyl legend:

Deprenyl Research then launched an initial public offering of 2.6 million common shares at $3 a share. The issue was underwritten by Wood Gundy Inc., which took 200,000 warrants to buy Deprenyl shares as part payment for its underwriting services. John Plaxton, senior vice president at Wood Gundy, and vice-president David Kassie are on the board of Deprenyl Research, as representatives of the underwriter.

The share issue is a tiny one compared with those normally undertaken by Gundy. And it couldn't have come at a worse time from a marketing perspective — investors are simply not interested in new equities after the Oct. 19, 1987 global market crash, and almost none are being underwritten. . . . Somewhat to the underwriter's surprise, the issue was oversubscribed...

Meanwhile the doctor who inspired the creation of *Wojeck* (currently in reruns) is looking forward to next summer. That's when a final updated episode of the 20-year-old series is scheduled to be shot, and the indefatigable Dr. Shulman says he has been promised a cameo role.

* * *

Do your cockles warm at the camaraderie, loyalty, the bonds stronger than Krazy Glue a new market venture forges? The ties of honor and fealty and common purpose that make the stock market go?

But ah, what a merry dance the partners are leading each other behind the scenes, while Virginia-reeling and smiling to each other's faces. Let us lift the veil on the worthy market players doing the backstage do-se-do to their corners all.

This is the postscript Morty writes to the chronicle of his first year:

When I originally set up Deprenyl, 200,000 warrants at $3 were allotted to Wood Gundy and 100,000 to each member of the board of directors. Art DelVesco said that he did not want Somerset's three representatives to get warrants and insisted that those 300,000 be assigned to Somerset.

Shortly before the issue was to come out John Plaxton called me saying that it was unpolitic for David Kassie and himself as directors of Wood Gundy to accept any warrants, and what he wanted me to do was to put their 200,000 in my name, "and somewhere down the road I'm sure that you'll have the opportunity to do David and me a favor."

Thus, when the issue finally came out, there were 300,000 warrants in my name, an equal amount in Somerset, 200,000 in Wood Gundy and 100,000 each to Geoff Shulman and Stewart Saxe.

When the stock got to $8, Wood Gundy began to short it, using its holdings in the warrants as a base. They sold 120,000 shares in this way and ultimately exercised the warrants to cover their short position. Until they actually exercised the warrants they did not inform me of what they were doing and I could not imagine where all the stock was coming from.

When I discovered what they were doing I felt aggrieved but I had given my word about Plaxton's and Kassie's warrants and was not about to break it.

Then providence struck in the form of Paul Parisotto, a bureaucrat at the Toronto Stock Exchange who called to tell me that because Deprenyl had applied for a TSE listing I would have to reduce my holding of warrants to 100,000 as this was the maximum allowed — I could either exercise them or cancel them.

By coincidence, the next night Wood Gundy was holding a dinner for the lawyers and clerks who had worked on the Deprenyl issue. Everyone got up to say a few nice words, and the Wood Gundy executives were waiting with some apprehension for my brief speech. It went as follows:

> I want to thank Wood Gundy for the wonderful job
> they have done. Without them I do not know how
> we would have sold the stock. Their efforts in that

140

direction were certainly unique. As for the aftermarket I am delighted to say that Deprenyl is now $8, and without Wood Gundy's efforts in the aftermarket I am sure it would not be at that level.

It is a pleasure to deal with people that are open and honest with you at all times and in appreciation for all you have done I have a gift here for you. As you all know, I was assigned 300,000 warrants in this issue and I am hereby donating back 200,000 of them to David Kassie and John Plaxton, or if they do not wish them, to Wood Gundy. The warrants have a value now of $1 million.

I handed an envelope containing a transfer agreement to John Plaxton, and sat down. He opened it and read the offer of transfer which was followed by, "In view of the fact that Wood Gundy requested that the shares I originally bought be put in escrow for one year I am making the same condition with these warrants. The TSE insists that they be exercised right away, so if you will send us your $600,000, we will send you the shares in one year."

John Plaxton looked like he had been kicked in the stomach, but what could he do? The next day he notified me that Wood Gundy was abandoning all claim to the warrants.

I then called my buddy, Willy Lebovic who, when the original issue had failed to sell, had helped me out by purchasing 150,000 shares at $3 on which he had made one million dollars' profit. I offered Willy the Wood Gundy options on the same terms I had offered them to Plaxton, with the proviso that I would release the escrow if at any point the market could handle the sale of the stock.

Willy accepted, and three days later the stock rose to $11 in heavy volume, and in my opinion it was the appropriate time to release the escrow. Willy sold 120,000 of the 200,000 shares and gave half the profit back to me. It amounted to approximately half a million dollars, and I used the money to set up the Parkinson's Charitable Trust.

The 300,000 warrants given to Somerset proved an unexpected bonus to them, and they were delighted to see that Deprenyl within days was trading at $6. They were happy to sell the warrants for $900,000; one-third of them were taken by Al Friedberg and the balance by White Knight Acquisitions. Within weeks the $900,000 investment was worth $3 million.

Four years later, the memory of it will warm one of Morty's darkest hours.

Ah, the Parkinson's Trust which I set up and which made millions of dollars, all because these guys are so damned greedy!

Jacqueline Le Saux was at the Wood Gundy dinner. It was a classic, most unique dinner which was given in our honor, supposedly, celebrating the success of the venture — and all this was going on at it. Jacqueline said it was the most weird thing she'd ever seen. People rushing off in corners of the room and all this whispering going on. She couldn't understand it.

And at the end of it Kassie and Plaxton: "We're not going to put up any $600,000 to redeem the warrants. You can have the damned things."

He backed it so strongly in the initial underwriting because, well, he backed it at $3 but he sure wasn't going to back it at $6! At $3 it's an interesting gamble, but the thing was now up to $6 or $8 or $10 or something. And his company was busy shorting it.

Oh, Plaxton's done underwriting for me since. Sure, he would be a couple of million bucks richer today. But he's got lots of money.

---

* * *

Meanwhile, in this autumn of its first year, Deprenyl, like the leaves, is turning to gold.

The orders pour in. The pills begin streaming out of the Roncesvalles basement. The rest of the business press jumps all over Deprenyl Research. The first *Globe* story will be the last friendly story for a long, long time.

Oh how the media tone sprouts fangs; how sharper than a serpent's tooth doth the press attitude grow. Typical is Bud Jorgensen of the *Globe*, in his "Street Talk" column, foaming at whatever moon madness might be that was packing would-be investors into the big stolid TSE auditorium to hear the Morty the Mouthmeister spin his dreams:

> Deprenyl drinks from the fountain of youth
> After pondering at length the extraordinary rise in the share price of Deprenyl Research, the drug stock being promoted by Morton Shulman, the conclusion can only be that he is selling the fountain of youth. How else is one to explain that Dr. Shulman is able to attract such a large crowd of brokers to listen to his pitch.

By this time, the market value of Deprenyl stock is about $50 million "on a fully diluted basis." Having gone public at $3 the stock is now $10.

Jorgensen snipes away at the lack of federal health ministry approval for the drug, Morty's blithe implication that the health minister himself has intervened to sweep the approval process through, and the dazzling promise Morty is holding out to the planet:

> Deprenyl has hoops to go through before getting full approval from government agencies in Canada and the United States. As seen by Dr. Shulman, however,

---

approval by the HPB is a minor detail. In his scenario Eldepryl will, over the next five years, be used to treat Parkinson's disease, as an additive to pet food, and as an additive in sunscreen lotions. . . .

There is no doubt that Dr. Shulman believes in Eldepryl but he would have done his cause more good by using a private company to do the research. As the situation now stands, however, market-makers have turned Deprenyl into a stock market game and veteran stock promoters know full well that the dream counts for more than results.

Jorgensen stays on Morty's case with short intense bazooka-bursts through the year. "Dr. Shulman," he writes in evident frustration, "has the zeal of a fundamentalist preacher when talking about deprenyl and certainly doesn't consider himself a promoter."

The fundamentalist analogy is right on: along with the evangelical zeal is a holy-roller devotion, the passion of the freshly healed true believer. Never has Morty believed so deeply in anything. They have called Morty sharpie names ever since he first appeared. In the old days it was a heady part of the game, quickening the pleasure of thumbing the nose.

But this time, for the very first time, it hurts. Morty is hurting. Every morning, in the endless hour just after he takes his 6 a.m. Eldepryl tablet, it is like climbing with great pain out of his coffin, the entrapping carapace of his body.

He believes, he believes with all his soul that now, at last, because he has put everything aside but his burning belief, they will put aside their bitter mistrust, and acclaim him for what he is.

As he says, " Eldepryl is what I am most proud of. It's my greatest achievement. It's the biggest thing I've ever done."

* * *

144

Morty's good buddy and investment confrere Andy Sarlos sums up the reaction to Morty, in a statement that perfectly characterizes the timeless, circular, insoluble conundrum of the market itself: "The problem is Morty's a promoter. He's a good promoter. Therefore he has a lack of credibility."

At 3 a.m. on August 29th, 1988 I awoke with a start and woke Gloria to say: "Eureka, I have it — the idea of my life. The market for Eldepryl in humans is small — let's sell it to the dogs!"

The next morning I outlined my idea to my associates, all of whom laughed initially and then began to look thoughtful. The idea of selling a pet food that would extend life was indeed novel. I immediately sent off letters to the presidents of seven pet food companies with my great idea and sat back waiting for the avalanche of offers. Six of them did not bother to answer at all. . . .

He will contact Ralston Purina, he will meet Dave Nichols and Galen Weston of Loblaws, he will survive a scathing article in *Business Week* and convince Ralston Purina to take a six-month option. He will acquire rights to market deprenyl for animals in all the Americas — north, south and central.

Now Jorgensen reports "the doggonedest rumor floating around about Deprenyl Research, after trading in Deprenyl "was halted yesterday and an announcement was scheduled to be made today." The week before the stock had gained $2.50 to $13.25 on a volume of 580,000 shares.

When Jorgensen confronts Morty with the doggone rumor — namely that deprenyl is being sold to a pet food company to prolong canine life — "Dr. Shulman's only comment was: "That's an interesting story."

In fact, Morty has quietly contracted a team of researchers from the University of Toronto, Dr. N. William Milgram and Dr.

Gwen O. Ivy, to replicate the study by deprenyl inventor Dr. Joseph Knoll that demonstrated statistically increased life expectancy in laboratory rats.

The stock continues to leap peakwards like a mountain goat.

He takes his fight for a TSE listing public. Fuming that the exchange has been pulling a dastardly stall he writes a penultimate steaming letter "withdrawing my application. I spurn the TSE."

Listing proved to be a major obstacle for reasons that had little or nothing to do with Deprenyl. We routinely put in our application for listing in Toronto and Montreal but the bureaucrats at each exchange were determined to humble me. At the same time as my application was entered in Toronto, there were two other applications put in: Lake Panask, a mining prospect in the Northwest Territories which quickly ran through the few dollars it had and is now insolvent, and Health Care, which was losing money rapidly and continued to do so. Although these two turkeys were listed routinely, Deprenyl was put through the hoops although we made money from the first day.

One routine objection was raised after another. Finally, Paul Parisotto informed me I had broken the law by breaching a section in the Ontario Securities Act which made it illegal to say a stock exchange application had been applied for. I had written that particular paragraph into the Securities Act 19 years earlier! . . to prevent the promoters of worthless stock from using a TSE application as a method of selling stock! In a fit of pique I withdrew the application entirely.

Even those brokers and fund managers who would follow him almost anywhere are begging him to cool it. Morty does know when it is time for retrenchment.

146

He writes a fulsome apology to the TSE's Paul Parisotto for "my part in the public imbroglio in which we became involved." The TSE graciously agrees to reconsider when Deprenyl has received full approval from the ministry of health.

Meanwhile, he insists he is perfectly happy to operate sans Exchange, since he has now learned a listing would mean Deprenyl Research's tax rate would jump from 25 per cent to 46 per cent.

By now all manner of dreampeddlers are lining up for Morty's attention.

Impotence cream? Toronto investment fund manager Dr. Morton Shulman says he wanted a sample to have it tested before he would consider putting money into Windsor-based Capsule Technology Group Inc. . . The cream was turned down when an employee reports, "it doesn't work and it tastes terrible".

At the end of the year Deprenyl Research has had a wild-mouse-ride on the market rails, hurtling to a $15 high, dropping to $8 when the TSE listing got stalled. Morty tracks his baby stock's behavior like a parent obsessed.

The stock was a rollercoaster from day one. It moved up steadily from its initial $5 trading level to reach $9 1/2 by the end of March. That day there was a raid apparently precipitated by the dumping of stock by Wood Gundy's trader, who began selling thousands of shares against their option. In a matter of minutes the stock fell to $6 1/2 and then slowly recovered to close at $7 3/4. . . . At the beginning of June it reached a high of $15 3/8 and then fell all the way back to $9 7/8. On two occasions the stock plunged as a result of panic among small stock holders. On each occasion this took place as a result of a misquote appearing in the press. As I write on September 24, 1988, it is at $11 1/4. . . .

The *Financial Times* runs a story headlined "Shut up, Morty"! He is "a hypester extraordinaire" who, "true to form, hyped the hell out of the stock, touting not only Eldepryl's benefits to Parkinson's patients, but the possibility that the drug might also have applications for Alzheimer's disease, that it might result in increased longevity in humans and pets, that there was evidence that it improved sexual potency."

To the charge that Deprenyl is just another way for him to make a buck, Morty angrily tells the *Times* he is "not making a penny out of it, doesn't draw a salary as the company's chairman, and has signed the 75,000 shares he holds outright over to Toronto Western Hospital's Movement Disorders Clinic."

"The stock is held basically by my friends, my family. My people are being hurt. I'm not in it for personal gain. I'm bringing help to people. What are they going to accuse me of? Playing God?"

Playing God? Who, Morty?

Morty also announces that men in Italy get Eldepryl prescriptions solely to boost sexual prowess.

With the brave candor that is the mark of a genius promoter Morty admits: "On the face of it, it sounds like snake oil. I can perfectly understand someone ribbing me about it. So why do it? Because it's right and it's true."

By the end of 1988 he can report first-time profits of $14,600 gross, before interest and income taxes, on sales of $60,500. He happily projects $18 million annual sales.

Meanwhile, Deprenyl has increased its stake in Somerset from 15 per cent to 29 per cent, and has a seat on Somerset's board. Morty would love to snap up the whole of Somerset, but instead the company strikes a formal agreement with Bolar and Mylan Pharmaceuticals.

And while pressing for full drug approval from the federal and provincial health authorities, Morty is shipping hundreds of pills a week on compassionate requests from physicians, out of cartons piling up in the rooms of the old Roncesvalles house, making a healthy mark-up on each pill, which he imports from Hungary for about six cents apiece.

But he is chafing at the thick cloud of disapproval and even deliberate misunderstanding he feels wafting from the media and the market. He is, he points out, also supplying the medication free of charge to patients who can't afford it; and pledging all his personal profits from trading company shares to the movement disorders clinic at Toronto Western Hospital.

In 1989, two years after first taking Eldepryl himself, a year after taking Deprenyl Research public, Morty is strutting and thriving and praising his savior drug as a modern miracle.

This is a major turning point in medicine, just as sulfa was in its field. This is a major turning point in controlling CNS disorders.

This is just the first drug in a series; this is just opening the gate. We may have found one time clock and turned it off. . . . The societal implications of this could be major. It could play hell with pension funds for instance. What if we're saving the aging population? That's a whole new ball game.

He has parlayed the Hungarian medication he wrestled into distribution in Canada into a pharmaceuticals company worth $40 million. Before he is done it will be valued at more than double that amount. The Parkinson's Foundation, initially up in arms, finds it is now willing to be soothed with an allocation of $5 million in Deprenyl Research shares. Why the change of heart?

Now, after all the years of struggle with the FDA and eight years of testing, the results of two major North American deprenyl studies are announced, to considerable medical excitement, in the last quarter of 1989.

In August, 1989, Bill Langston and his co-researcher James Tetrud report on their 54-patient study, which shows Eldepryl is "effective in actually slowing the disease, not just alleviating symptoms." By the end of August Deprenyl stock has zoomed up to $15.50.

In November, the big DATATOP study weighs in, to show the drug "dramatically slows the progression of Parkinson's in its early-stage." Deprenyl enhances the effects of l-dopa without the necessity for increasing l-dopa dosage: a major plus, in view of levadopa side effects, which can include psychiatric problems. "We're ecstatic. We're very delighted," says Morty's neurologist, Dr. Tony Lang, who is Canadian co-ordinator of the study. "We now have clear and powerful evidence that Eldepryl delays Parkinson's disease."

Patients on Eldepryl are reported to be free of serious symptoms almost a year longer than those who were on placebo. DATATOP establishes Eldepryl in North America as a breakthrough Parkinson's treatment that slows the debilitating progress of the disease.

But does this vindicate Morty, does it enshrine him as the hero he longs to be? Alas, no.

Morty can't stop citing all the more tantalizing and seemingly outrageous properties.

What is this thing called deprenyl? Everything from a Parkinson's miracle to a solution to aging, Morty claims.

What is this thing called deprenyl? Several company players and friends are taking it to boost libido.

Morty has bounced back, outraging everyone.

While Morty Shulman the Parkinson's patient uses Eldepryl to fight for his life, the world only sees Morty the promoter flogging his company's stock. No large drug company, let alone a one-man operation such as Morty's, has ever bulldozed its way into viable existence so quickly.

Deprenyl shares zip up to $17.38. Morty crows: "There's a $100-million market out there. If we only get half of it, that's $50 million."

In January 1990, he finally gets HPB sanction. They approve deprenyl for prescription in late-stage Parkinson's.

And March 1990 sees publication of *The Deprenyl Story*, by Morty's old buddy, business writer Alastair Dow. The cover blurb sings: "It is being hailed as a wonder drug, as a key to fighting the debilitating effects of Parkinson's, Alzheimer's and other diseases of the brain. Yet for years, patients in North America were denied access to this revolutionary treatment. Now the story can be told: of the scientific breakthrough that brought this new drug, the obstacles that kept if from those who needed it most and the hope it holds for millions."

In July, Deprenyl Animal Health Inc. — DAHI — is established "as a development- stage veterinary pharmaceuticals company . . . for the use of Anipryl in companion animals, first in dogs." Morty links up with a go-getting Kansas veterinary entrepreneur named Dave Stevens, who is pleased to announce, "The University of Toronto animal research team Drs. Milgram and Ivy have completed their rat-life studies in 1990, and the results, in part, have now been published. Although the Toronto scientists did not achieve the same degree of life expectancy as did Dr. Knoll, they did report a statistically significant difference."

Deprenyl first-quarter revenues for 1990 have outpaced total sales for all of 1989.

New president Jim Doherty, hired from the vice presidency of Connaught BioSciences, tells the annual meeting, "We have firmly rooted Deprenyl in the Canadian pharmaceutical marketplace. And 1990 looks like another good year." Shares close at $20.25; the high that month was $21.13. Investment income and a gain of $3.4 million from selling Deprenyl's stake in Somerset boost net income to $3.1 million.

Roger Odette, the ex-Dupont Pharmaceuticals executive who is Deprenyl Research's new deputy vice-president of marketing, says Deprenyl "will continue its strategy of purchasing the Canadian rights to drugs developed by foreign pharmaceutical firms, keeping the company's own research costs to a minimum." That month Deprenyl spreads its wings to purchase exclusive right to distribute Propola, a companion drug to Eldepryl, from Hoffmann-LaRoche Can.

And Baker Cummins Pharmaceuticals, wholly owned subsidiary of a company called IVAX which will figure large in Deprenyl's near future, sells Deprenyl Canadian rights to its sleeping medication Doral for $700,000 plus Deprenyl common shares. The drug is not yet approved for use in Canada.

Morty owns a total of 11 per cent of the company. Chinoin owns 10 per cent. Morty announces he is donating 10 per cent of his Deprenyl profits to Toronto Western Hospital's Movement Disorders Centre.

In November, Deprenyl is hailed in the Hollywood, *Florida Life Extension Report*, which bills itself as "the INSIDER'S report on efforts to prevent aging and rejuvenate the aging:"

NEW LIFESPAN STUDY WITH DEPRENYL
An inside report on the results of a new study on the effect on lifespan of today's most promising anti-aging therapy, and a discussion of how the FDA impedes the use of today's anti-aging therapies and the development of tomorrow's anti-aging therapies.

Other articles in this issue include "How the FDA Kills Americans", by depriving them of therapies they need to live longer, healthier lives, and by depriving them of information about these therapies. "Declaring the Right to Freedom in Healthcare: . . . endowed by their creator with certain unalienable rights . . . that among these are life, liberty and the pursuit of happiness."

And: "Declaring Independence from the FDA. Every member of the Life Extension Foundation should execute a document to declare his or her right to use any medical or health therapy of their choice. . . ."

On the establishment side, Deprenyl's potential also gets a cautiously glowing report in *The Wall Street Journal*.

And the company of players in the Deprenyl venture grow: ex-pharmaceuticals executives, entrepreneurial U.S. partners like veterinary entrepreneur Stevens; murky underwriters; a staff detective to track down the goods on folks trying to thwart the Morty machine.

By the spring of 1991, it seems the machine is going full tilt.

In March, Al Dow sticks it to the naysayers in a glowing newspaper story about Deprenyl Animal Health's plump and beauteous maiden share offering, and those who would dismiss it:

MORTY'S LATEST STOCK VENTURE IS NO DOG
Although there's been only the briefest mention of it in the newspapers, and although it's very unlikely that any stockbroker recommended it to you, the hottest stock in Canada this week was Deprenyl Animal Health Inc. Shares of DAHI (which is affectionately called Deprenyl Dog by Bay St. traders) come in a package: each package, or unit, consists of four shares and a warrant to purchase an additional share. The initial price of these units was $13.85. When the units came on the market, on Tuesday this week, the first trade was at $17.75. The units closed yesterday at $22.75. This is a truly spectacular performance. And yet, outside of the small community of stockbrokers and a few fortunate people who were able to acquire the units at the issue price of $13.85, who ever heard of Deprenyl Animal Health?"

The reason for the blank spot about Deprenyl, Al argues, is the Bay St. establishment's historic dislike for Dr. Morton Shulman by virtue of the fact that "he's smarter than your average stockbroker. So that when Morty has a conspicuous success when trading or promoting stocks and bonds, the Bay st. establishment doesn't like to acknowledge it."

Naturally, Al "discloses" his position as one of the fortunate few who got in on the initial $13.85 pre-market offering, which he sold the same day for $18. He also discloses that Dr. Shulman is "a close personal friend" — who provided the key material for *The Deprenyl Story*, his book about the fascinating deprenyl saga.

This kind of advocacy journalism by the few existing Morty-buddies is particularly disdained in the pristine business community — where business stories and analysts' reports are never, ever written at any but the longest, most rigid arm's length; where promoters never spread rumor but only crystalline gospel. . .and Santa Claus and the Easter Bunny visit Bay Street regularly . . .

* * *

July, 1991 brings the first big news of 5-ALA: Deprenyl Research is going after "a breakthrough cream to treat skin cancer that has been developed by Canadian researchers."

"It's a very significant advance," Morty is quoted. He has offered a "substantial" amount to three Canadian researchers: Dr. Jim Kennedy of Kingston Regional Cancer Centre, Dr. Roy Pottier of Kingston's Royal Military College and Dr. Michel Rinquet of Université de Québec, Trois Rivières.

The reports say the cream, called 5-ALA or simply ALA, has been used for three years to treat patients with basal cell carcinoma, a nonfatal form of skin cancer. It remains on the skin for three to six hours, and the affected skin is then exposed to RGO light.

ALA is Geoffrey's baby. Morty's good-natured little boy, after years of trying to show his dad he is a player, veering back and forth between his dermatology practice and his Deprenyl position, has brought home a big one.

It was Geoffrey, searching out a cure for warts, who stumbled on Jim Kennedy and his "miracle" treatment for basal cell skin cancer. At a McMaster University lecture in May, 1991, Geoff was transfixed by a Kennedy's lecture on the development of photodynamic therapy with the chemical called ALA.

This discovery by Kennedy, a university professor and "career scientist" biophysicist at the Ontario Cancer Treatment Research Foundation, chimed an epiphany for Geoffrey.

"He had an 80 per cent cure rate," Geoff later told a reporter. "I listened to him and I thought, this is fantastic. I stopped thinking about warts."

Geoff talked to Kennedy after the lecture, then hurried home to tell his father. Two days later, Morty and Geoff signed Kennedy to a letter of intent, beating out Connaught BioSciences by a hair, nailing down the worldwide rights in August. A furious Connaught President phoned a triumphant Geoffrey to berate him.

"The Shulmans moved very fast," Kennedy tells the press, "compared to the others." He and his Pottier had been working on the cream for a decade.

Deprenyl USA is set up in New Jersey "because our main focus for the skin cancer treatment is the U.S. market," says Geoff, "and we're better positioned to get the approval of the FDA if we're based in the U.S." It launches trials around the world: Buffalo, Boston, Leeds, Rotterdam, Oslo and two Austrian cities as well as in Canada.

In one of those significant notes for the future, it is tangentially noted that Kennedy is also experimenting with other applications of the process, with diseases "ranging from leukemia to endometriosis."

Although Canadian approvals are not in sight, a U.S. patent has been granted, and a development deal is signed with Medicis Inc., a go-ahead New York pharmaceuticals marketer. As Kennedy has noted: the Shulmans move fast.

These are the golden days. With the news of the 5-ALA acquisition, the stock takes off. On August 28 the share goes up $1.88; hits a dizzy high of $24.25. By September the Star's business section reports "millionaire Dr. Morton Shulman says his company is finally starting to get a little attention. No wonder. After neglecting Deprenyl Research since its inception in February 1988, brokerages are now looking closer as the company's fortunes soar."

In the last year the stock has zoomed 166 per cent, "easily making it one of the hottest stocks in town."

The company's profits have doubled in the last six-month period; revenue is up significantly, the stock split again a few weeks ago and the announcements for rights to drugs keep coming out. . . .

Morty feels the time is ripe to give his adversaries in the stock market establishment one in the eye. He draws up a classic, in your face, up your earhole nose-thumbing ad to run in the *Globe and Mail.* The headline is "Why are Canadian stockbrokers losers?"

> Deprenyl Research has never been recommended by a Canadian brokerage house or a Canadian analyst even though since the initial issue of Deprenyl at $3 per share, it has split 3 for 2 and multiplied 10 times! Canadian brokers prefer to recommend companies their analysts have carefully examined, companies such as Campeau, Dylex and Standard Trust.

The *Globe* refuses to run the last sentence, which contains what Morty considers his most exquisite, deathless parting shot: "As a result, Deprenyl Research Ltd. is making Canadians healthier and Americans richer."

(Morty simply repeats the line to the *Star*, which records it, along with the reminder that Deprenyl has made at least one Canadian both healthier and richer. In 1990, Morty made more than $15 million in "paper profits.")

By September, 1991, he has given about $4 million to the Toronto Western Hospital and the Parkinson's Foundation.

"You can only sleep in one bed and eat three meals a day," the *Star* quotes "the wealthy Shulman" as "joking," in a phrase that would emerge as a favorite of his in interviews to come.

David Saks, a respected senior vice president at the New York brokerage Wedbush Morgan, enthuses in print that he has "grown to consider Dr. Shulman an extraordinary and underappreciated entrepreneur," and Deprenyl "one of the most exceptionally attractive companies" he has come across in his 25-year career.

At which point, in November 1991, *The Wall Street Journal* finds it no longer possible to resist leaving its teethmarks on the Morty jugular, taking a good look at the medicine man, his saga, his stock and the whole damned thing, under strongly remonstrative headline "Shulman builds thriving drug concern, but his style alienates some investors".

A key point is the "investors" angle. It is this that counts and not the financially-boring questions of the drug's therapeutic merits or its potential for improving the human condition. In this Bud Jorgensen and his confreres and-soeurs have been speaking to the market nitty-gritty. It was the saleable dream that counted now — not the medical miracle, but the marketer; not the human benefit, but the financial bottom line.

In the lengthy front-page piece, the admonitory Wall Steet Journal ruminates:

> Maybe only Morty, as the thin, wiry founder of the company is known to all, could have generated so much hype and controversy along the way. His style as an investment adviser earlier in his career and now as a promoter of deprenyl have made conservative Canadians wary. The country's institutional investors avoid Deprenyl stock and no Canadian analysts cover the company.

In vain does son Geoff Shulman tell them: "For all of his career, there have been people who resented his success. He might get too enthusiastic about things, but he's taken a small company and built it into something very rare, an independent Canadian pharmaceutical firm."

The *Journal* does make the first-time point about the difference between Canadian and American perceptions of a Morty-type. Down there, he is not an irritating mouthy shyster, but the stuff of which entrepreneurial legends are born.

David Saks, Morty's effusive supporter at New York's Wedbush Morgan, enthuses: "He doesn't fit the mold of the traditional conservative investment adviser. But would Deprenyl be where it was today without his flamboyant style, without him behind it and promoting it? Of course not."

Morty gloats that the newspaper ad which gave the brokerage community such heartburn ran "without the knowledge or approval of other Deprenyl managers or directors." He repeats his hurt with the world's callous misunderstanding: "I was born and raised here in Canada. I've been a politician, a coroner, a doctor, and I thought my integrity was beyond question. Instead I hear comments about 'Shulman's stock scam.'"

The jab from the *Journal* seems to have drawn no blood. November 1991 brings the first evidence that Deprenyl has really arrived. Morty finds himself in a full-blown fight with a potential nemesis: generic copycats. Deprenyl and Chinoin launch a battle to stop a Vancouver company named Canguard from selling a cheap generic version of Eldepryl they want to call Parkinyl. They are suing Canguard for patent infringement. Canguard wants to sell its Parkinyl during "an investigative phase" in 1992, while it awaits regulatory approval of marketing applications in Canada and other countries.

Shades of early Deprenyl Research! Naturally, this raid is not to be born. Deprenyl shares have slipped back to $15 in recent weeks. But Canguard is only trading at 65 cents on the Vancouver Stock Exchange. Can anyone take such a piker seriously?

Deprenyl and Chinoin bring suit against Canguard for "unspecified damages," and request an injunction to stop them infringing on patent. Canguard is claiming the active ingredient in deprenyl is an old drug discovered years ago in Hungary, no longer under patent. Morty vows they are talking through their hat; later he will prove it.

Morty increases his Deprenyl holdings by 142,300 shares to 1,595,168.

The year 1991 closes blissfully with the company touted among the hottest pharmaceutical stocks. As the Star's business analyst says: "In Canada you'll have to look hard because pickings are slim. But the possibilities are there. Deprenyl Research headed by the colorful Morty Shulman, actually turns a profit. . . Its stock rose 14% this past week to $17.38 after reporting higher third-quarter profit and declaring an extra dividend. It's up 178% over the year."

Chapter Seven

The Parkinson's Years, Part II: Slide and Depression

Well then. Can 1992 possibly be anything but even purer gold than the years before?

Surely not.

In the beginning, all augurs well. Canguard backs off — drops plans for its undercutting generic. The stock cruises at the $21 mark; before the month is out, it will hit a psychedelic high of $23.50 Canadian. And the company has expanded. There's a series of brand new horses racing for profit carrying the colors of Deprenyl Research. There is DAHI: Deprenyl Animal Health; and there is Bone Health, with a new be-all and end-all osteoporosis medication in trials — both US subsidiaries of Deprenyl Research. There is another subsidiary, Memoral, conducting trials for Alzene, for treatment of Alzheimer's. And soon there will be Deprenyl USA — DUSA — with its 5-ALA PDT; a new photodynamic treatment being tested for skin cancer, quietly rumored to have spectacular possibilities for other cancer treatment as well.

And a lengthy negotiation is on the point of paying off — with a gold-plated Dr. Respectable to head up the burgeoning company and counterbalance Dr. MortyMouth.

Morty woos and wins as executive vice president of Deprenyl Research Dr. Martin Barkin, the eminent ex-deputy minister of health for Ontario.

I pursued Martin Barkin for three years, then persuaded him to come to work for me in half an hour. I told him in a year I would make him very, very rich.

Through the whole Deprenyl approval thing with Ontario I never met him. I kept phoning him and he wouldn't return my phone calls. I phoned him eight times. He didn't even return a single call. Finally I got pissed off and I wrote him and said, "Come on down; let's fix this damned thing up." He wouldn't. Even at that point I didn't meet him.

He got stock to come into the company, and an option on a million shares at $7. He'll get very rich from this. I think in five years he'll be a multi-millionaire.

In March, 1992, Barkin agrees to join the jolly ship Deprenyl as second officer if he is moved up to president and chief operating officer in June. It is a fascinating — not to say demonically inspired — joining of forces. Martin Barkin is a tall, portly and dignified 54-year-old with a distinguished background in medicine and health administration, and a tendency to flush dark red in temper. His interest in the business of medicine is as broad, and his ego as wide, as that of his diminutive new boss.

Barkin is a Toronto urologist and medical academic whose CV rolls richly off the page: President and CEO of Sunnybrook Health Sciences Centre, vice-chairman of the Ontario Hospital Association, president of the Ontario Council of Teaching Hospitals. Deputy minister of health for the Province of Ontario from 1987 to 1991, where he established, and was secretary of, the premier's council on Health Strategy, and chaired the deputy cabinet committee on social policy.

When Morty first began his recruiting campaign, Barkin had moved from government to the very bosom of the private sector as partner at the heavyweight brokerage firm of Peat Marwick Stevenson and Kellogg, as National Practice Leader for Health Care.

While at Deprenyl he will continue to chair Peat Marwick's Health Care Advisory Committee. He is frequently called upon by the editorial boards of both the *Star* and The *Globe & Mail* to expound on questions of health management, policy and marketing.

The pairing enthralls both Mortywatchers and Martywatchers. Murmurs a Metro Toronto health official who is both: "We all wish we could be flies on the wall for this one."

Remembers Barkin: "He called my partner at Peat Marwick and told him, 'I want to hire him as president of my company.'" While chuckling at Morty's nerve, Barkin smoothly recalls the achievements as coroner, gracefully complimenting "Morty's propensity for making statements that turn out to be true. It's: 'Oh there he goes shooting from the lip.' And he's always right. That's such a hateful characteristic! Morty's a voracious reader. He always has the facts."

However, for anyone who knows what to look for — and the Mortymouth is uncharacteristically not telling anyone who doesn't — there is one tiny black cloud in the blazing January sky, a minuscule cloud no bigger than a baby short-seller's fist.

It appears as a very small news item noting that Takeda Chemical Industries of Japan "has rejected rights to an experimental drug for osteoporosis being developed by Bone Health."

At the time it seems an insignificant puff on the deal-rich horizon of a growing pharmaceuticals conglomerate, as does a throwaway reference to the fact that Deprenyl stock has closed up 1/8, but with "one large block changing hands." It will take another month or two before the market chokes on that block, spits it back up, and reveals from whose ungrateful hands it was first flung. It will take several more months before the cloudlet blows into a tornado.

But for now all continues the rosiest. January snowshowers bring DUSA flowers. In the second-last week of January, still glowing from its November deal with Medicis Pharmaceuticals of New York to develop the Queen's University anti-cancer cream, Deprenyl Research floats a plumply billowing public issue on the market horizon. $20-million worth of shares and warrants are offered in DUSA to raise cash needed to get 5-ALA through U.S. and Canadian regulatory approvals.

DUSA is to be the base from which to peddle world rights to 5-ALA because Toronto simply isn't big enough to do the job. "It's easier to sell world rights from the U.S. because we're the backwater and they're the centre," Shareman Morty announces. "This will bring in substantial sums. It's going to be a lot of money." The share issue has been 184 times oversubscribed, he adds, vouchsafing that the sky is the limit, as usual, for those prescient souls who have plunked down U.S. $12 per unit. Each package includes two shares of DUSA common stock, plus a warrant, exercisable by May 19, 1993, to buy one more for just $9.

"But I'll wager you it will double," Shareman Morty dauntlessly thrusts. February sees the Deprenyl tiller set full speed ahead with Alzene, a "smart drug" derived from natural fatty acids, developed by Dr. Shlomo Yehuda at Bar Ilan University in Israel, another entrant in the timeclock-stopping sweeps. Morty's Alzene files show a fine flurry of missives between him, the ministry of health, and Deprenyl lieutenants trying ineffectually to rein in their boss as he goes galloping off in every possible direction.

To: Serge Lafond, Exec. Assistant to Benoit Bouchard,
        Minister of Health.
From: Dr. Morton Shulman, Feb. 17, 1992. URGENT.

The enclosed letter to Dr. Petersen of your Health Protection Branch is self-explanatory. Dr. Yehuda, discoverer of Alzene, is giving a public speech in Toronto on Feb. 26 at which time this whole matter will become public. Is it possible to get an appointment to see either the Minister or his Deputy before that time?

To: Dr. Catherine Petersen
       Acting Chief of Central Nervous System Division
       Health Protection Branch
       Ministry of Health
       Ottawa
From: Dr. Morton Shulman, Feb. 17, 1992.

I understand that the government has accepted our IND (Investigational New Drug application) for Alzene and we are now able to go ahead with double blind tests. For this I thank you — we will proceed as quickly as possible.

I was, however, disturbed to be informed that you have decided not to allow the compassionate sale of Alzene in Canada. I find this astounding inasmuch as you have allowed compassionate sale of a competing product manufactured for a U.S. company which has serious side effects, including liver complications, yet which has little benefit to the patient. This drug THA has been on the emergency drug program for 1 1/2 years!

Alzene is a perfectly harmless compound, being simply an extract from safflower and linseed oil. It is a food which has been consumed for hundreds of years. The only difference between our product and the natural substance is that we have purified and blended two components which are able to penetrate the blood brain barrier and wash out the cortical cells of their pollutants.

The two active ingredients linoleic acid and linolenic acid are freely available for purchase in health food stores (as you yourself have pointed out). The only difference is that they are in impure form and are of no medical help to anyone.

We have been shipping it all over the world except Canada
. . . We have not received a single complaint re side effects or
failure to improve the patient's condition. I do not want to be in
conflict with you. . . . I do not want you to think I am doing this
for profit motives. . . . I am in the process of setting up a Chair
at the Toronto hospital to whom I am giving $5 million. All the
monies I received in salary and bonus from Deprenyl Research
in 1991 has gone to the Parkinson's Charitable Trust, Toronto
General and Toronto Western hospitals. In short I am on a crusade and am not trying to make money.

In view of the above facts I am asking you to reconsider
your decision. I want to work with you because together we can
help a lot of people.

Memo to: Morty Shulman
From: Roger Mailhot, Deprenyl Drug Regulatory department.
       Feb. 17 '92.
Re: Emergency Drug Program with Alzene.

I had a lengthy telephone conversation with Dr. Petersen on Friday afternoon. Comments from the conversation are as follows:
 1) She will approve the 2 protocols that we have submitted.
 2) She warned me that she will not grant permission to release
Alzene for an Emergency Drug Program. . .

She has shown a great deal of determination during our
conversation. To quote her, "If Dr. Shulman uses the political
process to force an EDP on the HPB I will fight it all the way
and I will at least force a full disclosure on Alzene."

She claims that she is facilitating the initiation of clinical
studies and as a matter of fact making a favor by approving the
protocol for the study of Alzene in volunteers, consequently she
expressed that Dr. Shulman should be appreciative and should
not cause any trouble regarding his desire to have the Emergency Drug Program.

RECOMMENDATION:

They are on the verge of starting the review on Eldepryl as monotherapy. I would suggest that we don't force the issue of the Emergency Drug Program before we know the outcome of this review.

I know that you will be disappointed but let's examine what are our alternatives. I will be back in the office on Wednesday, February 19 and we will have the opportunity to discuss this further then.

From: Serge Lafond.
To: Dr. Morton Shulman, Feb. 18, 1992.

Thank you for your letter. . . . I am aware that Dr. Peterson is writing you to clarify the Department's position regarding Emergency drug releases for Alzene.

Note scribbled by secretary Ann Worobec on the bottom of Lafond's letter: *She did not write but phoned us permission to sell the drug.*

Why would she be determined that I not do with Alzene what I did with Deprenyl? Because nobody else does it. It means every other pharmaceuticals company will be after her screaming, "If he can do it, how come we can't do it?" Why the hell couldn't they do it as well? Well, they don't have the guts.

Every drug company in the world said, "How did he get permission?" There's 24 applications. It would have stood there for two years.

Two days after she said, "We would never give you compassionate approval," she gave it to us. And why?

Because she went to the minister and said, "This son-of-a-bitch is going to cause us trouble."

I still have the power to strike terror into their hearts. I'm the only one in the industry that can do that.

She calls me Al Capone. She still calls Roger Mailhot in our office and says, "How is Mr. Capone doing?"

Against all odds Morty has galloped back bearing the prize of HPB compassionate sanction.

Naturally Morty hurries to inform the press, exuberantly announces Deprenyl "has been granted permission to distribute Alzene upon a doctor's request to individual Alzene patients according to the Canadian Emergency Drug Release Program." The news gives Deprenyl shares, which have slid subtly from their January high, a healthy shove back from just under to just over $17.

The wording of the press release seems to madden the poor Health Protection Branch. There is nothing, strictly speaking, incorrect about what it it says, which makes it even more maddening.

"Deprenyl should not be saying Alzene has been approved under the emergency drug program," a ministry spokesperson complains. "The company is managing to give the false impression that Alzene has in some way been approved by the Canadian government when it has, in fact, undergone little, if any, testing in Canada.

"I'm a little concerned that they're sending press releases out saying this is now available through the EDP because it has always been available," the Health spokeslady adds with poignant confusion.

Morty, the soul of ingenuous reason, tells a reporter: "I don't want to get into a controversy about this. Health and Welfare has been very cooperative and helpful to us. I love them dearly, but whoever spoke to you misled you."

The Alzene file ends — how else? — with Morty having an incomparable last word.

Dear Dr. Petersen:

It is with some considerable regret that I must inform you that I will no longer be able to enliven your life or cause you aggravation or amusement. I am turning 67 next month and Dr. Martin Barkin is taking over the running of Deprenyl Research. He will be officially appointed President at the annual meeting in May. The company is keeping me on as a figurehead but, alas, my active duties will be limited to financing. I wanted you to know that over this past four years I did not want to cause you any difficulty and any differences we had I am sure resulted in both of us trying to do the right thing from different viewpoints. In any case I apologize for the many times when I am sure I was wrong.

I am sure you will find Dr. Barkin a far more reasonable man to deal with, but perhaps a trite [*sic*] — the typing is Ann's) duller. My best wishes for you in the future.

On March 14 the stock closes up 25 cents, at $17.50. On March 15 the Canadian Broadcasting Corporation announces *Wojeck* is back on TV, in a new two-hour special.

That day brings a major newspaper profile of Shulman, with a glowing account of Deprenyl's profit picture: shares that have "gone up 18 times and split twice, despite the naysaying of skeptics," a company which with its subsidiaries has a market value of "almost half a billion dollars." A pipeline of exciting products, including Alzene, and the exciting new Canadian discovery ALA PDT, the new photodynamic therapy for skin cancer uncovered by Geoff at that dermatology conference in Kingston.

There was a dash of lurid glamor, a remembrance of the Morty of glory days past, of one who "flaunted his conquests and kept a boudoir at his office, where he displayed pictures of the other women in his life."

So mesmerized is the reporter that she hurries back to her office to persuade all her friends to snap up the DUSA, quicker than quick. But underneath it all, the ground is crumbling away, and the January cloudlet builds to a thunderhead.

The *Star* piece — by then it was just damage control.

Chinoin had dumped a million shares of stock, without giving me any notice. That was the first thing that went wrong — our partners Chinoin in Hungary — to whom I had given a present of a million shares of stock. It was really a present, when the company came out, because I wanted their goodwill. They were our supplier, our supporter. I gave them a million shares and they dumped a million shares on the market. The people there didn't know me from Adam and they didn't give a shit and they started selling the stock and they just flooded the market and they drove it down from $24 to about $15.

And I barely got over the catastrophe when our big backer in the States, a guy from Wedbush Morgan, put out a sell recommendation in the middle of the day. And in March Deprenyl stock went from $22 to $12, and DUSA went from $15 to $3 1/4. And I tried to buy it, hold it up, and that was my big mistake. I blew $20 million in the next year.

Indeed, in the third week of March, seemingly out of the blue, James Reynolds, key West Coast analyst with Wedbush Morgan Securities, had flown in the face of his New York vice president David Saks' unabated devotion to all things Morty. Reynolds issued a sell advisory on Deprenyl stock.

Morty announces he is furious, hints Deprenyl may take the West Coast guy before the regulatory authorities.

169

It doesn't happen. Deprenyl stock sinks $2.62 to $15.25, flutters back up to $16.50. The ever-faithful David Saks continues to recommend Deprenyl.

But by the beginning of April, there has been a $10 slide from the January heights, and things start to get nasty.

A huge front-page *Toronto Star* piece in mid-April luridly paints Morty as Dr. Venal: rich, greedy and scamming the poor with unconscionable pill profits.

"Angry Parkinson's patients pay $2.31 for 6c pill" the headline shouts. Morty is said to be shamelessly blocking production of cheaper generic versions while sitting on "a whopping $10-million before-tax profit" and displaying hypocritcal hypersensitivity to criticism, "repeating over and over again he isn't in the drug business to make money but to help people, followed with several phone calls and faxes of documents showing evidence of his good works."

A Newfoundland Parkinson's sufferer is found to have complained about Eldepryl's price to the Patent Medicine Prices Review Board. "Why," the lady rages, "should we have to beg some rich man in Toronto for something that shouldn't be that expensive anyway?"

Only at the end of the lengthy story does a key piece of information appear — information that might have begun the story instead of ending it, and would make the roar of outrage against Morty Shulman ring a little hollow.

Here, the reporter briefly explains that Deprenyl is only doing exactly the same as every other pharmaceutical company. The difference is that the big private companies can keep it secret.

"Industry analysts say Eldepryl's huge mark-up is not unusual, that drug prices are never determined by company costs but are set as high as the market can bear. Finances of pharmaceutical companies are a closely held secret; most companies won't reveal the sales of individual drugs or break out what it costs to make them. Companies justify high prices in general by saying they are necessary to fund past or future research.

"The only thing different about Deprenyl is that the true costs — and true profits — have slipped into the public eye. It's only because Deprenyl Research was a new company with a single product that the factors behind the price of Eldepryl could be deduced by patients — and reporters."

The message in all this: you might say that Morty was once again paying the price he has paid all his life, for the same reason he has always paid it. He's getting zapped for letting it all hang out.

He's getting zapped for being too ebullient — or just too small — to anchor safely down there, deep underwater, with the establishment heavies.

As such, his protests get short shrift. The *Star* story goes on: "Shulman seems genuinely perplexed by the animosity that he, his company and his drug have sparked across the country. He sees himself as a hero, the small white pill his version of a strong white stallion that he will ride to the rescue of others suffering from Parkinson's. And he is frustrated that the public doesn't see the issue his way. 'I'm defending something which I shouldn't be defending,' he called the *Star* to say last week. 'This is not like selling baseballs. You don't get a licence to buy them somewhere, bring them in, mark them up and sell them.'"

The newspaper is obliged to print first a correction, then a retraction and an apology for two major factual errors which alter the thrust of the whole story: "A story in the April 19 edition of *The Sunday Star* concerning Deprenyl Research Ltd. and its founder, Dr. Morton Shulman, was premised on certain figures. Those figures were incorrect. The company says the 36c it pays for a deprenyl pill does not include its overhead and administration costs. According to the company's annual report, the after-tax profit on pharmaceuticals is only 15%. The *Star* regrets the errors and apologizes to Dr. Shulman."

Yes, the bloom is off.

A strange phenomenon is growing, assuming an immutable shape.

All anyone sees or talks about is Deprenyl, the company, as if deprenyl the drug didn't exist.

In the growing cloud of preoccupation over Deprenyl the company, the gathering strength and proliferating facets of deprenyl, the drug is becoming more and more incidental.

Deprenyl the drug keeps gaining new dimensions, but they seem almost dismissable.

There is news of another major breakthrough. On April 22 Eldepryl is approved by HPB for treatment of early Parkinson's; it is no longer officially restricted, as in the past, to be prescribed in conjunction with other anti-Parkinson's drugs for advanced stages of the disease.

This marks several large steps forward. Not only does it promise substantially delayed onset of symptoms, it also means a reduction in dosages of l-dopa, with its nightmare gallery of potential side effects after prolonged or increased use. It advances the great promise of the 1989 Langston-Tetrud and DATATOP studies.

Martin Barkin projects a doubling of revenue over next 24 months. He announces revenues of $13.9 million for the year ended December 31, 1991, and a profit of $6.5 million.

In May, the company announces the launch of its new star project. Bone Health, its new Massachusetts-based drug subsidiary, has begun a major clinical trial of its osteoporis drug One-Alpha D(2).

Results will be published in September. But the prognosis is so promising that, on May 22, Deprenyl Research issues to its investors a dividend in the form of one Bone Health warrant for each Deprenyl share. The warrant is good for the purchase of one Bone Health share for 30 cents, from March 1, 1993 to May 7, 1993; or may be traded at that time for 20 cents cash.

There is — surprise — a fierce scuffle behind the scenes with the Toronto Stock Exchange that goes all the way to the Securities Exchange Commission. The TSE has invoked a seldom-used regulation — capriciously, Morty is convinced — that says Deprenyl needed written confirmation from the Exchange before issuing its Bone Health warrants. The TSE regulators also jump on Morty for preventing sale of the warrants until March 1993. After the SEC steps in, the TSE and Morty agree on a compromise that allows the dividends to be credited, and traded, at the end of July, 1992.

Morty rages about persecution, Morty rages about harassment, about lack of appreciation. Appreciation is, at least, forthcoming from the cancer-cream research team at Queen's University, which is now foreseeing powerful new applications for ALA, thanks to Morty's infusion of cash and marketing know-how. With $200,000 in research funds from Deprenyl, the ALA team is investigating a variation of the ALA-light process which could produce a non-surgical alternative to hysterectomy.

A procedure like this could spare hundreds of thousands of women surgery commonly performed for excessive uterine bleeding. Jim Kennedy and Roy Pottier are being likened to Banting and Best, and Morty is getting kudos.

"In the past, we universities failed to retain the wealth produced by our inventions because we lacked the entrepreneurial infrastructure." John Molloy, executive director of PARTEQ, the university's research-funding institution, hails "Shulman's deal-making expertise" for keeping a Canadian drug invention home in Canada for its research. "We have money from Deprenyl for two new people," Kennedy tells a reporter, "but we have no space to put them."

Does Morty feel smart? He will be even smarter, and he will spread the brains around.

It is revealed that at the 1991 Deprenyl annual meeting in May, he recruited shareholders to volunteer for tests of Alzene as a smart drug. *Worth* magazine, a glossy U.S. bible of entrepreneurialism, comes north to describe the scene, one sweet evening in spring, 1992. It's a swell picture: the fancy dudes and dames rolling up to the Deprenyl storefront in the west end, smack-snug amongst hardware stores and Polish pastry shops, to give blood samples, take psychometric tests, and a 30-day supply of little orange capsules.

This spreading news is gaining Morty a firmer foothold in the dream-drenched world of life-extenderfolk. Life-extensionists from as far away as San Francisco are keeping files on Morty and Alzene. And his most admiring U.S. securities maven, David Saks, is in there cheering. "The possibility of 10, 20, 50 million healthy Americans using drugs to enhance memory functions. A very large investment opportunity." Deprenyl, he says, has "a classic profile for a risk investor.

"In the five years since the creation of his company Shulman has acquired the reputation of being able to make the drugs in its pipeline profitable at an earlier stage than might normally be expected, a skill that has proven attractive to investors."

Alas, the smart-seeds will not sprout the sweet fruits of genius at this planting.

Nothing demonstrable in the way of brain flowering is seen to happen to the hopeful Alzened shareholders; their brainpans seem no sharper of IQ than the placeboed. By the following April, Morty will be dauntlessly insisting it was because the dosages were too small.

And now, the storm begins to break.

The *Wall Street Journal* returns to the scene with a vengeance, turning both barrels on Alzene, and Morty, in the last week of August, 1992.

PROBLEMATIC PILLS
An unapproved drug for Alzheimer's gets a big marketing push. Proof Alzene helps is scant but that doesn't deter Deprenyl Research Ltd. Promoters defend methods.

Many Alzheimer's researchers doubt that Alzene, which hasn't been approved for sale in the U.S., helps the dozens of U.S. families who buy it by mail through a crack in U.S.

Right: MORTY DEAREST: Baby Morty, age one, gazes suspiciously from mother Nettie Shulman's arms in the backyard of her parents' High Park house, 1926.

Below: MATRIARCH MINNIE: Grandmother Minnie Winthrope (front row, next to bachelor-dentist son Lou) holds court with extended family, all living in her house. From back row, left: Morty, (age 10), Nettie Winthrope Shulman, Dave Shulman, Mac Robbins and wife Ethel Winthrope Robbins, Morty's cousin Doris Abiscott (later Doris Messinger), her mother Rose Abiscott, brother Billy Abiscott. 1935.

Right. OLD BOY: Longtime Chief Coroner Dr. Smirle "Big Train" Lawson, finally pushed to resign the year before his death in December, 1963.

Left: CORONER DEPOSED: Morty leaves for good, April 8, 1967.

NEWLYWEDS:
(above and left)
Gloria and
Morty Shulman
leave for their
Catskills honey-
moon, May 30,
1950.

Above: MACHINE-GUN MORTY: Posing with the semi-automatic .22-calibre piece he smuggled into the Ontario Legislature just to show he could. June, 1975.

Right: PARTY POOPER: Stephen Lewis at the Ontario NDP convention which elected him leader. Morty's button shows he supported Walter Pitman.

Above: COURT OF THE SUN KING: Gloria and Morty rule over a rental-hall Versailles at their third annual party, 1956.

Right: TV TERROR:
Host of The Shulman
File. March, 1981.

Below: UNKINDRED
SPIRITS: City-TV's
guiding genius Moses
Znaimer, left; theatre
mogul Garth Drabin-
sky, centre. The
inscription: "I seem
always to be lectur-
ing you, Doctor."

*Above: MONEYMEN: Publisher Ron Hume flashes a $10,000
advance for The Billion Dollar Windfall, 1968. Morty's mother
bought the most copies (three).*

*Below: WALL STREET WEEK: Host Louis Ruykeyser wel-
comes the star of The MoneyLetter, 1982.*

Above: HAPPIER DAY: Geoff, Gloria, Morty, Dianne outside the mansion; March, 1992.

Below: FAMILY TRUST: With son Geoff, Deprenyl Research President, March 1992.

import laws. But nobody doubts the promotional prowess of two young drug companies, a flamboyant Canadian entrepreneur and an obscure Israeli inventor that are touting the drug and investments in its prospects.

. . . Most users buy the pills on faith from Deprenyl Research Ltd., a small Toronto drug company. . . .

The story churns happily back into Morty's past: the LSD, the flogging of *The Happy Hooker* at 10 per cent discount from his office in the Ontario legislature; his "cult following" through the Hume newsletter, his best-selling *Anyone Can Make A Million* (mis-named as *How To Make A Million*. Even the *Wall Street* Journal isn't perfect).

Andy Sarlos contributes another priceless thumbnail sketch of Morty: "A person with strong convictions that has no time for unbelievers."

It seems Morty has been cutting through layers in his favorite time-tested ways to get Alzene into U.S. circulation ahead of the official approval process. There have been letters to American neurologists from Deprenyl Research, that warn "overwhelming demand" for the drug has caused a shortage." The FDA is no happier about this Mortyescapade than was Canada's Health Protection Branch before them. It issues a reprimand ordering Deprenyl Research to stop promoting Alzene.

Morty again denies exaggerating or law breaking. He faxes the FDA to assure them of the potential efficacy of Alzene.

Fax to: Mr. Brad Stone
          Food & Drug Administration
          Washington DC
          March 6, 1992

Yesterday I received a letter from Dr. Somers of Canada's Health Protection Branch indicating that you had complained to him about the Alzene information which I had sent to a number of U.S. doctors. I faxed you a copy of my reply to Dr. Somers. . .

Alzne's contents are pure extracts of linoleic acid and linolenic acid from linseed oil. They are absolutely harmless and innocuous and both acids have been available in impure form in U.S. health food stores for decades.

He stops sending letters to U.S. doctors; asserts, "I have done nothing more than inform my shareholders of events that might affect the stock."

The formula for having it both ways was working fine, for the second drug in a row. The publicity will speed the approvals process while letting Deprenyl Research do business by dealing the drug during the pre-approvals gap. For about a year before Eldepryl was approved for sale in the U.S. Deprenyl Research has sold it to American patients through the mail.

O tempore, O Morty. The *Journal* article says Morty offered to give the reporter's family shares in Bone Health, which at the time was due to be spun off from the parent company as warrants. Of course, "The offer was turned down," the worthy *WSJ* man notes.

All of it, the whole pattern of launch, incredulity, disdain, doubt, with growing reluctant acceptance — so reminiscent of the Deprenyl path — is starting to sound like something out of Elisabeth Kubler-Ross, that noted chronicler of the stages of death. Denial, anger, grief, acceptance . . . uneasy peace.

Why are they so committed to ensure that anything with the Shulman imprimatur must be bean-bagged?

The *Journal* story runs Tuesday, August 25, 1992; the next day, Wednesday the 26th, the *Globe* reprints the whole thing on the front of its Business section.

It is not a happy time in Deprenylville.

Dan Westell of the *Globe* follows with a close look at Morty's dollar-hedging activities.

He reports that Deprenyl's currency transactions top $514 million in a six-month period; that Danny Gordon, Deprenyl's broker at currency traders Friedberg Mercantile Group affirms: "He's on top of things. He's on the phone with me almost before I'm in the office."

Deprenyl, which reported revenue of $7.3 million in the six months ended June 30, did more than $514 million worth of securities transactions in the same period.

Martin Barkin says Dr. Shulman deals with Deprenyl's investments and then reports back on what he has done.

"We're not gambling on foreign exchange," Dr. Shulman says. "We hedge our net assets [of somewhere between $5 million and $20 million] because Deprenyl expects the Canadian dollar to fall."

This open avowal sits uneasily. Canada is stumbling towards a national referendum that is being bannered as the harbinger of its almost certain disintegration.

The land is short weeks away from what everyone has been told is the most momentous event of our time: the October, 1992 yes-no referendum on — well, no one is exactly certain what it is they're voting yes or no or maybe on, but each uneasy day drives the battered dollar lower.

But for Morty, as for hedgers and floggers the world over, the shaky economic and political situation comes to a focuspoint in the gleaming golden four-figure number that shows the downticking state of the Canadian dollar. As far as he's concerned politics is bunk, politicians are bonkers, and he couldn't be happier. Each tick is worth $1,000, every time the buck falls a point.

"It'll go down to 60 cents," he promises. "So what? It didn't do Mexico any harm. . . ."

* * *

Everyone with and around him talks the dollar. It dominates the first morning words between Morty and his perpetually-smiling Vietnamese chauffeur Luan Nguyen.

"Morning, Luan. How's the dollar?"

"It is down, Doctor Shulman, a little down."

"Made us 50,000 dollars, Luan."

"Is good, Doctor Shulman."

At the office, Ann Worobec holds her hand prettily out, turning it this way and that so the big opal glimmers in the light filtering through the bumpy old venetians. The dollar dealings will mean she can, make the final payment on the egg-shaped opal girdled with tiny perfect diamonds — a handsome $8 thousand-worth, in devaluing dollars.

Like the rest of the land, Morty waits breathlessly for the effect on the buck of each new pronouncement from the Charlottetown federal-provincial confab, which he likes to call The Charlatan Conference.

"Every time one of them issues a warning — down it goes! And up I go!"

What goes up, however, must come down.

* * *

7:45 a.m. on the first day of September, a soft balmy Tuesday morning exactly a week after the press blitz.

At 7:45 sharp, each soft September morning after his fall, Morty is there waiting, opening his arching oak front door as chauffeur Luan eases a boat-sized white Caddy limo into the Shulmans' curving driveway.

The only other car in evidence is Gloria's modest Honda, parked to the right of the turreted stone mansion like a prudent but pointless afterthought. Decades of publicity about the house's fabulous art-rich interior have already inspired more than a score of attempted break-ins. All failed — the house is better protected than a bank.

Morty moves to the limousine in a crabbed scuttle, hunching a little into his left shoulder, small and gray and thin in a gray summer suit.

I don't drive any more. Thank goodness I found Luan four
years ago. He's been a dream.

Luan wrote me a letter. "Dear Teacher," I still remember
it. "Dear Teacher, I come to Canada from Vietnam and I've
read your advisory column and I think you're very smart. I'm
running a limousine service having a terrible time getting
started, would you think of me?"

I've had hundreds of approaches but it was novel, I'd
never had an approach like that before. He'd taken my
course from the Hume *MoneyLetter* and wrote me this lovely letter and I wrote him and called him up and since then
he's been driving for me.

The timing was wonderful. At first I did it not because I
had to, but because it gave me the freedom to work in the
morning on the way to work. But then, of course, I didn't
trust myself to drive anymore. Although I'm fine now — I
could drive . . . I'm not sure that I'll remain fine.

Why impose that pressure on myself, anyway? It makes a
difference in the way I can function, the amount of tension. . .

It's barely an hour since he took his waking Eldepryl and lay waiting to feel his body begin to unlock. For an hour and more the
stiffness and slowness will linger and gradually drain away, like a
frozen plasticine figure warming, softening, becoming pliable.

His voice is still pitched low, creaky, swift, slurred and sibi-
lant. But his eyes, glittering and watery and alert, dart and
swerve like a flashing mirror of the mind that ticks impatiently
inside, waiting for the body to catch up.

My nights are all right. The days — I have one bad time. I
take a little rest after lunch, and immediately after the rest,
for about 20 minutes, I'm very, very slow. But the rest of the

179

day I start off — like this — in the morning, and by 9
o'clock I'll be rarin' to go and I stay good until 5-6-7.

In the course of the day I'll take my two Eldepryl and
about four Sinamet (l-dopa tablets). One long-acting one to
get me through the night. Keeps me going. Without those
drugs I wouldn't be able to get dressed in the morning, I
wouldn't be able to get out of bed, I wouldn't be able to
function. I wouldn't be able to do anything.

He has been bearing up and holding them off — Martin, Geoff,
Gloria, Ann, the skittering shareholders on the phones — all of
them snapping and fretting in the fallout over the newspaper
stories and the one-two thud to the stock.

The ticking mind spins and ducks here and there across a
wide troubled landscape, searching for small valleys of peace.

Life has always been good to me. I've never been sick. I
never missed a day of work in my whole life. And suddenly,
I couldn't do anything! I was doing everything, and being all
powerful. And I thought I was omnipotent. Omniscient. I
knew everything in the world. I was the smartest man in the
world, and I was the strongest man in the world. I thought I
could beat anybody, and do anything, and have any woman
I wanted. . . . Suddenly, I couldn't do anything!

In the office the girls and boys have already begun to trickle
in, make the coffee, prepare to keep up with Morty's day, a day
he is determined will unfold like all others.

So, I arrive at the office fresh, rarin' to go. There's a young
man at my desk. My secretary now has two assistants. It's

180

kind of funny: she's growing older with me, but she doesn't come in until 9:00 and she's got some young man who she's hired who sits at the desk who comes in at 7:30 or 8:00 and he holds the fort until she gets in. . . .

This morning, somebody will be there already at my desk, take a message. I'll answer any calls that have come in. And there will be appointments starting at 9:00, and the phone rings, and rings, and rings, and rings. At 8:30 or 9:00 o'clock Martin comes in for a consultation on what the day's going to bring and that's the basic outline, but you never really know what's going to happen. Each day it's a different crisis.

I'm still seeing patients, very, very few, perhaps three or four a day. Six mornings a week. People who have been coming here forever. I haven't taken new patients now in seven years. . .

What story would I like to be telling at this point? I don't know, I haven't really thought about it, I thought, whatever hasn't been told. . .

We're in the middle of the eye of this storm with Alzene. After the *Wall Street Journal* ran this horrible article, the one that the *Globe* picked up on. It went back through my whole life. It mentioned that I took LSD in 1964, when I was coroner. Just to say what an unsavoury character I was. They dug up every possible thing they could find. It was just terrible. There was very little about the company, but a lot about my sins, personality weaknesses — that went under unfair attack. And they got the facts wrong, Martin sent a letter but they haven't printed it, which is really aggravating.

Take action? Oh you don't get anywhere.

In the old days, politicians drank and came drugged to work — nobody said a word. They fornicated or they took too much drugs . . . personal sins were not considered in the public realm. But now, it's terrible. It's terrible for everybody and it produces standards that are impossible. You have to hire a president who was born, age 60, no sins. I mean people are human. We have human wants and needs and we all go through the same things. You have to have been born pure. Remain pure. Never lusted, never hate, never did anything. And you actually have no idea what someone is going to decide afterwards. Luckily I decided not to stay in politics. I was not a politician.

Seems to be getting worse every day. All sorts of people who you think are secure are not secure. It's very frightening. When Olympia and York — if they're going, who's safe? The whole real estate group are going down. We've been very fortunate it didn't impact Deprenyl, but that was a fluke. On Roncesvalles the whole damn street, every building, every building's up for power of sale except the ones we're in. It can't turn around because most of the industry's gone and it's not coming back. They kept the Canadian dollar high too long and we're paying the price. So now you have the bad bad news.

You know, Ross Perot's a shareholder in Deprenyl. Our biggest. Owns a couple hundred thousand shares. No, he's more than a shareholder. He's been up to see the company and he speaks to Geoffrey fairly frequently. — Well, he doesn't come personally. He sends one of his experts. They've been up three times. He phones from his plane. . .

The Canadian dollar opens in 10 minutes. But it will open unchanged. My faculty for money dealings — well, I consider myself of average intelligence and you follow certain basic rules. And you don't have to be a great genius to be good at the market. Look at Murray Pezim.

You have to have a knack for understanding people, the people that run the companies because there are a lot of crooks in this world and there's a lot of crookedness in this world, and you have to be able to avoid . . . well you learn you don't buy anything that comes out of Vancouver because they can't get in anywhere else so they go there.

Vancouver welcomes every crook in the world. The Vancouver Exchange has every fraud on it you could ever dream of. And on odd occasions some stock comes from 20 cents and goes up to 50 dollars — like Archer Communications — and then it comes back to 20 cents because they're all fraudulent. Maybe there's been an exception once. I can't remember one.

I get a kick out of dealing in money. It's like you're in battle. It's like the kick you get out of going out and putting on a knight's armor and going out to the joust and jousting off the black knight. You're beating the bad guys and that's part of it.

I always got great pleasure watching the movement of shares, so I finally decided I'm going to do it myself. And I built this company from nothing and I thumbed my nose at them as I did it, which I can see that Glen Adams at the *Globe* appreciated — and I ran a series of ads saying, "Fuck you!", and it sort of . . . it was a terrible mistake because this fury built up and when they finally got a chance to get even with me within the last few weeks, they all jumped on the wagon because our company's doing great.

But that didn't matter. They caused a panic, caused a lot of shareholders to be sold out and they got their revenge. But we're managing. It doesn't affect the company at all, but they sure hurt a lot of my friends.

I can guarantee that the company's being run well. I can't guarantee what the stock price will be.

I thought I could. I thought at that point I was running a company so well, that makes so much money, there's no way they can hit me. And it turned out the strength of the shorts was stronger than I was. I thought I could beat them all put together.

What happened was the shorts started hitting me so I developed what I thought was a very clever — it was a very clever scheme to cut them off at the pass and I found to my

horror when I — it was perfectly legal — but when we went
to institute it, the Toronto Stock Exchange intervened against
us with the commission and they made it so difficult. We
could have won if we'd persisted but it would have cost
hundreds of thousands of dollars in legal fees.

So they gave me a dilemma where I could either persist
and win at tremendous costs to the company or admit that
they were stronger than me and throw in the towel and
make a compromise. And so we compromised. They were
more relieved than I was and signed each of the joint statements like everything's fine. But everything wasn't fine
because if I'd been able to get away with what I wanted to
do it would have bankrupted a lot of these short sellers. But
the short sellers were members of the Toronto Stock
Exchange. And they were stronger than I was.

I found that the person leading the complaint was a
senior executive at our underwriter.

I don't know if it was illegal. It was certainly immoral. I
wrote a letter to the Exchange saying, "Would you mind
checking to see if he was short at the same time as he made
this complaint?" and they didn't even answer my letter.

Pretty wild. It's the Wild West out there and that's why
the public is so disillusioned of the stock market. Because
here you have a company whose earnings have increased
every quarter since we began, never been in the red, don't
have a cent of debt, our dividends have increased every
quarter in the last 11 quarters. Yet they hammered us down
from 24 dollars to seven dollars in a matter of six months.

I fought back — with any and every bit of energy I had
and I wasn't strong enough because the combination of
forces was just so great: the newspapers — except for the
Financial Post; the so-called analysts, who can be sold for a
nickel; and the brokers. It was to their advantage to make
money by forcing the stock down. And they were determined to force it down. And they forced it down regardless

of how good our earnings were or how big our dividends were, nobody cared.

Who profits out of all that? Shorts, professional shorts, and the newspapers, and envious columnists that love to drag down the successful; and the advisors that get free trips from companies they recommend.

The feeling is exactly the same as when I first went after them all, when I was chief coroner. Exactly the same thing! Like layer upon layer, just a layer of black ice.

At some point you reach the point that you just can't do it any more and you have to either compromise or get bankrupted. Lose your job — because the newspapers are all against you and the reporters tend to mistrust someone like me...

A reporter at the *Globe,* Dan Westell, is being fed stories by Alex Winch, of Grange Securities, who's our largest short seller of Deprenyl stock. And when it was proved he was being fed the stories, I investigated to see if there was a payoff. But he wasn't being paid off. We went through everything. We went through his bank accounts, we went through everything and he's clean as a whistle. He's just a dedicated reporter who doesn't like people who've made money. He's got a house two blocks from here with a huge mortgage. He would love to bring me down. And I don't know what he's mad at me about.

He's a holy roller. He has no money and I gather he feels people that make money easily and particularly if they boast about it, have to be bad. I represent, I think, everything that's bad to him.

No. I don't think anti-Semitism is involved. None. I don't think so because they don't attack Martin Barkin and he's Jewish. I mean he is a more acceptable type of Jew. I think I represent all that is bad.

Whether I'm Jewish or not is quite irrelevant. I'm arrogant, I'm successful. I don't pay homage to the establishment and — it's my basic "screw it" attitude. It drives people crazy, this feeling that there's nothing that could faze me. I wanted to put that picture — the one up on the wall, of the three girls and me in bed — I wanted to put it on the cover of the Annual Report. Martin nearly had a heart attack. I told him, it proves Eldepryl works. Anyway, only our heads are showing! Rest is under the covers.

Yes. The thing people don't seem to be able to forgive is people who don't lie down and die when they should. Because most people are knuckling under in big and little ways at so many points in their lives because — most people don't have a choice because — many of them have children, responsibilities. During the coroner thing, I could always go back and be a GP and I could always make a good living.

It's true, people can't bear to go from up here to down there. I know the feeling. When they fired me as coroner, I walked out of there and I had this sinking feeling, what will I do for with the rest of my life?

But still never rolled over and died because of it.

Well, as of this morning, I will not be allowed to talk to the press. I will not be allowed to talk to analysts, and any ideas I have I will have to take across the road to the Management Committee. And the only thing I refuse to give up is the investments. I'm keeping that under my control, come hell or high water.

But I gave up all the rest because everyone agreed that all this trouble is because of these crazy articles that are appearing. The crazy articles are appearing because 25 years ago I did this and 30 years ago I did that. And so they start any article on Deprenyl Research by saying, "Chairman Morton Shulman said . . ." and then they go back on the LSD I took and the *Happy Hooker* books I sold. The fact that it was 30 years ago is irrelevant.

I always have been, some would say insanely, up front. Outspoken is the word I would use. But from now on our spokesman in this company is Martin Barkin. If the press are to be spoken to or analysts are to be spoken to, he is the one who will speak with them. They're not going to let anyone get near me. They've got two people taking phone calls saying, "You can't talk to him."

It's going to be a lot less interesting, yeah. But absolutely better for the company which is really what it's all about. . . .

Every company in this whole country hedges the dollar. That means if you have access to Canadian dollars, you buy U.S. dollars to offset it, so that in case the Canadian dollar goes down you don't get killed. And I did it and every other company does it. But no other company's ever gotten written up on the front page of the *Globe & Mail* for doing it.

That's what that was all about. The big article in The *Globe* made it appear I was gambling in currencies and was going to blow the whole treasury. But there's no gambling at all. There's no risk and that article was really a watershed. If they can hang me for hedging . . . General Motors does it, but nobody ever writes about it . . . I just couldn't believe it. I realized I couldn't talk to the press anymore.

Why is it so important to them to bring me down?
Because I'm different.

Why is it that when a black moves in they burn his porch, or if a Chinese family . . . anywhere where the majority, I mean, when everyone's one way and someone's different, it causes suspicion, it causes envy. I live like a king, I have all these women who adore me and it drives everybody crazy.

Yes, I have always projected this feeling that nobody's going to make me cry. That whatever hurt, you never show it. I try not to. They perceive it as arrogance. If one played the game and appeared to be hurt, and beat your breast — it's non-productive. It gains you neither sympathy or gain or anything.

It's far better to appear to be a winner. If you appear to be a winner, somehow you are a winner. If I walk into the bank, they loan me money — even in these bad times. But if I had a reputation as a loser . . . fat chance!

This town and this establishment is very unforgiving of weakness. Especially from anyone whom they perceive as an outsider. That's very, very true. I learned my lesson early, as the coroner.

A person has to be a member of the Old Boys or old whatever it is. You have to conform or appear to conform.

Can a person ever become powerful enough that they can get past that?

I thought I was.

Oh it's a blip, but it's a very painful blip and it's cost millions and millions. Well it's cost me $15 million dollars — personally! It's cost the company — not directly, but indirectly — because if we want to raise money now we've got to work from a base of $7 dollars rather than a base of $20 dollars. So that if you start thinking you're all powerful, you're suffering from megalomania.

But anybody can be brought down. Because of my arrogance and because of feeling of omniscience and omnipotence, I've been able to get away with things and make successes that no one else has ever dreamt of. We have had two drugs brought into this country and approved within two days. No one, no drug company has ever had a drug approved within less that two years.

And I did it by, I guess as my mother would say, *chutzpah.* I called the minister and said, "I've got two speeches to make tonight. Which one should I make? The one saying you're a hero for allowing this drug in the country or the one saying all of you sick people will remain sick because René Bouchard will not allow the drug in." René Bouchard is human, he's running for election. He says, "Make the first speech."

You're supposed to sit around and wait your turn.

I had two drugs which I was convinced would help all sorts of human beings. I knew the first one would help because I'd taken it myself and it had done me so much good and I was too impatient to wait and I wasn't going to wait.

There have been a series of articles that were written about Eldepryl which appeared four years ago, written in the *Globe* in 1988 saying exactly the same thing as they're saying about Alzene today: "It doesn't work. It shouldn't be in a stock. He's lying. He's exaggerating. All doctors have agreed it's useless." And now they can't say that any more because it's be proven so we're going through the same thing with Alzene.

You know who denounced us first? The Parkinson's Foundation. But they've come around. They took the first step. They phoned, apologized and I responded by giving them five million bucks. I'm a bit of a sucker.

Because they are — in the case of the Parkinson's Foundation — these are dedicated people whose lifework is with Parkinson's. They've given their whole life to working on this terrible disease and mitigating its horrible effects and some idiot comes out of left field and says, "I have the cure." Their first reaction is, "He's nuts!"; and their second reaction is anger; and their third reaction is the fear that they're going to lose their jobs.

I must give these people credit, particularly Grazyna Bergman, who denounced me as a charlatan. She phoned one day and apologized and as a result I gave them a lot of money and they honored me. Hal Jackman, Lieutenant Governor, had this little event for me down at Queen's Park. He said, "If someone had said to me 20 years ago that I'd be in the Lieutenant Governor's suite honoring Morton Shulman, I would have called for a psychiatrist.

Well, today I'm not worried about it anymore, about

what the stock is going to do. I'm going to start moving up the secondary stocks.

The fact is there are no profitable biotechnical drug companies in Canada. They all need money. We're the only drug company making money.

We're the only one paying a dividend. We're the only one making money.

We're doing wonderfully and people are so jealous and we've been approached by the big underwriters. Lehmann Brothers.

The big people. And ultimately, in February, we will list on the New York Stock Exchange and de-list in Toronto and I'll thumb my nose at them. Because the New York Exchange has agreed — as of February '93, I figure. As long as our '92 earnings are higher than our '91. And I think they're going to be higher. I'm sure they are.

A lot of doors have been closed in my face, but usually I kick them in.

I was told I could never be chief coroner. I was told I could never be an MPP. I was told I could never get approval for this drug, Alzene.

If I was told I couldn't have something I wanted then it was almost a certain guarantee that I was going to get it. Well, there certainly was a major effort.

I expanded to fill all the possibilities. If there was a power vacuum I'd grab it, and this drove people a little crazy. They never quite knew when to stop me, or where to draw the line, and I would sort of — slide around behind.

I never hated anybody in my life. I think I was motivated by personal revenge — but revenge and hatred are very different things. I never hated Arthur Wishart, the attorney general who brought me down when I was coroner; I thought he was a fine gentleman, but I wanted to get back at him. . .

Until I got this damned Parkinson's I enjoyed the heat. I always thought, "Oh God! here we go again" — because I knew I could best them in a debate and I could best them in facts and I wasn't afraid of them. But I'm losing it now, unfortunately.

I'm still not afraid of them.

I believe in truth. I believe in doing the right thing.
I believe in getting even when I see things that drive me crazy.

How do you tell the difference? I don't. Sometimes they get mixed up. That's the trouble.

I'm usually on the side of the angels.

I don't do anything wrong. Never.

Never.

There is someone out there in the big doubting financial community who does esteem Morty for being the Canadian unicorn he is; one who would see the hedging, the chivvying of bureaucrats as the marks of exciting individualism and potential for greatness.

This diviner is one Richard G.D. Lafferty, known as a great shaggy individualist of an investment analyst himself, nesting away in a tiny office at Lafferty, Harwood and Partners.

For Lafferty, like Wedbush Morgan's Saks, Shulman is a burry little diamond hedgehog; much like Lafferty himself, whose plummy verbose and occasionally malaprop paragraphs of analysis read like a cross between Dickens, Yogi Berra and Conrad Black.

"There are not many people on the Canadian scene," he writes in his August 27 newsletter, clearly savoring every single syllable:

"... with the energy and ability to pursue original ideas. Dr. Morton Shulman is among these. Because he disturbs the conformists in the medical field, the financial markets and the red neck politicians he arouses wrath and mean retaliatory vindictives. Through his own mischievous humor he tends to egg them on with the result a credibility image has occurred.

"Be that as it may, he has successfully pioneered the use of Eldepryl as a therapy for Parkinson's disease. He created the parent Canadian company to develop and market pharmaceutical products for the central nervous system, dermatological uses and osteoporosis.

"This company [Deprenyl U.S.A.], which is listed in Canada and the U.S. was established to develop and implement the regulatory steps required to obtain marketing approval in the United States for dermatologic applications of ALA photodynamic therapy. . . . This is the skin cancer area that is increasingly coming into world focus because of the sun and ozone situation. . . ."

"A great deal of work has to be done before it is broadly applied but the principles appear to be clearly established as long as one can gain access by light to the affected areas. FORECAST: This is the investment in and the pursuit of an idea. There are many hurdles to be crossed but there is enough satisfactory evidence. . . ."

The news of the Lafferty nod has buoyed Morty. His recycled 1970s orange paisley tie seems bright and shiny, his speech and body control is improved hugely over that of the day before.

He has only been told about the Lafferty recco; the newsletter is only sent out to the biggest of big cheeses, he says excitedly — you have to be turning over $10 million a year, and you can't ask to be cited — oh no! And this is one of the most important respected analysts in the business. . . . Tonight he intends to go home, raise a glass of wine to Mr. Lafferty and his great acumen.

* * *

Lafferty or no, the bottom is falling out.

DEPRENYL PRICE SLIDES AFTER CRITICAL STORY
IN U.S. PAPER

The stock dropped 38 cents to $7.63, bringing to 9 per cent the decline so far this week. The tumble began Tuesday after publication of a front-page article in *The Wall Street Journal* that was critical of Deprenyl and its marketing of Alzene. . . .

Martin Barkin has used all his political savvy to smooth the waters. "The only thing that's happened in the last two weeks is that Morty has been the subject of news articles," he tells reporters. Barkin also issued a press release which took the unusual step of predicting Deprenyl's pre-tax net income from pharmaceutical operations would be $1 million in the 3rd quarter compared with $728,000 in the same quarter a year earlier.

But notwithstanding, analyst Michael James, Health Care analyst with Montreal-based Dlouhy Investments, expects the stock price to keep falling . . . while "defending the worth "of other products: a good future for Eldepryl, "and the 5-ALA drug they are developing is going to work, I'm very confident of that."

Autumn is on its way.

The Deprenyl caper is rapidly ceasing to be fun.

To Market, To Market, or Shorting in a Limo with Luan

The time: 7:45 a.m., December 9th, 1992.

The place: The block-long white Caddy limo heading to pick Morty up and take him to work, driven by Shulman chauffeur and market disciple Luan Nguyen, who is explaining his short position on PetroCan.

SK: So it doesn't make you nervous, huh?

LUAN: No, no, not yet. If a week more, stop trading big volume, and nothing happen, I can't remain in it. But, right now, no.

SK: Well, there was a story yesterday that they're trying to prop it up.

L: Yeah, they try to sell, but they're looking for buyers now.

SK. How much did you get involved?

L: About 5,000 shares.

SK: 5,000 shares, but you don't own them, you're shorting them, right? Whatever that is. Some day it will become clear to me, when I'm old and smart, I suppose.

L: The market, it's hard to understand.

SK: It's impossible. Really, I'm very admiring. You never were involved in anything like that back in your home?

L.   No, never.

SK: Only when you started taking the *MoneyLetter*. When you started that, you were still involved in the grocery business?

L: Yes, yes.

SK: What gave you the idea of taking the stock course?

L: When I work in a company. I used to work early every morning, and I saw some people, they try to study to become more involved in stock...And I say, "Why is that?" and they say "To make money." So one day I get the *Toronto Star* and I get inside, an ad that says "You really become a millionaire" and "How to Make Money in the Market" and like that.

SK. Ah. It was a newspaper insert, from Hume.

L.   And I said, "Very interesting," and "I will study and make money". It was very exciting and I love it more everyday.

SK: How long did it all take?

L: Every two weeks they send one or two letters and, if you study like that, maybe one year there would be about 31 or 32 lessons.

SK: And there was basic information on how it worked, and then there were specific tips on things to invest in?

L: No. That is different. That, you get *MoneyLetter*, so I get it. I get it until 1990. I'm upset with them because the Deprenyl Research, going up too much from $3.00, then go up, up, up, every year, but they didn't recommend.

SK: Oh, Dr. Shulman was no longer involved with the *Money-Letter*.

L: Yeah, and I said, "Oh, that's not for me any more" and so I quit that.

SK: What was the first thing that you ever invested in?

L: In mutual funds. In the Hume Fund, but I got out before the market crashed. I got out at $14 and, after two months or three, four months, the market crashed, that fund is

---

195

going down too much. I still left there $1,000...until I get out, that's only 800. That one lost money. After the Fund sold to somebody else.

SK.: Were you already married at that point?

L: No.

SK: I was going to ask you if your wife got nervous. You got married not very long ago.

L: No, three years.

SK: How did you meet your wife?

L: I met my wife in Canada. Someone recommended her to me.

SK: So. PetroCan had set $8 for its issue. But people are buying it for less than that. Now, how does shorting it work?

L: It is softening now, the market, value right now still almost $7, almost $7.82, 83 cents, and they stop sell, and now they sell on the market at that price and, later on, they stop to sell . . . and then they make $1.00 on $8.00 if they sell right now.

SK: O.K. They'll sell right now.

L: And they buy later on, they buy low.

SK: Oh, they buy it back low. O.K. So that what Dr. Shulman has done is basically he's pledged to cover, say, a million shares at $7.80, which are really being sold. So, without putting out any money, they're selling them on his behalf at $7.80.

L: The guy he trading to, he get very good trade from commission and the trading too. For the regular, for me, if I want to stop sell, if I buy the stock, right. I must put all the margin mark-up. That mean, they borrow me, they lend me money, so I pay around 50% or 70%. They lend me 30% of it.

SK: So you have to put down that much.

L: Not to buy the stock. But, to short the stock, you have to put up 150%.

SK: Oh, you have to put up more?

L: Yes, 150%, if it was me, but if it Dr, Shulman, it different because he got lot of trading.

SK: So he might have to put up — ? We'll ask him what he has to put up.

L: Maybe he don't have to put.

SK: Maybe he doesn't have to put up anything. Maybe his credit is good enough.

L: Right, right.

SK: So that he says to them, "Put me down for a million shares" and then they sell them, in his name, at $7.80, without him putting up any money, so that they then hold the money that they've made —

L: He doesn't put money in maybe because, I think, in his account, enough to cover.

SK: He has enough to cover, or they know that he's good for it, yeah. O.K., so a million shares of the stock are then shorted, are then sold at $7.80, right? So there is, whatever it is, $7 M in that account, and the shorts count on it dropping more so that, when it goes down to $7, they then go and buy —

L: Buy. Now, he doesn't have anything. He borrow.

SK: He doesn't have anything, so he's selling something that he doesn't have, in effect.

L: But the short-sellers, they borrow the stock and give it him to sell. So, after low, he buy and give them back, that finish that transaction.

SK: So, in other words, like, if they sell the $7.8 M worth today, he, in effect, he has $7.8 in his pocket. When it drops, then he'll buy $7 worth and he keeps —

L: No, he didn't get any money now, no.

SK: No, but it's as if it was his?

L: Yes, and until he sell or he buy back and he give back, then O.K., that's how much he have and how much he have to put up to pay them, if he lost.

SK: But it counts on a selling transaction and then a buying transaction. . . . Oh, good morning, Morty. Luan and I were discussing this extremely elusive concept of short-ing. "He has it. No, he doesn't have it."

MS: I'll be happy to give you a comprehensive lesson at your convenience.

SK: Uh-huh. Now, as Luan was explaining, in the shorting sit-uation, on your credit, the broker will have, in effect, acquired the right to sell a million shares.

MS: He will have sold them.

SK; He will have sold them, O.K., without you ever having bought them. But, I mean, strictly speaking, if push ever came to shove, that's what you would have to cover.

MS: I would have to buy it back. He who sells what isn't his must buy it back or go to prison. Who was that great American?

SK: Um, Boesky?

MS: (laughs) No. Maybe one of the founding fathers. George Washington.

SK: So when the stock drops —

MS: You hope that the pressure will break up the syndicate, or lower the price. And, let's suppose they break the syndi-cate today. The other brokers that have it are going to rush to sell and, when they're rushing to sell, I'll be buy-ing it back. Now, with a little luck, I'll buy it back at $5.

SK: Uh-huh, and then, on the basis of that sale which you didn't have to pay for up front, I mean, —

MS: I didn't buy anything, so —

SK: No, I know, I know, but still, you'll wind up, if it goes for $5, you'll wind up pocketing —

MS: About three million dollars.

SK: And the whole Catch-22 and the terrifying and exhilarat-ing part of shorting is that as Luan said an ordinary per-son would have to put up 150% to short.

MS: Well, it's 150%, but it's really only 50% because you get the proceeds of the short. You have to put up 150%, but

---

198

you get 100%, so you only put up 50% The beautiful situation, the ideal short, is something where there's no risk on
the up side because, the nightmare is that, for some reason, the stock will go up to about $10 and you'll be forced
to buy it and you'll lost $3 M. So that's why this is the
ideal short. Everybody's got stock to sell. There's no
chance of it going up.

SK: Because, if it goes up, you're liable for it, not at the price
that you pledged, but at —

MS: I have to buy it. If they get up to $10, I'm in trouble. But
that's why this is such an ideal, I short rarely because I'm
not a gambler. But this is an almost sure situation.

SK: I see! . . . But, for a lot of people, this is a way of life.

MS: Oh, there are professional shorts. They'll short anything.
They're like those guys you see on planes with briefcases
going to gambling casinos all over the world, doing nothing but gamble. I always short sure things.

The risk here is an eighth of a point. If worse comes to
worst, I buy it back at $8.

SK: And then what? You're stuck with this huge —

MS: No, you don't have any stock. All I'm buying back is —
look, I've got nothing. If I sell 100 shares short today at
seven-and-seven-eighths and I buy it back tomorrow at $8
or at $6, if I buy it back at $8 I lose the commission, plus
an eighth of a point, but I have no stock and I never will
have any stock.

SK: Aha. I see . . . Hm. O.K., now I almost understand shorting. What are junk bonds?

MS: Junk bonds are bonds issued that have no — Well, bonds
are supposed to be debt and shares are supposed to be
equity. And the bonds, in theory, if you buy shares —
you're gambling; if you buy bonds — you're investing.
And, if Deprenyl Research was to issue $10 M worth of
shares and $1 M worth of bonds, the bonds that are in the
first column all are assets, so there's no risk. But junk

bonds are bonds that are issued in such a profuse quantity that they exceed the assets of the company. So, in effect, you're buying equity, instead of safety.

SK: Well, I mean, then is it really is like Zero Mostel in the movie *The Producers*, where he sold investors 150% of a play he was counting on to fail?

MS: There's a chance. What they're hoping is, with junk bonds, is that the company will do so well that it'll earn enough money to pay them off. Usually, it doesn't.

SK: Aha. Mm-hmm. If only this ingenuity could be turned to the good of mankind.

MS: Well, I'm told that Ivan Boesky was very kind to charities. To his dog, to all his children.

SK: Right. I see. Heavens to Betsy! Now here on your little stock screen, this is D.E.P.L.F.'s position on Petro-Canada common, price $7 7/8, and there's 393,750, yeah, bucks here, $2500 commission . . . and the net is 391,249.50. So that's your on-paper position on Petro-Canada.

MS: That's at that broker's.

SK: At that broker's. And how much have you got altogether?

MS: Quite a bit.

SK: So the whole office is following the *Business News* fairly closely. And should it wind up going up instead of down, everybody will share the —

MS: There will be hara-kiri. The worst thing that can happen is that nothing will happen.

SK: Yeah. I see . . .

The Parkinson's Years: Part III

48 Hours

One of the ways Morty tries to have a small amount of fun in September, 1992 is by contemplating a partnership with a notorious anti-abortionist evangelist named Reverend Ken Campbell.

"Odd couple meets over abortion pill" chortles the *Globe*'s Dan Westell, moving from his normal business niche to a choice spot up front in the news section. "A series of letters, faxes and phone calls late last month saw the two men negotiating to become co-chairmen of Lobby for Life, a nascent group aimed at convincing governments to spend as much on alternatives to abortion as governments spend on ending pregnancies.'

The good reverend is known for his hell-fire and damnation lectures on a wide range of modern iniquities, from rock concerts by Prince to Charter of Rights protection for homosexuals. Campbell claims that Morty agreed to pour bucks into his anti-abortion lobby if he in return agreed to endorse RU-486, the controversial French abortion pill, which Morty might be thinking of marketing in Canada. The profits from marketing the abortion-inducing pills would be turned over to fund the financially floundering anti-abortion lobby Choose Life.

It smells like a wonderfully aromatic stew. But Morty says the reverend fire-breather, whom he describes as an esteemed friend, has it wrong. The reverend insists Morty has it wrong. Although the subject will flame up again a few months hence, for now the matter flickers enchantingly, and dies.

But this is only the 3rd of September.

On the 5th comes the announcement that Purdue Frederick, the Canadian division of a U.S. drug company, is ending an 18-month-old agreement to market Eldepryl in Canada.

The official announcement says this is a mutual decision [with Deprenyl Research] because Deprenyl Research is acquiring the expanded sales staff it needs to market all of its own growing product pipeline.

On September 18th Bone Health gets a huge kick in the shin.

SmithKline Beecham announces it is dumping One-alpha D(2) because it feels preliminary data from the clinical trials did not demonstrate a significant difference between patients treated with the drug and those taking placebo. SmithKline transfers its marketing rights back to Bone Care International.

Deprenyl has a 14 per cent interest in Bone Care and holds 381,500 shares of Lunar Corp., the U.S. pharmaceuticals company associated with Bone Health. The announcement knocks Deprenyl shares from just above $7 to $6.63. The future of Bone Health is pronounced "uncertain."

If Deprenyl investors bail out of their Bone Health warrants, it could cost Deprenyl $3.4 million, instead of the $5 million it was counting on reaping. On September 19th, Deprenyl shares hit a 52-week low of $5.38.

Barkin tells the press the company is "paying the price for Morty's seeking — and getting — so much publicity. Deprenyl sure gets a lot of press attention," Barkin says ruefully.

The company has decided to "tone down its image notably by keeping its chairman and founder, the flamboyant Morton

Shulman, out of the limelight. "There is no question that Morty Shulman has tried to keep the media eye on this company and that has not always been the best policy for this or any other company."

Barkin adds that the evidence on which SmithKline based its pullout from Bone Health is "pretty flimsy."

Two days later Deprenyl shares clunk down to $4.70, totter back to $5.38. DUSA lurks around $6.75. Chief Financial Officer Ed Foster emphasizes the company is still in great shape financially, well able to come up with cash to redeem the Bone Health warrants if need be.

On September 23rd a special Deprenyl Research Limited board meeting is called.

* * *

"Shulman and Deprenyl may be in for a change. Board meeting today expected to address relationship," headlines the *Globe*. Dan Westell writes:

> For what may be the first time in his life, Morton Shulman has been rendered speechless. The co-chairman and single largest shareholder of Deprenyl Research Ltd. is not taking calls from the media, in what seems to be an attempt to remove one factor from the volatile mix that has kept Deprenyl stock in a state of agitation.
>
> He has told at least one media executive that the company will hold a press conference tomorrow to announce changes resulting from a board meeting today.
>
> But his secretary of 33 years is emphatic in denying that he will leave the company.
>
> "He'll always be here at the very head for as long as he can speak."

None of Morty's circle ever describes his state of well-being as anything but tip-top, even on his very worst days. Showing no pain has always been, one of Morty's firmest tenets. So Ann's words have an ambiguous, prophetic and dolorous ring.

Westell skips past her words to scroll the number-clogged screed of Morty's market dealings, those dealings that have swamped all awareness of the life-giving drug behind them.

No more $500-million romps through the currency markets in six months.

No more follies like the Morty-maneuvered purchase last summer of 380,000-plus shares of Lunar Corp., a share purchase that took U.S. $2 million out of the company coffers.

The Lunar purchase has taken a large bite — larger than Westell knows — from Deprenyl's resources and its stock standing.

But now Westell voices the nub of Bay Street's complaint about Morty:

> "Both deals are classic Shulman; both have in different ways come to haunt Deprenyl, which calls itself a pharmaceutical company but which makes most of its money on financial transactions."

(In the rich elastic tapestry of market ethics, whose warp and weft is too complex for most students of ordinary morality to fathom, the ways you are permitted to make money may seem limitless. But this particular way is a no-no.

Not always, but in this case.

(Not in every case like this, but in every case like this that involves Morton Shulman.)

The Westell piece continues:

> Dr. Shulman has been an active and, by all accounts, highly successful investor and speculator for many years, but Deprenyl represented several departures for him.

First, it seemingly began as a labor of love. Dr. Shulman. suffers from Parkinson's disease, and Deprenyl's initial business was distributing a previously little-known drug, Eldepryl, that has greatly helped patients suffering from the degenerative nerve disease.

Secondly, Deprenyl became a public company, which imposes certain rules and regulations on its officers and directors. Deprenyl has had at least two disputes with regulators since early summer.

And while Deprenyl has had modest success making money from drugs, it has had a stunning run in the stock market. The price hit $23.50 Canadian in January before beginning a slide that took it to yesterday's close of $5.37.

While he has a lot at stake — about 1.6 million shares at last report — certain aspects of the company's business appeared to be left totally in his hands, in a way that a private company might leave vital functions in the hands of one executive. . . .

But Deprenyl's days as a currency trader are over, and its equity transactions may well fall under much tighter control. The company announced on Aug. 31 that it had appointed Sen. Stanley Haidasz and retired investment executive Martin Seigerman to serve on an investment committee. . . . It appears the committee was formed too late to oversee the multiple daily calls Dr. Shulman was making to his currency trader.

The market was still absorbing the currency deals when Deprenyl disclosed it owned 380,000 shares of Lunar Corp., a U.S. company that lost $6 (U.S.) a share in one day's stock trading last week. Dr. Shulman did the Lunar trading, Dr Barkin said. The stock was bought over the summer when.

Lunar traded for between $15-21. It closed (Sept. 22) at $9.50 on NASDAQ.

The official press release comes the next day: "Martin Barkin Named CEO of Deprenyl Research. Morton Shulman to Remain Chairman."

The announcement, put in Morty's mouth, rings with uncharacteristic corporate phrases like "consistent with our management succession plans" and "the company entering a new period in its history."

Morty is to remain co-chairman of the board of directors, but "the entrepreneurial business approach used to launch the company is being supplanted by a greater focus on professional management and strategic planning. Dr. Barkin's background and management style make him the ideal person to take over leadership of the company."

Dr. Shulman, a postscript says, "will be available to answer questions, but only between 10 a.m. and noon on Thursday Sept. 24, 1992."

He will give no sign that Martin Barkin and the Deprenyl board have moved to demand Morty turn over his power, shoved him out as CEO — insisting, and finally getting, a written pledge that he will cease activities and speaking on behalf of the company that he carved out of thin air.

The day after Dr. Barkin is elevated to CEO, he sends a letter to Shulman asking to have Shulman's salary as CEO diverted over to himself. Shulman gleefully replies that he is happy to turn it over in full, "But, as I have never drawn a salary as CEO, it will not be of much help to you". Morty personally takes the letter over to Barkin. Barkin reads it, turns red in the face and rips it into little pieces.

The *Star* runs one of its more recent file pictures. The heavy drunkish eyes, the grin a rictus, and gray. Old.

Barkin tells reporters there will be a brake on Morty's currency activities, which will be supervised by two outside advisers. "Shareholders have to be confident such things are being closely monitored." And, "while Shulman's health is good, the company is definitely looking at succession planning. We accept the fact that Morty is 67 years old . . . and we are taking a look at succession planning as it deals with his son Geoff."

The king is dead; long live the kings.

The shares close up 13 cents that night: $5.50. The industry analysts express their approval. Confidence reigns, sort of.

* * *

Four o'clock in the afternoon, Wednesday, September 23.

At the end of a long day, Morty is waiting for Luan to take him home, playing and replaying the day's infamy like a phonograph needle stuck in a groove.

Nobody would talk to them, so the *Globe* interviewed Ann yesterday!

I'm having a press conference tomorrow and I told them, Send me anyone but Westell. I won't talk to Westell. Since May 19th, Westell has been going after Deprenyl and me. [For comfort, he turns to his stock monitor. Perks up, just a little.]

I've been driving the dollar down! I'm one of the first in Toronto. People do it in Europe, in the U.S. How many Toronto dealers in currency are there? Wait a second. [He punches through a call, puts it on the speakerphone, barks a name at the secretary who answers.]

Danny Gordon. He's in a meeting? . . . Somebody else then. It's important. Everyone's in meetings. Then get Danny Gordon out just for 30 seconds. Tell him it's urgent. . . . Danny, give me the honest truth on this, it's for my biography. How many other dealers in Toronto are trading dollars? [Gordon pauses, laughs. His voice is a mirror of Morty's: short, sharp, no bullshit. "That's a hard one. . . . Individuals? None. Banks, a couple."]

Okay. Thanks. . . . That's news to me. That's a surprise. [Morty laughs weakly.]

Roma Dzerowicz, Deprenyl Research business coordinator, pearly pink and round of face, climbs into the limo with Morty. A soft perfumed presence that somehow manages to be peach and pink and no-nonsense all at once, she is bound for a launch party for Sylvia Fraser's *The Book of Strange*.

Morty and Luan tell each other it was a good day. The dollar went down half a cent.

Morty's speech is slow, sluggish and dry, his eyes red and face gray with the stress of the day. The attacks, all the attacks: why, who, wherefore?

Suddenly, there's a whole article on the hedging activities of Deprenyl Research. A little 50-million-dollar company. Why so much attention? Who benefits from the attacks on the company? The shorts benefited. Alex Winch called and said: "I'm going to destroy the company and eliminate you."

The company is doing wonderfully. We're getting lambasted because of the vendetta against Morty.

It's affecting thousands of people: patients, people with stock. Why does the Ontario Securities Commission harass only the people buying Deprenyl Research? Debbie Worobec bought 1,000 shares and they came to investigate her; said, You bought 18 minutes before such a such a press release. But that release was bad news for the company! Percy Parks, my bodyguard bought 20 shares and they went to interrogate him. In his hospital bed in Belleville!

"It's been a difficult time," Roma agrees softly, talking of the mood in the office, all the attacks on Morty and the stock in which they all have so heavily invested. "We try to think positive. But it can be tough. Demoralizing. . .

"Are you coming to the book party?" she asks.

"It's been a terrible day," he says.

"Maybe I should ask for my salary in U.S. dollars," says Roma.

He puts a hand on her round knee, leans on her like a child resting for comfort against his nanny.

* * *

Moving like a stick man, he gets out of the car and lets himself in his front door. Luan drives off, taking Roma to the party.

"Gloria! Hello, I'm home."

The long living room, lapped with paintings, hangings, antiques, is empty and quiet.

"Gloria! Gloria, I'm home."

Morty sinks into a pale Louis XVI chair. On the coffee table is a copy of Sylvia Fraser's new book.

A moment later, with a flurried shuffle on the stairs, Gloria appears, in dark straight skirt, white silk blouse, and furry slippers. She is frowning, impatient, but containing it. "I'm here. I'm here. Hello. We expected you to dinner twice before but you disappointed us. What would you like to drink? A glass of white wine?"

She hurries off, returns with two glasses of wine, a pewter glass of water, a silver bowl of almonds, her look still harried.

"Morty, when would you like dinner? You know I won't be joining you."

Ten minutes, he says.

The time is just 4:48.

"Do you have 10 minutes' worth of questions? Wait a minute." He makes his way upstairs, returns with papers stuffed askew into a copy of *ArtNews* magazine, launches slurredly into a story of foiling Boris Yeltsin at Sotheby's. . . . "Gloria. Do you have the Gotha watch book?"

Gloria hurries in, harried again. "It should have been with the other — I'll look. It should be . . ."

"Never mind, Gloria. Not important."

"No, I'll take a look, but I don't know if I can find — "

"Never mind, Gloria. Gloria, never mind. The Germans have agreed to buy back three historic pieces. The clock, there, and two antique guns. " He gestures at a glass case of weapons that look like blunderbusses. "Gloria! The Germans have agreed to buy the pieces on our terms. A million dollars."

"You say they're buying the pieces, Morty? Which pieces do you mean?" She is in, fretfully, again, flicking on display cabinet lights.

"The clock and the two antique rifles. Not the duelling pistols, the rifles."

His stance has stiffened, body flinging in stiff jerks as he speaks or moves his arms. He has a pattern of arm movement as concealment: flinging one crooked arm across his front, or behind his back, or over the back of his chair, camouflaging the involuntary movements with deliberate ones.

"You're saying those two and you're pointing, but which ones do you mean? There are several different guns in there. Do you means these, or these?"

"Those," he says, flinging his arm again.

"I still don't know which you are pointing to," she says, speaking with special precision.

She vanishes from the room again.

Morty drinks half his glass of wine, leads the two-person march into the dining room. It is not quite 5 o'clock. The large empty bright room is lit by early evening sun through three windows over the garden. An antique English oak table with room for a dozen is set for two, one to the far end, one to the right; linen placemats with hand-worked sprigged edging.

From the kitchen pantry at the far end comes the sound of Gloria's voice on the phone. The house is profoundly empty, it feels inhabited by no one.

"Oh, you're in here. You said 10 minutes and it was 20." For the next 12 minutes Gloria darts in and out with plates of food, one course overlapping another. There is cabbagey broth in china bowls, a platter of rusks and cheese, two large plates of appetizers; a murmuring about having to get ready to go out, about Gloria's desire that Morty have wholesome food, about not being sure just what to cook. The appetizers of beautifully arranged smoked salmon, sauce, asparagus and an unidentifiable brackish-green vegetable are barely touched when two more big plates appear, each with a large dry chicken leg and a single boiled potato.

The time is 5:12.

Gloria sits at the table briefly and feverishly. She is to go out, her best friend Sylvia is having a book launch, and Morty was to have come . . .

"I had a terrible day," he says.

She wasn't sure what he would want to eat, so she went out and got these chicken legs, free-range chicken, because it would be good for him to eat some plain healthy food, but, as she sees he's enjoying the smoked salmon, would he like more of that, instead of the chicken? — and the herbed bread is very good. Watches as he takes one bite.

"This is fine, Gloria, this is plenty, it's fine."

But is he not going to eat the chicken? The chicken she went out and bought — although it would be good for him, if he doesn't want to eat it . . .

She takes the chicken plates away. "And I have some fruit salad for you." There are chunks of fruit in glass bowls, she removes the appetizer plates of still-unconsumed salmon bits, and is back out and in again, plunking down a thick red book with more papers stuffed inside: The Gotha clock book, a history of his German clock which Morty put together himself, just 12 copies, a couple of them given to museums. He is spooning down fruit salad as he speaks, recounting, hardly intelligibly, a story of the deal he pulled off for a wonderful snuff box from *A la vielle Russie*, a luxe antique dealer's in New York, only $80,000 . . .

"That shouldn't go in the biography," Gloria interrupts. "I

don't think it would be appreciated if that went in. I hate this book. I hate it," she says with intensity.

"Don't worry, Gloria. Maybe like Stewart says it won't come out till after I'm dead and gone." Stewart is daughter Dianne's husband. Morty gives a slurred cackle.

"But don't you understand that even if you're gone the fall out will cover the rest of us," she says. She shakes her head, still angry. "Morty gouges," she says. "He gouges. Like that business with the turkey and *eye* magazine.

"*Eye* wanted to know what wine to serve with a moderate Thanksgiving dinner and he told them he would serve a Lafitte 1961!" Morty finds this uproariously funny, but Gloria shakes her head again. "It wasn't necessary," she says. "It wasn't necessary." She vanishes to get ready for her party.

After all the years of smiling stories for the press, this year Gloria has for the first time gone public with her displeasure.

Telling a reporter who was doing a profile on Morty that he is "spoiled by his mother and his wife." That for 42 years he swallowed Gloria up while she stayed home "facilitating Morty's every need for 42 years. It's the kind of personality he had, his enormous energy, he swamped me."

She had much to contribute, Gloria told the reporter, there is much she longed to do, but Morty stilled her song.

"I went to the NDP Waffle convention in Winnipeg and I came out of there with so much to say and there he was and he just went on and on — he never stops talking — and I realized I would never have my say. It's a great loss. He squelched me. But I have nobody to blame but me. Morty doesn't understand why I should ever have been angry at him. He is as good as he can be. He does the best he can with every moment. He's a fighter, such a fighter. He has never once complained about the Parkinson's."

But Morty is restless at night, roams the house, moves from bed to bed, wakes her up. "I've always been too aware of him." And now, she says, he's very dependent on her. She's not getting enough sleep. "Morty rents a villa and takes a crowd of people. It's a week of 'adore-Morty.'" She smiles. She ends on a gallant positive note. "I'm the worker bee. But I'm not complaining. I have been well rewarded. It's a fairy tale life. . ."

* * *

It has become a sore place between them, this public dissatisfaction of hers, particularly now. Now they are both coming out with it. He does waken her, he does lean on her, does have her transcribe his 3 a.m. brainwaves, filling sheet after sheet of yellow foolscap with her neat schoolgirlish hand, because no one can read his writing any more, including himself. But he returns to the sore place often, poking at it again and again.

Gloria is — she's supportive externally but internally she's told me I'm wrong on every issue. She thinks my judgment is very bad. For the last 30 years she's thought I've done everything wrong. She always criticizes me. — She always agrees with whoever says anything on the other side! If I disagree with my son she says, You should do what he says. She thinks Geoffrey's always right and can do no harm, and she thinks I'm always wrong and do no good!

It's not a question of rationality; it's a question of male-female relationships.

We had a lot of very dramatic, exciting, romantic early years; other people were struggling, we were travelling across the Gobi desert. We had a wonderful 20 years and she became disenchanted. I don't know why. She was fine, she was lovely, she was apparently happy — she was nice to me. I don't understand.

She has, in the last 10 years or so developed terrible financial insecurity. So I transferred the house, put it in her name — there's no mortgage on it. I bought annuities that can't be touched. And she's still financially insecure.

213

She never went to university, only high school. I grabbed her off. She could have taken a job as a model, took one for a few months — oh yes, she was beautiful, I was jealous of her, I didn't want her modelling. I was jealous of her, but she was never jealous of me. Totally tolerant. She's wonderful as far as that goes, she's perfectly tolerant, she gives me a lot of space. She's very secure in herself. Very secure in my loyalty to her. And I wouldn't do anything disloyal to her, I would never — betray her. . .

My daughter Dianne is something else. She actually became me. Except she's worse than me because with her there's no greys — everything is black and white. I see a lot — I can compromise.

I know how to compromise. Dianne can never compromise, she storms ahead. Damn the torpedoes.

She's an environmental lawyer and takes everything very seriously. She never lost a case when she was a prosecutor with the government and she's never lost a case since she went into practice.

When other lawyers see her show up in court they tend to relax because she looks like a frail child. Then, they can't believe what she does to them. When she worked for the Department of the Environment, I went down to hear her give a speech to a group of lawyers. the room was packed and she gave a carefully reasoned argument. When she concluded, she said "You will now hear the other side of the argument from (prominent lawyer X) who will disagree with me. I feel dutybound to warn you that he has now defended 17 cases which I have prosecuted, and he has lost them all.... do not pay too much attention". The lawyer flushed red, rose to his feet, opened his mouth and nothing came out.

Her most disruptive case was after she was transferred from the crown attorney's to the public trustee's office, where they thought she would have nothing to do. Couldn't stir anything up. So she's sitting over there going through old files, and finds a case in the docket of a lawyer who had swindled his clients 15 years ago and gone to jail.

She got it in her head that that money should be owed by all the lawyers in the partnership. Everyone said, No, you can't win." But she did. Went to court, won the damn thing, caused absolute catastrophe because by now some partners have retired, some have become judges, and the amount of money now mounted up, because of interest, to millions and millions of dollars.

To add to the consternation, Dianne was 8 3/4 months pregnant with her first child, Rebecca. The judge said, "I hope you're not going to have that baby in court and stain my carpets."

Before the appeal could be heard she was transferred to the department of energy, where a special cabinet meeting was called after she began demanding that presidents of companies found guilty of polluting be given jail sentences.

She's . . . she's a devil. I'm very proud of her.

She won't talk about me. She dodges having anything to do with publicity about me but she's learning the value of it for herself.

Oh, she was difficult as a kid. She was wonderful the first two years and then when she started meeting other children she was — she had a very unhappy time, a very unhappy childhood. We had terrible troubles with her and she was unruly and disobedient and did not recognize anyone who wasn't smarter than her. She had problems with her mother. Didn't see eye to eye on anything. Couldn't get along with other children and it was very difficult for her, very difficult for us and . . . it all turned around when she grew up and became a lawyer and met other great people. Was acknowledged and wrote all these books. She got her PhD without getting an MA and did the whole damn thing in six months.

I had my IQ tested when Dianne took her Mensa test. I made the mistake of trying to compete with her. She whipped me terribly, whipped me. She had an IQ of 175. Mind-boggling. Mine is 163 which is fairly . . . not bad. It was the first time I realized I wasn't the smartest person in the world. . .

My son Geoffrey is more measured; he's bright. He's not as brilliant as she is, but he's bright. He's a mixture, a mixture of Gloria and me. Geoffrey is a gentle soul and he's always been bright, above average, but amiable. He doesn't have the sharp edges that Dianne has. Everybody loves Geoffrey, which is good in a way. It can make you vulnerable. It can make you soft, too.

He's president . . . he was president of this company. He's now co-chairman; the president and chairman of DUSA, which runs the ALA. He went back to his dermatology practice for a while, but he's actually given it up and moving in here, full time.

Geoffrey works at a more measured pace. He doesn't have the passions. He won't be — what drives him crazy is the way I go off and get an idea and do it without discussing it with him. He says, "All I ask you, Dad, is to discuss it with me". He says, "We're a team here," and he's a more normal human being. . .

You know, what Gloria would love is for me to get the Order of Canada. Been trying for it for years, wasting Gloria's time and money. Sylvia Fraser has written the applications. They're never going to give it to me. Last year there were 168 nominations, 167 appointees — I was distinguished — extinguished. Same with the Order of Ontario. Year after year.

Never. A small bet? Maybe after I'm dead.

I don't care for myself. But Gloria would be thrilled.

———————

Ready to leave, Gloria has smoothed the edges down. She praises Morty's stamina, tsk-tsks at the way people ask lugubriously about him. "People do this careful composing of the face, and ask" — she mimics their grave tones — "'How's Morty?' I say he's fine, just fine. The harder things get the better he is." She gives instructions on how to spot the signs that Morty is fading and the visit must end. "When he stops bubbling, when he starts looking as though he's listening intently, that's the time to go."

"I didn't want to go to the party because I didn't like Sylvia's book," he confides *sotto voce* when she has gone. "What's it about? I don't know. I didn't like her last book either, the one about remembering her abuse as a child. I don't believe it," he says."Don't tell Gloria."

Upstairs he leads a tour through a colony of console phones; sometimes two per room, a map of his restless nighttime travels. There are glasses of water with striped straws, little dishes of pills placed beside chairs and beds. Half a dozen beds: one in the library anteroom, a double bed in a small room to the right, in the farthest room, which was once the master suite, a huge round bed, looking unused. There is also a daybed, and another couple of single beds.

Which is his, which hers, any of them?

"We sleep in separate bedrooms now; we have been for three years. It was a gradual thing," he says. Since I have been taking Sinimet I tend to wake up and wander from bed to bed, and Gloria was not getting any sleep.

The room with the round bed, built *Playboy* mansion fashion in the '60s, is dotted with a collection of antique and handcarved merry-go-rounds. "My toys," he says. Turns on each of them, one by one.

Is there anything not part of a collection, bought simply for its solitary self?

Now the magician's snuff boxes; gilded and gemmed.

A picture of one he says he would give anything for, priced in the catalogue at $3 million U.S.

He talks about counting blessings. About conquering. "This Parkinson's is a nuisance," he says. With the laugh, but not loud. "It's conquered me."

217

"I've been lucky enough to be supported by people who love me," he says. "Gloria. Debbie. Kim. Ann. I've had a sybaritic life. There's nothing I would change, nothing I would do any differently."

He is not bubbling anymore.

It's time to say good night. Let the ramrod will slump, let the driven body relax.

He has not even begun to reveal the extent of the disaster that is now upon him.

Morty only tells disasters when they are past, and melted into the chalice of a bright new triumph-to-be.

* * *

In October, Morty gives a relentlessly entertaining and upbeat speech to the Toronto Board of Trade Entrepreneurs' Club.

He calls it, meaning the title to be thoroughly ironic, "The Rise and Fall of an Entrepreneur."

I am a most unlikely entrepreneur. I began very late at the age of 62 completely by accident. Prior to that point I had a series of odd jobs. I could not hold a job. Every four years I would be fired or I would get bored and quit. I never had to meet a payroll and for 35 years I had one employee — my ancient and faithful secretary.

In 1987 I started a new company in an industry that has been a failure in Canada and I've had the most exciting, productive, infuriating and absolutely horrible five years of my life. I think the horror climaxed some weeks ago when my picture appeared on the front page of the *Wall Street Journal* in an article purportedly about Alzene, a new drug we are developing for Alzheimer's, but much of the article described my character defects in great detail. The *Globe & Mail* reprinted the article the next day.

Being an entrepreneur in Canada is a much admired and praised profession. The one thing that is not tolerated is success. This is the Canadian disease.

A broker told me a story the other day of the man walking down Fifth Avenue carrying a bucket of lobsters. He came to a red light and put the pail down to rest. Another man waiting for the light said to him, "You'd better be careful, those lobsters will climb out of the pail." He replied, "No they won't, they are Canadian lobsters; if one gets near the top the others will pull him back down."

In 1982 I developed Parkinson's disease and by the spring of 1987 I was so disabled that I was desperate. My doctor told me of a drug called Eldepryl which was effective but was only available in Europe. I had a supply flown over and within days I was feeling normal.

I was so impressed that I wrote a nasty letter to Jake Epp, then Minister of Health, demanding to know why he did not allow the sale of Eldepryl in Canada. He replied, "I wish it was sold here, no one ever applied."

That was the day I became an entrepreneur. I contacted the company in New Jersey which had the Canadian rights, Somerset Pharmaceuticals, and I asked if I could buy in. The girl on the phone replied that they were in the process of selling 15 per cent of the company because they were broke, but they had just received a one million dollar offer from DeGussa, the German distributor. I replied that I was willing to pay more than DeGussa and would fly down the next day. The lady asked if I was bringing my staff. I replied, "Of course," and then phoned my bridge club where I recruited three shills to come with me.

When we arrived it was a weird scene. There was a long hall with an office at each end. In one office sat Don Buyske, chairman of the company, and in the other office sat the president, glaring at each other. They had not spoken for seven years and hated each other almost as much as they hated the moneyman on the board.

I introduced my companions as my accountant, my underwriter and my medical consultant and for the rest of the morning I travelled between the two offices trying to make a deal. I offered them $1.25 million in comparison to DeGussa's $1 million.

After talking to my pseudo-experts the president said: "We cannot go with you, we have to go with DeGussa. Your extra $250,000 does not make up for their expertise. We are running out of time and money and have been working on this for nine years." I pulled him aside and said, "If you go with DeGussa, 10 years from now you will have a great medical company and you will still be working for those bastards Buyske and the moneyman. If you come with me I will raise the offer to $1.4 million and I will buy your personal shares for $1 million cash and you will be gone in two weeks to enjoy life." He bit, and one week later I owned 28 per cent of Somerset.

I was not sure what to do next. The moneyman represented Johnson's Wax. He disliked me at first sight and he made it very clear that he wanted to sell the company to anyone but me. I came home and my next-door neighbor John Plaxton saw me running around the garden and suggested that I do a public issue in Canada and his firm would underwrite it.

Two weeks later I signed the contract with Wood Gundy which called for the public issue of 2,000,000 shares at $3 a share, the company to be called Deprenyl Research Limited.

This was October, 1987. The issue was due in November of the same year and when the market crashed, John called me to say that he had to kill the issue. I replied, "Do not kill it, I will be responsible." By the end of December only 300,000 shares were committed and I was desperate.

On January 2nd I got lucky. A doctors' convention in Toronto was being addressed by a Dr. H. from Ottawa University on the topic of Parkinson's. I went to his lecture, learned that he was being sponsored by Sandoz Pharmaceuticals and listened to a one-hour praise of bromocriptine, which happens to be manufactured by Sandoz. Bromocriptine is truly a dreadful drug. I tried it. The drug made me faint, vomit and totally disabled me without helping the Parkinson's.

At the end of Dr. H's speech I asked him, "What about Eldepryl?" He replied, "Nobody knows about Eldepryl; it has only been tried on 12 people." I said, "That is not true." I had papers that showed it had been used successfully on 30,000 people. The meeting ended in a shouting match and I was thrown out.

Come the next morning, Wood Gundy's switchboard lit up. All the doctors were trying to buy. The order book was filled that day. I got my $6 million and I was in business.

I hired one employee, the prettiest girl I could find, gave her a desk in my basement, and announced to the world that I had the cure for Parkinson's. The reaction was not very favorable. Dr. G, Canada's most famous neurologist, called it a stock scam. Toronto's most prominent neurologist, Dr. K, said, "I will never write a prescription for Eldepryl." Dr. H said it was useless and it would never replace bromocriptine. I went down to the Parkinson's Foundation and was thrown out bodily with cries of rogue, cheat and malpractice ringing in my ears. They wanted nothing to do with me.

So I began travelling across the country from little town to little town talking to small groups of Parkinson's patients about Eldepryl wherever I could find them and spreading the word. A few of them insisted that their doctors write the prescription and they got better. They told their friends and sales began to pick up, reaching the then-amazing level of $500 a week.

Then the big companies began to call. Sandoz came

and laughed. The president of Searle struggled through the mess in the basement and said he had seen an operation like this once before in Mexico. The Mexicans were selling iguana oil.

Finally Dupont sent a representative, one Roger Odette, who carefully looked around and said, "You've got a gold mine here. Don't sell to Dupont, hire me and I will build a huge company for you." I did and he did.

The first day he was with me we flew down to the States to try to find a partner to help buy out Somerset. At the border the customs officer asked, "What do you do?" I replied, "We are drug dealers." Roger turned pale and the customs officer said, "Go right through; we give priority to drug dealers."

Things were improving steadily but slowly when to my absolute amazement one day the headlines of *The New York Times* reported the findings of Dr. Langston's study in California that Eldepryl not only controls the symptoms of Parkinson's but also slows the development of the disease. Suddenly and briefly I was a hero. Dr. G, Dr. K and Dr. H began to write prescriptions for Eldepryl. I was approached by the Parkinson's Foundation and all was sweetness and light.

A year ago I was approached by Phil Frost, president of Ivax, a Florida-based pharmaceutical company. Phil said to me, "Morty, I have bought the rights to an incredible drug that seems to restore memory in Alzheimer's disease and may improve memory in normal individuals. I would like you to purchase the Canadian rights. This is the biggest thing you are ever going to see in your life and I want a million dollars for it."

I am approached to buy new drugs every day of the week, so I did not get too excited, but I told Phil to send me the literature. Two unpublished double-blind studies arrived the next day and I was blown away. The results were fantastic. I immediately phoned Phil and said, "I will buy it." He responded, "It is $5 million." I protested: "But you said $1 million yesterday," to which he replied, "That was before you said you loved it." We worked it out and I actually paid him half a million dollars cash and stock and promised to pay another $4 1/2 million if we ever get full sales approval which will probably be some time long after I am put in an old folks' home.

I announced the drug, filed an IND (application for investigational new drug status) with the government and asked for volunteers to test it.

The response was exactly the same as with Eldepryl. The same doctor in Quebec, without testing the drug or knowing what its contents were, said it was worthless and denounced it as a stock scam. The Alzheimer's Society would have nothing to do with me, and a host of hostile articles appeared in the press supposedly discussing my new drug, Alzene, but containing a litany of my past sins, a dissection of my personality defects and most common, an accusation that there was something seriously wrong with Deprenyl Research because it had no debt and made the money to buy new drugs by making capital investment and by hedging in currency.

Cangene, Allelix, RML, QuadraLogic, DIME, Hela, Biochem, Biomera. Did you ever hear of any of these names? They are the other Canadian owned drug companies. They produce neither earnings nor dividends. Their share prices have fallen drastically over the last six months as has that of Deprenyl Research — but have you seen any critical word about any of them in the press? No one attacks them because they are good Canadian models. They are all in debt and lose money.

I was determined when we started this company that sick patients would not go without Eldepryl because of money, and following that policy we have now supplied at no charge over one thousand patients since we began, but you will not read that in the *Globe*. We have taken thousands of sick people and improved their health to the point that they have left hospital or nursing homes and returned to home or work, and we have innumerable grateful letters in our office attesting to this. But you will not read that in the *Globe*.

We have put 60 Canadians to work at well above the average wage; our lowest-paid employee receives $26,000 plus stock options. I have donated over five million dollars to Toronto hospitals — you won't read that in the *Globe*.

Deprenyl rapidly outgrew me. Two and a half years ago I knew that I needed a professional to take over. I wanted someone who was bright, young, ambitious, energetic and had government connections. There was only one person who fit that role in Canada, Dr. Martin Barkin, Deputy Minister of Health for Ontario. Over a six-month period I called him 12 times and he never returned my calls.

The company was expanding so rapidly that things were getting out of control. We had over 50 employees and the business had crept up from the basement to occupy the entire building. We solved the problem by renting commercial space up and down Roncesvalles, and now occupy three buildings on Roncesvalles Avenue. I found my new job running a company a nightmare.

I made one more call to Dr. Barkin. This time he took my call, we met for lunch and I made him an offer and he accepted on the spot. He made two conditions: 1) He will run the company and will not be anybody's front man and; 2) He will be the sole spokesperson of the company to the press.

Strangely, it turned out well. He is a tremendously competent man. He does not draw lightning the way I do, but all in all, he is a total disappointment to the press, who cannot get him to say the outrageous things I used to.

Thank you.

It is a bravura performance.

But by now, the memory of Morty in the exultant summer of 1989, year two on Eldepryl, Morty strong and outrageous, contrasts cruelly with Morty approaching winter 1992; a driven exhausted and over-medicated shadow.

By now, his symptoms held with more difficulty in abeyance, upping his dosages of l-dopa and Eldepryl to buy extra energy, Morty is grappling for control of his proud Canadian mini-pharmaceuticals empire. Willing himself to believe he can reverse the overthrow that began in September; his board, headed by his son and Martin Barkin, turning on him, abrogating his precious control, getting him to promise that Barkin and only Barkin will be company spokesperson.

Early in November he plays out with his no-nonsense Tyrannosaurus-Rex secretary Ann a diverting comic-opera reminiscent of the old days.

Doggedly behaving as though he were still ruler, in spite of all the newly crowned heads at the palace across the road, Morty is courting another government star for the Deprenyl board: federal Health and Welfare's prescription drug director Dr. Jacques Messier.

Morty is insisting on employing the good old time-tested techniques of courtship — faxing the upright object of desire into submission with a sparkling lure of stock-option riches:

* * *

"The average man lives with his mistakes," reads the latest fax Morty dictated to a reluctant Debbie:

> The intelligent man recognizes and corrects his errors. If you had accepted my offer last week, you would have made $275,000 so far.
>
> I respect your sense of loyalty and look forward to having you join us.

Ann is balking. The ancient-and-faithful secretary has never treated her master with the respect due a hero millionaire, but these days she is particularly on her mettle. She and helper-daughters Deb and Kim mill and mutter as Morty roars.

"Ann! Did you send that fax?"

Ann stomps to his doorway, fists planted on her hips, enunciation like hammerfalls.

"Are we *sure* this is what we want to say to this nice man? This is a *very* nice man, we *like* him and we want him to come here and are we *sure* this is the way we should talk to him?"

"Send it!"

"Deb and Kim both feel you should get another opinion on —"

"Sssh!"

"Have we checked with Dr. Barkin?"

"Send it!"

"No!'

"Send it!"

"I'm not sending it unless Dr. Barkin —"

"Copy Dr. Barkin and send it! Now!"

The fax is sent.

Messier never replies. He has already accepted a job with Novopharm Ltd., a major generic-drug competitor of Morty's.

The waning days of Deprenyl's fifth autumn have turned sere and cold.

Even as Morty was delivering the upbeat entrepreneuring speech, the whole thing was slipping away.

Down there in the market depths are Deprenyl millions sunk into Bone Health, which looked to be one of Morty's most promising new acquisitions.

It is not the news of the Bone Health fall alone that precipitates the dive in shares, nor Deprenyl's Morty-invested losses in Lunar.

As much as anything, as Westell has divined, it is the market finally taking its revenge on all of Morty's insufferable early success, all of it, all together: being both the user and the producer and the promoter, somehow keeping all the balls in the air and, for a long giddy time, earning a handsome return; and most insufferable of all, crowing about it repeatedly and publicly.

In October, in November, the creditors pounce. Five of his six brokers call their loans. Morty is confronted with $5 million in margin calls.

Overnight, he is bleeding. Hemorrhaging.

It started four weeks ago, when there was a raid, the stock was down to $3.80, everybody called my margins, everybody called my loans, and I was beset. I didn't know where I was going to raise all the money to pay everybody off at once.

Oh, it was terrible. It was terrible . . .

For a few moments he rallies. Takes a shot at trying to sound as though he's still having fun.

Oh, something funny happened on Hallowe'en. There was a party at Anita Wortzman's, and Sylvia Fraser had made me, for my birthday some years ago, a pair of fur trunks. X. asked if she could borrow them and she bought a fur brassiere to go with them, and came to the door trick-or-treating — and she was wearing practically nothing else, just those under a cape — she came trick-or-treating to the door and Y. said: "How could a woman that fat have the nerve to show off her ugly body?"

But there is little fun to be had. He is playing desperately for time. The Bone Health research results, he says, may have been misreadings because of a technological wipe-out.

Someone forgot to put the goddamned batteries in the machine monitoring the readings on bone density. They plugged it into the wall but didn't realize the batteries weren't in it. It ruined the readings on bone density and the stock collapsed and it looked like we lost four million dollars up front on one of our major drugs. The stock fell to $3.80. I was pushed out by my board, we lost all this money and it was a hellish week. And we sent all the stuff back to Bone Health and that's when the machine problem was discovered.

University of Connecticut was doing a two-year study on 60 patients, completed the studies, sent the X-rays and all of the material out for analysis and then the analysis showed nothing. The charts were not sorted. The X-rays and the charts were matched haphazardly. They had the wrong X-rays with the wrong patients. The study was done properly but the charts weren't filed with the right X-rays. They still know what the results are, so we're optimistic.

SmithKline, not so optimistic, stays out, leaving Morty raging and stammering about skulduggery and backstabbing and lack of appreciation.

The stocks were struck a mighty blow and I was responsible for the whole damn thing and they dumped on me — everybody — the press, the board, the management, although they're taking a slightly different attitude now. And that's when the Deprenyl investment committee got called in. The investments were taken out of my hands, so that's cost

228

$300,000 so far because of losing out on the Canadian dollar position. Meanwhile, all the millions of dollars of all the people who bought Bone Health shares got wiped out.

It sort of looks suspicious. I think the insiders from Lunar are buying. The buying is very heavy. . . .

The press and the analysts jump harder.

On November 15: "At the wacky end of the scale is Deprenyl Research Limited," jeers the *Financial Times*. "Despite the stock's drop from 52-week heights of $23.50 to $6 last week, the firm still has a staggering 160-multiple. Deprenyl is dear because it does little R&D (research and development) in Canada. It is concentrating on selling drugs that treat Parkinson's disease. In the firm's defence, it also has marketing arrangements in place for drugs being developed by European firms."

They're valuing the stock by dividing the capitalization by the R&D, which is crazy! Who decides it? Idiots who write this for $30,000 a year. Business writers. Nobodies. People who are successful at it don't write business tips; only people who are failures. I mean, I can't get (Vancouver moneyman) Peter Brown to write a column on his secrets. So you get Andrew Willis. Andrew Willis, multi-millionaire? Nobody. And giving bad advice week after week in the worst financial paper in the world.

Five days later, he is almost feigning equilibrium.

Today is November 20th. A very important day in my life.

Because today at 11:30 they're coming from Lunar and they're going to tell us whether the Alpha-D-2 works or not.

Today, this morning. You're talking to a man who has 10 or 20 million dollars at stake this morning. They're flying up to tell us. I can't believe they would fly up to give us bad news. That would just be ridiculous.That wouldn't make any sense. So I'm optimistic. . . . But I don't like the action of their stock the last couple of days, it's come down.

It's not a good indication but we'll know for sure very soon. It is not a good indication if stock goes down. Somebody always knows. There are no secrets in the market and someone should be buying. Anyway, we'll know in a few hours.

Did I sleep all right? Oh, yeah. It doesn't bother me. Nothing is worth losing sleep over.

Not much.

The Lunar-Bone Health bigwigs come and leave in a mildly positive haze. There is more evaluating to be done. Nothing can be stated with positiveness.

It will be left to the gods of the market to see whether it all shakes down positively.

Meantime, within two days, Morty has had to come up with $5 million to cover those margin calls.

With 48 hours to make good, all his friends and contacts pooping out, he has scraped money together from Gloria's secret life savings, offering to sell off paintings and antiquities for a song, scrambling madly to put together new backers, new bankers, calling on every source he knows.

On November 23rd, he will offer his tremulous thanks to a terrifyingly tiny band of saviors.

And now, finally, he tells the story of the disaster; a disaster he swears he has averted.

It is the real story behind Morty's crunchtime brunchtime, tucked off to one side at the once-carefree Sanssouci restaurant in the faltering Sutton Place hotel.

This Sunday I've booked a brunch for the people who stood by me. The people who came and offered money — very few. Gloria, of course, my son, my daughter, and Debbie, and two surprises, although one shouldn't be a surprise. Al Friedberg, who was wonderful, but the one I really want to be there is Don Morton, my new banker, who saved me.

I said if I hired the Sanssouci for the people who let me down, I would need the entire room and we'd have to hire it four weeks in a row. But, we're taking one table for 11.

It's never fallen through on me yet. No, and it never will again. I won't get in that position again, I'll tell you.

How did it get to that? The company is doing so well and the company is so successful that I did something which I had never done in my life before. I guaranteed all sorts of people millions and millions of dollars, and my friends, some of them turned out not to be friends. I was very disappointed.

A very wealthy friend of mine offered me about two million dollars cash and stock, and neither the stock nor the cash ever arrived. One day I said to my underwriter, "I've got a real problem." He says, "Well, Mort, I've wanted that piece of property you own for some time. I'll give you $300,000 for it." I didn't want to sell it but I was desperate and I said, "Okay, you've got a deal, as long as you give me the $50,000 tomorrow and the other $250,000 the next Friday, it's a deal." It never arrived.

I sent him a letter and I said, "Of all the people in the world, you're the last one I ever would have dreamed would welch, but it's okay. I bear no grudge."

They all thought I was going down. They all thought that. The guilty were punished and virtuous were rewarded.

But I've paid everybody off. I don't owe anybody a penny now. I emerged with some millions of dollars of the spoils. It was terrible. I kept it very buttoned up. Yeah. One does not advertise one's weaknesses because if Don Morton's superiors at the bank had known I was in trouble, they might have called my loan.

It was a shock, a terrible shock. I thought that nothing would surprise me at this point — but, no, I'm still surprised by people who I suppose are great friends and when the crunch is on, they're not there.

There were millions of dollars at stake, control of a company that's worth a quarter of a billion dollars and I almost lost the whole goddamned thing.

The powers that be in the company found out about it this week and tried to push me out, I'm sorry to say. They have since paid for it. The two chief antagonists did not get the raises they were supposed to get and had their activities curtailed.

It was a lot simpler when I was riding alone. Yes it was.

I'll never be in that position again. Never. I'm never going to trust again. I'm replacing the two men on the board. I'm putting two new people on the board who I can trust completely and make sure that I'll never lose control. I lost one fight so I'm not going to lose another one.

No, actually I almost lost to the board. It was very close. I'll replace them. I did it once before. My first board move, when I first formed the company — I signed a deal as if it was my company — but in the board meeting, they voted me down. I replaced them one at a time over the next three months. Kicked out all the people who voted against me and put a new board in.

Well, there's going to be a turnover now. It will be the second turnover. The only thing I demand is loyalty. They didn't have it. But you know who was wonderful was Al Friedberg. He was great. I was in real deep shit and he wrote a cheque for two million dollars. I will owe him forever. If he hadn't come through, well, I would have had to, I was desperate. I would have had to sell the house, I guess.

But I survived. I won.

Now I've put an executive committee in to supervise them. The executive committee now supervises Martin . . . yeah. . . .

The start of this whole terror a month ago, that cleared up yesterday, was Lunar. The Lunar disaster.

I put all this money into Lunar and Lunar was worthless. The drug didn't work. I bought $8 million worth of Lunar with Deprenyl money and Lunar was a fake. It didn't work; only it did work.

That was when SmithKline pulled out. A great disaster. The stock sold at $3.80. I was pushed out of my job as chief executive officer. They tried to push me out of my job as chairman. And I lost control of the investments. It was a rout.

It was at that point that, before the different news about Lunar came in, I was rushing around trying to get people, to raise the money.

I offered the stock. I had no cash. So I was trying to get people to buy Deprenyl stock or — loan me money or take a position with me. And those 11 were the only people who stood by me and helped. Albert Friedberg, for example, bought a million dollars of Deprenyl U.S.A. and Deprenyl Research from me. It gave me some cash to work with. I needed to cover $5 million, in 48 hours.

If I had not . . . well, they could have put me into bankruptcy. No, they couldn't have put me into bankruptcy, but they could have embarrassed me mightily. I could have been forced to sell my house. Because I owed money on margin to the stockbrokers and they all called my credit the same day, with one exception. They all closed in. "You have X shares here. You owe so much money on it. We want to be paid today."

Six brokers. And the brokers were friends, the individual brokers were friends of mine and they didn't want to do it but they were ordered.

Denise Petican at Marriott had faith. Then, Albert saved me. Well, Albert and the Canadian dollar. Albert and Mulroney. I had an open supporter and a hidden supporter.

Yeah, that saved me.

Several million in margins, over two or three days. This was not a coincidence. I think one of my friends at the Toronto Stock Exchange orchestrated it because each of the brokers, each of them were my friends, and two of them said they had received a visit from the auditor of the Toronto Stock Exchange that day.

Gloria had hidden away $375,000 she hadn't told me about and she wrote me a cheque, and Debbie gave me her money, not a lot but she gave it to me, and Ann came to me and said, I'll mortgage my house — which I didn't let her do. And Denise took in stock from the other brokers and paid them cash for it. She put herself on the line.

Every dollar counted and I was struggling like hell. I tried to sell the clocks. That guy came for from Germany, he took two; the one we had discussed and another one he saw there which he wanted. He gave me a damned good price. And I sold four guns. But, that's all I had to sell. So, thank God, at that point it turned, and I'm trying to get my other clock and I'm trying to get my guns back.

I had just spent a million dollars and bought 12 Colvilles and I figured I should be able to get $600- to $700,000. I would have sold them for $500,000. Ultimately, it could have been sold but, "ultimately" was of no use to me. That's when I went back to the original owner. He said, "I've got no cash." The million dollars of mine was gone, long gone, to pay debts.

There were very embarrassing experiences. One chap promised me $100,000 and then disappeared. Then there was the question of the non-buying of the lot I owned, and then his firm shorted the stock as well.

It was a nightmare, but they will all be repaid!

Chapter 8: The Parkinson's Years: Part III

First of all I was temporarily saved by these people and then I started making money because the Canadian dollar money started pouring in. Because I had lost the company's money, I was forced to do the investing individually. I couldn't do it through the company any more and, as a matter of principle, I hadn't been doing it personally. And so — now I was doing it for myself again. The dollar dropped and I went short and the money just came pouring in in vast amounts. The last two days I made — how much did I make, let me call Danny Gordon — I made $77,000 over the weekend.

It was Don Morton who was the last, pushed me over the top, so, between Denise covering and Al Friedberg and Don Morton, I made it to the five million . . . and then, then, I got a phone call from Lunar saying, "There's something crazy going on here. We just received the files from the University of Connecticut and the first patient we looked at was on placebo and he put on 11 per cent bone." Meaning: the osteoporosis drug isn't working, but the placebo is...which is impossible!

That was three weeks ago. And I said, "Well, how can that be?" And he said, "Well, it can't be." He said, "I'm flying up to Connecticut right away." So he flew up to Connecticut and everything was okay there. At that point, I'd virtually written Lunar off. I mean I thought it was going to take a five-million-dollar loss. The stock was down $8 and everybody was shooting at me, the *Globe & Mail*, the board of directors, Martin, Geoffrey. They thought I had lost my judgment. They said, How could I bet the whole company on Lunar, which is in effect what they thought I had done, but. I knew the drug worked! It had been tried on 10 people, which I knew about, and it worked. It had been tried on hundreds of animals, it worked. And it didn't make sense that it couldn't work and they could get no results.

Then people started making their money back, Lunar started going up. The Bone Health warrants, which were

235

down to 20 cents went to 40 cents which indicated that something positive was going on. And Deprenyl, which was at $3.80, went up to $7.00.

I didn't get the real proof until Friday. But in the meantime, people had started to make their money back. Those who stayed. A lot of people got sold out. All sorts of our shareholders were either sold out on margin calls, or lost faith and gave up and sold their stock. It was terrible.

These were new stockholders. There's a whole new stockholder list. There's hundreds of people, thousands. But, if you look at those shareholders now, and compare it with three months ago, it's a whole new list. It's turned over completely.

Yeah, all the bargain hunters were jumping in at the bottom and some who had stayed with me from the very beginning gave up because, with the stock gone down to $3.80, it didn't make any sense. And there was a rumor going around that we were going broke, and it sure looked like it. The rumor went around that I lost everything in Lunar. And I remember, Alex Winch phoned me and said, "I'm going to destroy your company and I'm going to ruin you." And the *Globe* ran these terrible stories. Dan Westell wrote a story, given to him by Alex Winch. . .

Everybody's been paid back. Oh yeah. Gloria — she'll get it back tomorrow. And the same with Debbie and the other people; Debbie, I've given her money back already.

Ann can pay off her ring. She wanted to buy a ring and she lost money in the stock market, so she put $3,000 down and another $7,000 to pay. So, on Monday, I put her money into five contracts. She made the balance she owed out of the Canadian dollar.

It's not possible ever to get to the bottom of who is operative in helping a panic like that get going. I'm going to take action. There were actual damages. The 100,000 shares of Lunar that I was forced to sell. And then we have an unlimited amount of internal damages because of the disrepute that we were thrown into. Now, whether I have a personal suit is moot because I have no contractual relationship with them. But, if I had a personal suit, I could sue them, if I get legal advice, for a lot of money.

If anyone would have told me Lunar was a dud eight weeks ago, I would have thought they were crazy.

I kept saying, "We're having a wonderful quarter" and everyone said, "Bullshit." The story went around that I was going personally bankrupt and the company was going to close down. I wondered how they could see a company close down that has no debt. I kept saying, "We have no debt. How can we go bust?"

Obviously, there were various parties and forces trying to do it to me, but nobody was listening to me. Nobody believed me, after that Lunar disaster. I had staked it all on Lunar — and Lunar, SmithKline said — was worthless. I was being jumped on already and this was the final disaster. It turned out to be the triumph, but it looked like the final disaster at that time.

I was in shock when SmithKline brought out their report. It just didn't seem possible. And the market overreacted and brought our stock all the way down from $20 to $8.50, which is crazy. In the space of three days, or two days. I thought, this is insane because the company is a solid company.

My other stocks had suffered from the fallout as well. I was now down to about $8 and Deprenyl fell all the way to $3.80.

Deprenyl money invested in Lunar was $5 million. No, I think it was $8 million. I put the entire treasury into Lunar. It seemed like the safest and best bet in the world. The company is earning a dollar a share, it's been in business umpteen years, it's got Hector De Luca as the head of it, it makes the osteometer machines which are in wider and wider use because every woman past the menopause is now having her bone density tested and, to boot, they had a chance of finding a cure for osteoporosis.

And I was right but, through a missing battery, the whole world almost came apart. And then all the brokers called in their chips which meant I had to put up the cash. Just under five million I had to find. That's what I was putting together in bits and pieces that way.

Don Morton and Denise and Al Friedberg were the big three.

And then my wife found her stash. (Laughs.) She had $375,000 she had hidden away and hadn't told me about it, saved out of her $50 a week allowance. (Laughs.) And she ran the house on that, too! A few bucks a month I gave her, and no accounting. It just shows the miracles of compound interest, hahaha . . .

Yes . . . everything is good. The Canadian dollar is down, substantially. The Deprenyl shorts are on the ropes. There'll be heavy buying coming in today and Monday. Our financial situation is great. Our sales are great. We're heading for another record quarter. Lunar is moving back up again, and all is well with the world.

———————

November 27th, 1992.

Unbelievably, the very week after the breast-beating brunch at Sanssouci, a fairy godfather materializes, a market wizard with the power to bring the expiring stock instantly back to life.

It is Martin Barkin who has drawn on his connections with some major FOOM — Fine Old Ontario Money — to bring the shaman in.

Martin belongs to a hunt club, cheek by hindquarters alongside some of the FOOMiest in town. One of these is the chairman of X-X, a major international underwriting firm. It is this market god whom Martin has persuaded to come hear Deprenyl's pitch.

The chairman and a couple of vice-presidents of X-X have attended, heard and expressed enthusiasm; the kind of enthusiasm that could turn the most grievously stained, spotted and fallen shares into units of the most upright, churchworthy respectability.

These FOOM connections are so far beyond Morty's lifelong sphere of deliberately chosen equals that he is deliriously, deeply bedazzled.

Martin Barkin got us this meeting with X-X and he was absolutely wonderful. Three top guys. I wouldn't be able to reach guys at that level. They wouldn't even listen to me, and when they left, the chairman said, "I had no idea as to what you were doing out here. I thought you had one hot drug, you got lucky, and it would play itself out and that would be the end of it. I had no idea you had a pipeline and the whole thing."

The first time I've seen Martin in action and he really knocked them dead. I said, "Martin, how does it feel to get up and give a better presentation than me?"

The difference between him and myself is that he can get the audience. I can't get that audience. — He hunts with the chairman. Hunts whatever you hunt with dogs. He shoots things. So he had a chance, hunting at his hunting club to get to the chairman, and he got his ear, and managed to get him to listen. I could never get someone like that to listen to me. That's what I brought him for.

I never had any doubt about his abilities. But . . . I sat there silent and amazed. We went out clapping each other on the back. This is going to give us the prestige, the stature — It's a big step up. — He got us X-X!

They asked questions about everything, about our research, about our staffing, building up new drugs, how do we compete with big companies? All the knowing questions, and he had all the answers.

It's a major coup to have them listen and an even more major coup to have them announce publicly that they're

---

going to, which is what they're going to do next week, apparently. They're going to be our underwriter.

That's going to give everyone a major shock. I wonder how Dan Westell is going to write that one up? It doesn't matter. No way he can damage that. He'll turn tail. Nobody's going to attack X-X.

God, what a difference a week makes. Unbelievable. What a difference a month makes. It seems like last Sunday was decades away. The stock is going to be very strong today, I expect. Things trickle very quickly in this market and the Lunar news is wonderful. . . .

It'll be tough on the shorts. They have my deepest sympathy. Because they're going to have their balls squeezed off!

———————

Two weeks later, Morty's troops are placed on an unexpected Sunday alert.

Usually he only works five-and-a-half-day weeks, finishing after lunch on Saturday.

But early on Sunday, December 13th, Morty makes several peremptory calls, and at 10 a.m. the majestic white Caddy disgorges an uncharacteristically dishevelled Morty, drooping in a baggy green tracksuit, at the door of his office. Ann, summoned even earlier, waits within to type some emergency correspondence.

———————

Dear P [Ann briskly types from sheet after yellow sheet of foolscap, transcribed in the wee hours in Gloria's patient hand]:

I write this letter with considerable sadness. You've been a good friend and a fine broker and we've worked together for 20 years without a single disagreement or harsh word.

Despite your loyalty and reliable service you've given me, I've no choice but to close my accounts at X-X.

———————

240

It's not your fault nor is it mine, but on Friday an incident took place which, coming immediately after the anti-Semitic incident in New York, makes me very uneasy.

Three weeks ago our president Martin Barkin arranged for three of X-X's senior officers to visit Deprenyl and examine our operation in detail. They were very impressed, and it was their suggestion that Deprenyl pay X-X a retainer and that they become our investment banker and underwriter.

This is very important to Deprenyl because it would have represented a major upgrading of our brokerage support. Last Friday the vice-chairman of X-X phoned Martin and cancelled the deal giving as his reasons that Deprenyl had bad vibes in the market.

An employee in his department told me the objection was not to Deprenyl *per se*, but to me personally, and that an unfortunate comment was made about my about my personality and my racial origins.

X-X has a perfect right to accept or reject any client it wishes to, for any and no reason, but in these bad times I have an obligation to support brokers who support my companies. Please transfer the contents of all my accounts as soon as possible to D. at Y-Y. I hope we'll have the opportunity to do business again sometime in the future.

———————

Although he is trying to rev up, Morty is pushed; the forced edgy facade is costing him. His voice, which often becomes clearer and more resonant with a hit of positive adrenalin, is strained and breathy and slow.

———————

Mmm . . . very bad, very unfortunate. They shook hands, there was nothing in writing, just shaking of hands — they phoned Martin and said, told him — and Martin was shocked, he said to me, "This man's been a friend for years;

———————

241

someone got to him. We knew that there were bad vibes, that's why we wanted them. We discussed that. That we were going to have to change all that."

And then, uh, shortly after I phoned someone who I know, who works down there, and said, "What happened? When the three guys walked out they were sold." And he said: "A senior executive said at the office today: 'We're not going to have that, um, aggressive Jew working — with us, are we?'"

(Morty tugs at his crumpled sweatshirt, and at his equilibrium. This must not appear to be a rout.)

Every day it's something. It's a tough world and it's hard times, and everybody — envies success and, and — they must find it infuriating, they're probably saying, "That sonofabitch Shulman, why should we assist him, he's been so much trouble in the past?"

Have to build the barricade a little higher. It aggravates me. Because I thought when we got Martin in here all these problems that I had personally would be over because I had stepped out of the picture and he could deal with them and he could handle them and we shouldn't have any troubles but, obviously, that isn't — isn't true.

It's not a serious problem it's an unnecessary problem, he adds hoarsely. And, above all:

It wasn't an anti-Semitic crack; it was a crack about me, not a comment on my ancestry. Martin's a good Jew, I'm a bad Jew.

He gives Ann another underwriter's name. A Morty equal; a banker who has gladly done business with him before.

Tomorrow, tell him I want to see him. Tell him to bring his president with him. Or his vice president. Ask him if he'd be interested in being our underwriter.

The way I fight them is pull the money out. When he comes here on Monday I'll tell him what happened with X-X and remind him I got two million dollars at his place, so they'll think twice before they reject. . . .

Meanwhile, down in the cheery land of Kansas, Deprenyl Animal's Dave Stevens is feeling his oats, and going for a larger portion of them.

Ann is to administer a sharp reproof to him also. Stevens, too, will have his money cut off.

"Are we faxing it today or tomorrow morning?" she asks.

"Send it today. Ruin his Sunday," Morty says.

He's trying to seize control, having great success down there and I think it just went to his head. He started to make his move same time as Martin did.

Morty allows himself a thick, bitter chuckle. He has seen all this on the horizon. But he believed that while he was around, the fortress was strong.

The thing is, it's becoming a big empire and people, people think the head of it is weak and and so they try to grab on. It's like, uh, when Tamburlaine died. Everybody grabbed onto the Roman empire.

I thought it wouldn't come till after I was dead.

I thought they'd move against Geoffrey.

I didn't think they'd move against me.

Morty will move the pieces, he will promote, he will create supervising committees, he will rebuild a safe, dependable wall of support, with enough sturdy bricks to make up for the chinks and fissures, he will . . .

Ann is impatient to go. Her husband, the Griselda-like Russ, has called twice: the family is gathered for a pre-Christmas brunch and, after all, they do have some claim on their mother-provider's time. Even Luan has been released for the rest of the day.

Morty is shuffling through papers on his desk for, on the bright side, the FDA is endorsing deprenyl for pets, and so is the *National Enquirer*.

Have to show you the copy of the article. It's very exciting. Outside of the front page, which is a joke, the *National Enquirer* has a very good scientific report. They've done stuff on us before. About me, about Parkinson's, deprenyl. With a phone number. We got a lot of calls. . . .

"All right leave!" he barks at Ann. Hikes up the sagging green sweatpants, shuffles to the door, waiting for a taxi to take him back to his rich and empty house.

And the lost market wizards of X-X?

Does the bad-vibes bad-boy triumph over the cruel FOOM's anti-Mortyism?

There is a short sharp game of bluff-match-counterbluff.

A week later, the FOOM wizard and his viziers pay one more visit.

"Think I'm gonna have a new broker announcing himself tomorrow," Morty predicts, cawing with revivified laughter. "They'd be crazy not to — I've never, in my entire career never yelled anti-Semitism. I have personality defects and, it's not because I'm Jewish that all these people hate me. This wasn't being anti-Semitic; it was an accurate description! Difficulty for them is how unfortunately he worded it! I have no grievance against them. Whatsa point? They're just the same as all the rest, it's just that they got caught."

But the FOOM hold firm. They have only come to demand the identity of Morty's source. When he refuses, they pack their portfolio of magic underwriting dust and leave.

"Thing is now, I'm just amused, I don't know what, if they piss me off — there'll be trouble," Morty warns.

He insists that the reluctant Ann ("Shouldn't we show this to Martin?") fire one more missile to FOOM headquarters:

I'm very disappointed in your reply. You offered no explanation as to why your firm withdrew its offer to be our investment broker and underwriter. You offer no amends; you offer no denial of the allegations that your senior officials do not want to be associated with people of my type. Your sole interest seems to learn the name of my informant and punish him or her.

I had no intention of escalating this matter publicly but if you insist on investigation it must be an impartial one not an internal one. If you wish to follow this course simply inform me and I will turn all the the information over to the Ontario Human Rights Commission. In my opinion this would not be advantageous to X-X. Meanwhile kindly transfer all my funds as previously requested.

What happened after that?

Nothing that Morty is telling. Except to note that he can call the FOOM at X-X anytime for advice in assessing other underwriters for him. They are, he says, always wonderfully helpful and polite. Which seems to be perfectly fine with him.

* * *

On December 16, Deprenyl shares close at $6.40, down from $7.

We could get a panic, Morty ponders. . . .

On December 22, he grants a lengthy interview to magazine writer John Lawrence who says he is doing a profile of Deprenyl for *Saturday Night* magazine: the story of a year in the waning life of the stock.

Morty is cool, flung-back against his chair, articulate and only moderately slurred. The fall began, he smoothly tells Lawrence, when Chinoin, the Hungarian parent company that developed deprenyl, suddenly dumped 500,000 shares.

"I bought up stock. I blew $20 million," he says, throwaway, as though he were talking about play money. Has the problem abated? Lawrence asks. All over now, Morty assures him. Canadian short sellers are amateurs — they did some damage but the worst is over. He adroitly fields questions about Alpha B-2 and Alzene: since he is now not a chairman of Deprenyl he is not supposed to know the business of his son Geoffrey, who is. Also deflects a question about the upgrading of Martin Barkin to CEO: did it take place ahead of schedule, as Barkin himself had told Lawrence was the case?

Morty opens his gray-green eyes wide. "Oh no," he says with a perfect semblance of ingenuousness. "Not ahead of schedule. He's been promoted exactly as planned."

When Lawrence suggests Morty has created bad vibes because, "It's one thing to promote drug; another a stock," the repentant drug lord lowers his head in sporting acceptance of the rebuff.

"I promoted both the same way," he acknowledges, "but I was mistaken. People reacted badly because no one had ever promoted a legitimate drug before. Of course it was hard for them to believe me about deprenyl."

Lest anyone be lulled into believing the Mortymouth has been permanently muted, he gets in a shot at his most persistent nemesis, the *Globe*'s Dan Westell. Westell is "a newborn Christian (*sic*) who doesn't like people with money."

Lawrence doesn't flick an eyelash. But then, he has the whole thing on tape.

* * *

And 1992 comes to an end.

Morty has involved, alienated and perhaps recaptured his son; rediscovered his grandchildren, reawakened, he swears, to the meaning of life . . . with one eye always on the international stock tables.

He has drummed himself in, been drummed out, and tottered back to the door again.

He has turned control of his worldly goods — almost — over to his wife, his autonomy — to an extent — over to a board of directors.

He has been forced to relinquish control of his company, pledge to shut up in public; down to the last of his assets.

Is this the end? . . .

The faithful little world of bottom feeders depending on him: his family, his circle of stock-suckers, Ann's kids, her friends' kids staffing his warping office operation are watching and worrying and losing faith as he seems to get weaker.

The good-hearted ones sigh, say: "Okay, the rollercoaster ride is over."

"I've got my ring," Ann says, "I've got my house, I've got my stained-glass window, I've got my Colville, I've got my car. It's been a good ride."

Outside, as he seems to be losing steam the sharks of all size are circling.

By rights, he shouldn't be here at all.

But . . .

Stay tuned.

There is at least one more chapter. At least.

The Springtime After the Fall

April 20, 1993

A gray, chill afternoon.

Eighteen days ago, the deposed but not quite demolished founder of the kingdom of Deprenyl celebrated his 68th birthday.

Today he is sitting in his office — his old office, on the unrenovated side of Roncesvalles Ave., exactly where he first hung out his shingle 43 years earlier when his heart was young and gay.

He is waiting for the world to absorb the official news that today hit all the papers: the announcement of Morton Shulman's total retirement from Deprenyl Research.

The phone rings fitfully.

"Nobody from the Deprenyl office across the street has called," Morty says to Deb. Shakes his head. Turns, away from the light.

"Lash...got in my eye," he says into his handkerchief.

248

"Ann!" he calls suddenly. "What did I get for my birthday?"

Ann appears in the doorway with the fiercest scowl she can muster; pummeling to hold off the fuzzy demons of self-pity.

"Your birthday? You got that nice pillbox from Roma, we dedicated that stained-glass window to you, you got . . .you got all sorts of nice things. It was a wonderful birthday!"

"It was a terrible birthday. Worst since I was two years old and broke my leg."

"Aw! Look how sad he is. Couldn't have his court jesters at his party! Look how sad he looks; see that baby picture of him on the wall? He's got exactly the same expression, just like that!"

A blurring eight-month-old Morty in a baby smock sits plumply, stares lugubriously, from a fading blow-up on the cluttered wall above Ann's desk.

"Thought I'd be here forever!" he says, rallying. "Thought I'd be everywhere forever. Be chief coroner my whole life!"

Punches on the speakerphone.

"Happy retirement! Been a pleasure," says a plummy male voice.

Over the wire from New York it's Deprenyl's original stock-schlepper, the betimes reviled Marty Meyerson.

"Saw the write-up in the *Wall Street Journal*. It sounds very nice! You sound like a new man. Onwards and forwards! So you'll keep in touch . . ."

"Knows I'm still where the action is," Morty says.

"Martin will make a success of it. With his brightness, energy and ambition. Be very cautious, won't make any mistakes.

"Less exciting! You're not gonna get a fountain of youth. May get a better cream to help eczema."

Relations between the two Deprenyl giants might be warmer. Evidently Barkin expected Morty to disappear in discreet silence, and has expressed his chagrin at finding this not to be the case.

Just yesterday, Morty found it necessary to fax his piqued protègé:

Dear Martin:

One of the reasons I left this company was so I would no longer be in a position where people could tell me what I could or could not say.

Please do not phone to lecture me again. It is the opinion both of myself and my counsel that I did not breach the confidentiality agreement and the conversation between two friends that took place had nothing to do with my position in this company. For that reason I did not inform you or anyone else about it when it occurred.

I ran DRL for five years without the need to keep any secrets. We managed reasonably well. So far as I know I am not in possession of any confidential information.

Incidentally, Dan Westell just called me to compliment me on my press release. He said how refreshing it was to deal with someone who was truthful and how he had become a Shulman fan and was going to miss me — I was mightily touched.

If you are going to take offense every time I make a public speech, you are going to be in a constant uproar. I think very highly of you but I am afraid you have been associating too much with Jacqueline (Deprenyl lawyer Jacqueline Le Saux) and have lost your sense of humour. Incidentally, I have never described you to others except to praise you. I regret to hear that the courtesy is not always reciprocated.

There is one letter from the fancy Deprenyl offices across the road: from the worthy Roger Mailhot, offering uplift from the scriptures:

> Psalm 55 says, Cast your burden upon the Lord and he will sustain you . . . Our grace at the meal often includes you, dear Morty.

Who's actually going to own Deprenyl? Geoffrey'll be the chairman, and — nobody'll own Deprenyl. It's a public company and — I'll have more shares than anybody else but I won't control it.

People here have been easing themselves away from me. — They figure the power's gone and they're trying to sucky up to across the road. Everybody. Ed Foster, who is the chief legal officer, said, I've gotta get, I've gotta move, he said to me: 'T be quite frank, I've gotta move across the road, I gotta be close to the source of power."

I'm isolated here. But, he'll have to have 'em give me my kitchen upstairs back! Ripped out my kitchen, changed it to a Deprenyl office.

The new Deprenyl rulers are threatening some of Morty's most cherished staff.

But to no one's surprise the unseated chairman has a whole new fiefdom in the works, the corporation papers already being drawn up by longtime faithful Mortylawyer, Harry Malcolmson.

The Safety Corporation.

It turns out that Morty has been planning it . . .well, for weeks. Months.

What will be the business of Safety Corp?

"Number 1: Eternal life. Number 2: a secret project."

Eternal life is to be contemplated with the potential aid of a team at Dalhousie University, who are looking to raise cash for a research project into Biological Substances for Growth and Survival-Enhancing Effects on Human Brain Cells.

As for the secret project, Morty is talking of ringing in one of the few Canadians who can match him for instant controversy: Dr. Henry Morgentaler, who the year before had been bombed out of his abortion clinic in downtown Toronto.

I've offered Deprenyl Research $6 million for the Canadian rights to use ALA in uterine problems.

Morgentaler's already called me. He was gonna be on the board but Geoffrey vetoed it.

Actually I contacted Morgentaler. — Was over at my house the other Sunday. Very enthusiastic.

Geoff is concerned. He's concerned that I would go announce that I had a wonderful new drug for, uh, (whisper) ABORTIONS, and that this would cause him all sorts of trouble with the regulatory authorities.

Talked to Geoff. And uh, we ironed everything out. I made some changes he asked, every change he asked. Took Morgentaler off the board.

Morty rallies still further.

In truth, as he now comes to think of it, he planned the whole thing, was engineering his separation from Deprenyl all along.

It's been, gradually generating and, uh, the situation became impossible last month. I decided that, uh, life is too short to spend the time fighting 50, 100 employees now, with subsidiaries, and I was so exhausted at the end of the day that I thought, Fuck this! I thought, This is crazy.

So I'm taking — two employees with me immediately and three more in 3 months . . . Luan, and Ann — that's what this separation agreement is: — Ann, Luan and Kendall McAlister will be available one hour each — and Deborah of course. And Iole.

It was the final straw. I wasn't getting any pleasure; I wasn't having fun any more! And, uh, I'll start all over again, I'll have two or three employees, a little company.

It's going to be a hot issue, the stock's coming out at $5, I'm already getting bids of 8, and 10; I've got three brokers lined up — they're dying to give me the money; and this is going to be a drug that — this is going to be Deprenyl all over again. This is a BIG drug.

It's called The Safety Corporation. I wanted to call it The Last Hurrah! Hahaha...

Oh this'll be fun. This'll be fun. It's — all the things I do well, and, I won't have a million employees that I have to —

Where? — Here. At 378 Roncesvalles. I own the building. I gave Deprenyl Research the right, it says it all in here, they can stay as long as they want, but they have to give me my kitchen back! haha, because, they ripped out the goddam kitchen!

The phone rings some more.

"Hello. Morning. Yes all sorts of important news, I've been trying to reach you desperately since Friday. We're doing an underwriting and I want to give you a chance at it, or to participate in it, but, uh, you've gotta get in touch with, uh, what's his name, Ken Williamson and tell him if he wants it he's gotta move quickly. It's headed by Barclay's and First Marathon's taking a piece and — they want as much as they can get and so does, uh, uh, Standard, but I'll protect you if you can move quickly — .

Yeah, I'll try and — get something to you today.

Called The Safety Corporation. Yeah. Yeah. It's — has the rights to the use of ALA solving uterine problems. 'Kay, I'll get it down t'you right away. Cover it. Thank you. Cover it. Cover enough to get me in. Buy it up. Mm-hmm. Right."

Later that morning there is a meeting to discuss security arrangements, should it turn out that Morty is going into the *(whisper)* abortion-cream business.

To handle it, here is the invaluable Percy Parks, private

detective and security expert par excellence. Tall, tan, blow-dried, craggy but cutehaired; in tweedy bulky jacket.

PARKS: I think since just this building is involved — oh, your house too, okay, so I'll set up — tell you what I'll do is, I'll put together today — I've got a good idea of, I've roughed it out here but I want to get together with the necessary agencies — what cameras, if we decide to go with them. Prob'ly want something with the monitor inside and then so, okay — yup, we'll have one in to monitor, and we'll have time-lapse on it.

MORTY: There's a meeting with Deprenyl Thursday and then I'll be able to tell you — on Thursday that it'll be acceptable.

P.   So what I'll do then, I'll get prices and everything on the camera equipment, and once Thursday comes then we'll say go. . .I also, before, if this happens I'd like to talk to your limousine driver too, that picks you up, we'll make different arrangements, for the pickup and dropoff; we still want him here to make it look like it's the way it's always been; but if we have trouble I don't want, you're not going out the front door into a crowd, we'll take you out another way and the limousine can be there and they can think that everybody's come into the limousines.

M.   Sneak me out.

P.   We'll just move you in and out that way. So that's it, I'm gonna talk to the guard company, get you some people on the streets with cameras, in case we have trouble, just for the first few days and see how it's gonna go. And uhh . . . I guess that's about all I need right now, I just wasn't sure what, if everybody was involved or just this building here or both or what. Okay. So, are, cough, the Deprenyl people still gonna be in here. They'll be moving out, okay. Cause . . .

M.   We're keeping, to start with, Ann, and Deborah, and Luan. And I'm going to offer later on, Kendall and Iole Fabbro.

P.   Okay. Okay. Well, that's not . . . too difficult.

M.   Deprenyl, as far as I know, are going to use the upstairs for storage.

P.   For storage, okay. The only thing that I want is that, if we do run into a problem, a lot of people on the street out here, whoever's in here needs to identify who is allowed in the building and who is not, cause how do you know, hey.

M.   We have to change the, uh —

P.   The alarm system,

M.   The alarm system, because —

P.   Yuh. That's a rinkydink system, this system you have in this building is not worth, snuff anyways.

M.   We may get off lucky and . . .

P.   Yuh. Right. But —

M.   But maybe — when they realize what's going on —

P.   Exactly. Some morning y', you come in here and 'r be a whole buncha people with placards and — alla rest of it.

M.   I don't mind placards, long as they don't bring any bullets.

P.   Yeah no, Haha, yeah, after that doctor gettin' shot inna States, 'r —

S.   And bombs, they bombed one clinic in town here.

P.   Yuh. Yeah, well that's what we're — hm, ahem, well, if you say, if it's all go on Thursday well, we'll just cover it . . .

* * *

None of this comes to pass.

The uterine applications of ALA fail to pan out.

By July, 1993, suitors hoping to link up with Morty in a quite different sort of gamble are showing up at the old Roncesvalles digs, with that brand new Safety Corporation sign on the door.

The Parkinson's Trust gets itself a license to run charity casino nights.

Safety Corp. will be supplying scratch-and-win gambling cards to benefit the Parkinson's Trust further.

That will be yet another hurrah. Not the last one, either.

Chapter Nine

Slaying the Generics Dragon

November 10, 1992

SK: What sort of person would you say brings out the worst in you?

MS: Feminists. Before feminists any guy who pushed me — I hate being pushed. If he hit me, I hit back harder. I learned, never defend yourself. When someone tries to blackmail you, always ask for a few days to think it over.

I've never picked a quarrel in my life.

Barry Sherman, Eugene. They both own Canadian generic drug companies. They've both come after me here since I've been in this business, and I didn't defend myself. I went after them.

Barry Sherman called me in two months after we got our license to sell deprenyl and said, "I want you to license me the generic rights. If you don't, you're first on my hit list and I'm going to put you out of business."

That was the biggest mistake he made.

How did I manage to right that imbalance? I don't think I'll tell you that story. . . .

Toronto Star, July 11, 1993

SHULMAN VS. SHERMAN:
THE DRUG ENTREPRENEURS FACE OFF

Take two aggressive, multi-millionaire entrepreneurs accustomed to noisily getting their own way. Add the potential for millions in revenue from a potent pharmaceutical. Throw in a batch of lawyers. Make that two batches. Stir and stand well back.

Morty Shulman and Barry Sherman.

The daddy of Deprenyl Research, and the prodigal upstart who heads up the huge generic drug conglomerate called Apotex, Inc.

They stand, thinly smiling, side by side, in separate newspaper photos. Two no-holds-barred all-Canadian go-getters, separated by a little less than a generation, joined in clamorous battle for the same prize.

One fine day in May, 1993, Barry Sherman announced he was bringing out a 40 percent lower-priced generic version of Eldepryl, and that there was nothing Morty and his folks could do to stop him.

What made it particularly galling for Morty was the fact that only two weeks earlier, Deprenyl had confidently announced that Eldepryl would be safe for nearly three more years from the depredations of the generics — protected by a brand-new regulation that gave extra teeth to Bill C-91, the Patent Protection Act.

Had the world spun a degree or two differently, you might have imagined Shulman and Sherman as allies.

Both self-made Toronto millionaires who had blossomed from shy half-orphaned overbright youths; each given to showy public displays of temper and muscle, each hell-bound determined to do it his way.

Naturally, Morty and Barry hate each other like poison.

Here on the July newspaper page is Morty, 68, gray-haired, deeply lined, wearing both belt and suspenders to keep his trousers from twisting and slipping down his shrinking concave waistline. And Sherman, 50, pudgy cheeked, permed, pouched eyes behind aviator glasses too large for his round baby face, white pharmacist's coat bellying out below. File photos because newspaper libraries overflow with pictures of both men; no need to take fresh ones in these straitened economic days.

Neither man's smile reaches his eyes.

Holding off the West Coast generic upstart Canguard was a breeze. The Apotex machine would be something else again.

* * *

Barry Sherman, raised by a mother who was widowed when her son was 10, got a Ph.D. in systems engineering in a brilliant, record three years from the Massachusetts Institute of Technology. A scientific star, he told interviewers he "stumbled" into the drug business after "the sudden death of his mother's brother, who owned a pharmaceutical company called Empire Labs."

Young Barry had worked summers in his uncle's lab. He bought the insolvent company from the trustees with an accountant friend, resold it for a profit. They started Apotex in 1974, sledding flatly along until they hit the jackpot a dozen years later with the Health Protection Branch's approval of their lucrative generic copy of a major brand-name blood-pressure medication.

Sherman is described as "a shy high school whiz kid who only got noticed when he directed his teachers to mistakes he'd found in the math textbooks."

Barry's childhood friends, like Morty's, express amazement to hear their tongue-tied old buddy holding forth on the business stage.

Politicians and bureaucrats harassed by Sherman describe him, like Morty, as "a man who likes to exaggerate."

259

Many Sherman tenets have Shulmanesque overtones.

"I have no patience for incompetent bureaucrats. I tell them exactly what I think and it's usually not what they want to hear."

Or: "Others in this industry operate differently, but I don't think it's the right thing to do to kiss people's asses just to stay on their good side. It's better to say it like it is."

And, Sherman's professed disinterest in money qua money: "In my early years in business I was motivated to make enough money to be financially secure but I'm far beyond that now. Quite frankly, I'd rather give the money away than waste it."

Barry Sherman is a man who goes for it on the same scale as Morty.

Apotex in 1992 is a $500 million agglomerate, and has played a major role in the transformation of the copycat drug game into a serious force.

Sherman has been taking on several of the biggest pharmaceuticals companies in the world. Burroughs Wellcome, Syntex, others who have enjoyed carte blanche in pharmaceuticals pricing are screaming foul at this merciless new free-market development.

These hugely profitable multinationals, rolling in biotech gold, are massively aggrieved by these latter-day cream skimmers. The big boys who have controlled the field from the start are crying the blues. They put up the money to search the labs of the world for pharmaceutical gold, to buy the brains that discover the drugs, to pay the shot for the trial and error, the protracted clinical testings and endless government approvals; and, in exchange thus far, their reward has been to mark themselves up whatever profit they saw fit.

Markups in the order of 500-fold on raw costs are taken without a blink, and generally don't ever see the light of public scrutiny. They are private companies, after all.

Now come the generics, easily synthesizing the biggest profit makers and slapping their version on the market with none of the costly preamble. The price to the consumer will be lower, but not the genericist's profit margin — his going-in expenses being so much less.

Deep into this fertile field ploughs Barry Sherman, seemingly announcing copies of patented drugs at the rate of one a month.

He is mimicking Burroughs' anti-AIDS AZT. He is all set to go generic with Merck Frosst's Vasotec, a mega-market heart medication that is the largest-selling drug in Canada.

In July 1993, Apotex will get a federal court ruling allowing it to proceed with its copycatting. The generic version will hit the pharmacies "as soon as we get it packaged up."

Barry Sherman has had his sights trained on selegeline, the chemical generic of Eldepryl, for a long time, and now he means to bag it for Apotex.

Within months of Eldepryl's HPB approval as a recognized Parkinson's medication, in January 1990, Apotex signalled its interest in cloning the drug.

Morty had, of course, earmarked the generic threat from the very start. As part of his push for HPB sanction he hooked into the pharmaceutical industry fight for the passage of Bill C-91, a new law to beef up patent protection against the accursed generics.

With the biotech boom of the late 1980s attracting a passel of upstart generic pharma-prospectors to the modern-day Klondike, the fight over the new legislation raised quite a dust storm.

But the brand-namers mustered more clout than the generics. In 1992 Bill C-91 became law, giving the multinationals twice as much precious patent protection for new drugs as they had had in the past. Some drugs would be safe from cloning for as long as 20 years.

Apotex, which had seen its sales quadruple since 1986, protested that the new legislation would cripple the company, reduce it to shark-bait for razor-toothed multinationals. The renovated Apotex was not only copying some 45 existing drugs but, they swore, preparing to find some new ones of their own.

In the meanwhile, Apotex was throwing itself into court to find loopholes through which to stitch down claims to several mouthwateringly profitable copies of brand-name drugs.

In late 1992, Morty is throwing himself into high gear against Apotex.

Burroughs-Wellcome hired a detective — I don't know who it was — and got some terrible information about Barry Sherman and gave it to the FDA. The FDA raided his place in the States and he's had all sorts of troubles ever since.

You see, guys like that are all bad men, and you will always find something on them.

Most people are weak. They wait and see and hope it will all go away. We don't cave in.

I won't hear from him again. I don't think I'll hear from Barry Sherman again.

Morty has been bombarding all his political contacts, pushing every political, emotional and patriotic button he can dream up. The hamstrung Deprenyl board, thinking their esteemed founder safely put to pasture, only gets to read the missives after they have been sent. Over in the respectable pharmaceuticals office on the other side of Roncesvalles Ave., they are torn between shrieking and cheering.

* * *

March 1, 1993

Dear _____: Can you assist us in getting a 10-minute appointment with the Minister of Health. As you know, Deprenyl Research Ltd. introduced Eldepryl to this country after it was available in Europe for 20 years. No one else was willing to do so because of the lack of patent protection and the initial outlay of $6 million with the danger that the generic copy would destroy the investment shortly after it received approval. We made the investment in 1988, received approval to sell the drug in 1990, and since then:

We have paid $18 million in corporation tax, we have refused to set up subsidiaries in the Cayman Islands or Barbados as the other drug companies have done, and I believe we are the only public Canadian drug company that is paying taxes.

We have supplied our medication free to anyone who cannot afford it. We have donated $5 million to the Parkinson's Foundation. . . . I have turned over all my profits to the Toronto Western Hospital and the Toronto Hospital foundation. We have put 80 Canadians to work scattered from coast to coast.

After barely three years we are facing the onslaught of generics, and as 95 per cent of our income comes from Eldepryl, there is a real danger that we will be forced out of business or at least forced to drastically cut our employment. Where we paid millions of dollars for the right to sell Eldepryl in Canada, generic copiers pay nothing. We advertise — they do not advertise. We employ detail representatives — they employ no detail representatives. We simply can't compete. . . .

We would appreciate anything you could do.

* * *

In February, the Morton and Gloria Shulman Centre for the Study of Movement Disorders opens in a modestly gala ceremony at Toronto Western Hospital.

In March, 1993, a Private Member's Bill is introduced to buy Eldepryl patent protection until 1997.

"What, no statue? No horse, no sword?" quips a delighted Morty.

Late in April, 1993, he scoots a flyer to pharmacists, bearing on its cover APO — the Apotex logo — with a big X through it:

"It's Time To Substitute. If it has APO in the name it comes from Apotex. Apotex is owned by Barry Sherman."

Deprenyl Research has done very well and has been a good citizen. It now has a pipeline of 10 or 12 original products, but these will take another two or three years before they produce meaningful profits. Meanwhile, 90 per cent of our income comes from Eldepryl. There is a cloud that threatens our future. Apotex, a large wealthy Canadian generic multinational generic company (sic) is trying to market a generic copy of Deprenyl. Deprenyl is just one more drug to Apotex but to Deprenyl Research it is survival. If Deprenyl Research is not successful, no one will risk the millions necessary to bring new drugs like Eldepryl into Canada.

Send Barry Sherman a message by not dispensing APO products. There are many other generics available.

(Dr. Morton Shulman has resigned from all his posts with Deprenyl Research and its subsidiaries. This folder is being sent out as his sole responsibility; no one at Deprenyl Research has contributed financially or has been informed of this action.)

On April 27, 1993, Morty sends "A Letter to My Friends" on stationery of The Safety Corporation.

I no longer have any connection with Deprenyl Research Limited but I am, I believe, still the largest shareholder. For those of you who bought stock because of me, I want to advise you that I am increasing my position to its former level and purchased 400,000 shares last week.

There is an article in this morning's *Globe & Mail* on page B3 which is of great interest. [It] refers to the hobbling of generics. This new regulation protects

Deprenyl's marketing of Eldepryl for some years to come and in effect guarantees the company's market in Canada at least until 1996.

Best wishes,

Morton Shulman,

President, The Safety Corporation

They passed an Order In Council! We've got protection for 30 months after a full application is made to produce a generic. We've won the war against the generics!
[Morty bursts into creaky song. "Happy Days Are Here A-gaaaiin!"]

The *Globe* story that day describes a new federal regulation that extends the drug-patent protection extended by Bill C-91. It closes a loophole that allowed generics to quietly begin development of patent-drug copies before a patent has expired, and go on working while the whole thing is battled in court.

Now the generic company must give notice of intention to the patent-holder, and will be prevented from selling its copy for up to 30 months after court action is commenced.

This is the 30-month safety shield Deprenyl has happily invoked.

But barely two weeks later, here is Barry Sherman making a counter-pronouncement that Apotex means to produce Eldepryl by a process that has nothing to do with the patented Deprenyl method.

This means war.

Since that nose-thumbing announcement about Sherman's beyond-the-law Eldepryl knockoff, Morty has had his prescription pad stamped with the words *Do Not Fill This Prescription With An Apotex Product.*

Sherman applies for an injunction to stamp out the stamp.

Morty changes the stamp to *Fill Only With Brand Name or Novopharm Product*, throwing a mouldy fig to the company that is Apotex's major Canadian generics competitor.

It cannot be that Apotex fears profit erosion from a boycott by Morty's three dozen declining patients. Evidently a deeper imperative is at work. Apotex files for a fresh injunction against the new wording, too.

Morty tries, and fails, to have Sherman charged with insider trading, claiming Sherman was shorting Deprenyl stock on the eve of his clone-Eldepryl announcement.

On May 21, Apotex Inc. serves Morton Shulman with notice of a $1,100,000 suit for defamation damages.

Morty has come up with a ton of — strictly confidential, what else? — paper documenting the hail of injunctions from brand-drug companies strewing the path that Apotex and its U.S. subsidiary, Barr Laboratories, are gouging in the U.S. pharma landscape. Even the FBI is on the case.

The story is too good to keep.

I'm not a professional shorter; I short very rarely, once every three or four years. One time I did it when it was spectacular, what I did was short Barr Labs, because that was a sure thing, too. Barr Labs is part of Apotex. Mmm, Barry Sherman's company.

Around the end of '91, I took a pretty hefty short position because I had the sensation that his company was going to run into trouble.

What did I make on that? A lot. That shorted at $30 and it settled at $6.

Did I ever tell you my story of Barry Sherman?

I was summoned by him in 1990, a few months after we got approval from the HPB for Eldepryl, one of my brokers called — Arnie Polan from Scotia McLeod — and said, "Barry Sherman would like to see you."

I said, "Who's Barry Sherman?"

"Sherman is one of the richest men in Canada. He makes more money than anybody else. He's got the biggest generic drug company. He wants you to see him. He wants you to come to his office."

He took me and Arnie on a tour of the place. It was wonderful. State-of-the-art; it's a monstrous place, and he said, "I want Deprenyl and I want you to sign a contract with me and give me the rights to produce a generic competitor in June of 1993."

This was February 1990.

I said, "Why should I give it to you?" And he said, "Because, if you don't, I'm going to knock you off." I said, "What's this crap I always read in the paper where you're saying you're a patriotic Canadian, and you drive down the price for the multi-nationals?" And he said, "Never mind that bullshit; I want it and I'm going to have it and you'll get a 5 per cent royalty and I'll give you $50,000 in advance, or you'll get nothing and I'll take it."

So, I went and hired Percy Parks, who went to work on him. Sherman made a lot of money legitimately, but he was greedy, and he was running an operation from Nassau called Silver Bullet Pharmaceuticals, and he was advertising in American magazines — "Prescription drugs at half price, no prescription necessary, send your check to Silver Bullet" — and when detectives traced Silver Bullet back to Toronto, it was just a mail drop.

The money was sent there, came back to Toronto and was given to D.

D. took it over to Apotex and he would take shipment of all the drugs from Apotex.

And, somehow, the situation went into the hands of the FDA. Just — somehow!

You don't know how delighted we were. And he had problems and he was too busy to worry about me.

About two weeks after that, I got a phone call from the owner of a Canadian drug company — a charming young man — inviting me for lunch, and when I arrive, an ex-employee of mine (Mr. F) is with him. Mr. F was the man we hired to submit our applications for Deprenyl to the drug approvals branch. And he shows up with this owner.

Mr. F, after he got through with the application and we paid a lot of money for it, about $100,000, gave us back our application form and, we thought, all the copies. But, he kept one. He's now gone to work for the other company and supplied the owner with our application that would contain all the information, all the tests. If you were making an application without this information, it would take you three years.

The owner said, "I would like half of your company." He said, "Mr. F is now working for me."

Mr. F didn't deny it. They were very good friends.

You can't sue a guy for that. He hasn't done anything illegal, they hired him. It's business.

I was very shocked, very shocked, and Mr. F was very uncomfortable sitting there. He didn't want to be there.

But the owner needed him there to show me that he had the goods.

This was 1991. And I was a little upset. The ownere said, "If you don't cooperate with me, I'm going to produce a long-acting Deprenyl for a fraction of what you sell it for, no research costs."

I said, "Let me think about it."

I used the same detective, Percy Parks, he's a great detective, and put him to work. A week later, he ushered a fellow named B. into my office. B. was the former chief financial officer at this company.

He said he quit because the owner was paying for his personal expenses through the company and giving gifts to his girlfriends, using company funds — a very expensive necklace. And he wrote a sworn affidavit.

I called the owner and said, "Let's have lunch again." And I went and I laid the affidavit in front of him and he was smooth. He said, "No problem. I never intended to produce Deprenyl in the first place. Let's be friends."

I said, "My detective's expenses were $7,000," and he said, "I'm not paying the expenses, but I won't produce Deprenyl." I said, "Okay."

About six months later, I got a phone call from Dave Musket, who is an analyst in New York, and he said, "There's a chap (the owner) out here trying to raise some money for a U.S. underwriting," and could I give him my opinion on the company.

I said, "Let me call you back in 10 minutes."

So I phoned the company and got the new chief financial officer on the phone and I told him the whole story and I said, "I've still got this file here and it's cost me $7,000." He said, "I'd like to buy it and pay your expenses," and I said, "You're going to send over the $7,000?" He did, immediately.

I sent him the file. And I told Dave, "Don't do the underwriting."

Percy Parks is a real gem. He's known me for 30 years. He's in charge of security here now. He's the one who came in as my bodyguard.

Was the owner ever aware that I put the jinx on him anyway in New York? I don't know.

It would be more fun if he did. . . .

Well, I learned! . . .

Now, I don't know who sent this, but someone sent an anonymous letter to the FDA. I got a copy of it.

Yes: how fortuitous! This is the U.S. Federal Drug Administration. It's about Barr Laboratories. A subsidiary of Apotex — Barry Sherman's company.

This was November, 1991. See, it says: "Silver Bullet Marketing, 335 Ormont Street in Toronto," and 335 Ormont is owned by Barry Sherman, and the illegal operation is managed by his partner Alan Shechtman.

"After the money is received, Silver Bullet ship the pills to Buffalo where they're picked up at the General Post Office."

Well, a hundred FDA officers descended on Barr Labs, and the stock was $30-odd, and I'm told that Barry tried to protect it by buying 400,000 shares, and it went to nothing and they were, temporarily, partially shut down. They screwed him up. Barry Sherman is a ruthless man. It was lucky for me it happened.

He was well connected; he had two Congressmen who fought for him, but nothing helped.

"FDA moves to shut drug maker". That's the *New York Times.* "Two legislators challenged the punitive move against Barr Labs. Representative John Dingle, Democrat of Michigan, and Alphonse D'Amato . . . suggested that FDA officials may have threatened to punish Barr Labs as retaliation for the company's part in uncovering corruption and fraud that led to criminal convictions of five former FDA officials. . . ."

Then I ran this ad in the *Globe & Mail,* with a bunch of headlines from American newspapers:

> *Generics Case Guilty Pleas. Widening Inquiry on Generic Drugs Focuses on Switching of Ingredients . . . Hospital Bans Many Generic Drugs . . . The Generic Drug Scandal . . . Hospital Stops Using Generic Drugs . . . FDA May Withdraw Another Drug Approval*

Look who's been making a lot of headlines.

Many generic drugs have claimed they are as effective as brand name medicines, at less cost. They don't always live up to the promise. In fact, some hospitals in the United States have stopped using generics altogether. To be sure that you're getting what your doctor prescribes, ask him to write "No sub" on the prescription. Because there's no substitute for good health. . . .

The ad has the Deprenyl Research logo — "A Canadian company dedicated to a healthier Canada" — and "This advertisement paid for by Morton Shulman,co-Chairman, Deprenyl Research Limited."

This year I got Arnie to go back to Sherman, get him to back off. Offered him a big block of shares in Deprenyl Animal Health and DUSA — would have made him a fortune. He won't even listen. Says if I want him to leave Deprenyl alone I've gotta pay him 10 million bucks!

May 31, 1993
[Lawyer's memo]

Spoke to Arnold Polan on May 31, 1993. I introduced myself to him as a solicitor for Dr. Morton Shulman.

Mr. Polan's comments were that indeed Morty Shulman had asked him to meet with Barry Sherman. . . . The meeting was very congenial and Mr. Polan confirmed that the object of the exercise was to see if Mr. Sherman would not compete with Deprenyl.

Mr. Polan had several options by way of proposal including giving to Mr. Sherman some shares of an entity known as Deprenyl Animal Health Inc. Mr. Sherman was not enthusiastic.

Mr. Polan asked him what would it take for Apotex to stop developing and producing in competition to Deprenyl. Mr. Sherman said that likely he would make about $10 million profit and so if Dr. Shulman wanted to stop him, it would cost $10 million.

Mr. Polan was not sure that that was a serious number. Mr. Polan reported this to Dr. Shulman.

On June 19, 1993, the *Globe &Mail*'s front-page story is "FBI probes big Canadian drug firm. Apotex products sold to U.S. residents without prescriptions."

Canada's largest pharmaceutical drug manufacturer, Apotex Inc., is being probed by the U.S. Federal Bureau of Investigation to find out how its generic drugs are reaching U.S. residents who do not have prescriptions for them. The FBI and the U.S. Attorney's office in Baltimore are looking for evidence of violations of U.S. federal laws involving mail fraud, wire fraud, money laundering and the unlawful distribution of unapproved drugs. The RCMP have been helping the FBI with its investigation.

A U.S. District Court judge ruled in Atlanta in March that the export of the drugs from Canada to the United States involved "false representations in furtherance of . . . business interests" and represented a "threat to public health."

Besides Apotex, the FBI probe includes the company's president, Bernard (Barry) Sherman, 50; his brother-in-law, Allen Barry Schechtman, 45; and Mr. Schechtman's company, Silver Bullet Marketing.

In an affidavit sworn in February, Mr. Sherman said he believed the Atlanta lawsuit was launched to punish him for making cheaper drugs available.

. . . Christopher Mead, the assistant U.S. attorney in Baltimore assigned to work with the FBI, said he would not comment "other than to request information on how you obtained" an FBI report on the investigation of Apotex. . . .

The *Wall Street Journal* also splashes the story high and wide.

On June 29, the Associated Press reports from New Bern, North Carolina:

Jury selection began yesterday for a patent infringement lawsuit that will determine whether the anti-AIDS drug AZT can be made and sold as a less-expensive generic drug.

Burroughs Wellcome Co. of Research Triangle Park, NC., filed suit against two would-be competitors, Barr Laboratories Inc., a subsidiary of Toronto-based Apotex Inc., and Novopharm Ltd., also of Toronto, after they applied for U.S. permission to manufacture AZT. The drug now is made only by Burroughs Wellcome. Last year Wellcome PLC had revenue of $388 million (U.S.) worldwide on AZT including $195 million in the United States.

On July 20, Merck Frosst Canada Inc. announces it will fight Apotex all the way to the Supreme Court of Canada to block any generic version of its $120 million-a-year heart medication, Vasotec.

Merck gets an immediate, interim halt on generic distribution, and gives notice it means to pull out all stops to keep the ban in place for as long as the court case can be kept alive.

As the month draws to a close, Barry Sherman, his plate full, his defamation suit against Morty only one of a score of litigations, has much to occupy him besides Deprenyl.

With any luck, he will remain distracted for a while at least.

* * *

SK: If you were asked whether you think you have flaws, an impediment . . .

MS: Impetuousness, urge for revenge, weakness for pretty girls.

SK: But those things can be strengths as well as weaknesses.

MS: Well, my strengths are my weaknesses. No, there's nothing I've regretted. I think I've done the right thing right along or, at least, the best thing. You always have choices and you never know where you would have gone if you had taken another route. But I don't think I've ever hurt anybody deliberately.

I don't get caught up worrying about whatever might have been different. It's a fact of daily life. What's done is done.

I've never been to a shrink, no. I'd never been to a doctor at all until I got diagnosed with Parkinson's. Not for 50 years. . . .

Outside the public arena, I have no enemies. Don't think anybody can say that about me. . . .

I have no personal enemies. Don't think I've ever done anything bad to anybody. . . .

My public enemies don't know me. I have all sorts of public enemies but none of them know me. And they don't know they hate someone that doesn't exist.

SK: And you don't have any feminists in the office, do you?

MS: No. I have one shrew and a dozen lovely young girls. One old shrew.

SK: I think all the women in your life are actually incredibly protective of you, and from one another.

In fact, I think that is the secret of your success. Each one thinks that she's your only armor.

MS: That's true. [Laughs.] Well, we've had some wonderful experiences.

Chapter Ten

The Bestowal

May 16, 1993

From the four corners of Metropolitan Toronto, the Morty circle is gathering.

The impossible has happened.

Morty is to be inducted into the Order of Canada.

He has just gotten the news and of course it is all strictly confidential, but . . .

"To honor our dear friend Morty," Roma Dzerowicz's faxed invitation reads, with her usual precise directions to their pleasure patch among the semi-working farms and nouveau-gentry estates in the Halton Hills, between pretty Milton and the puppy-breeding townlet of Rockwood.

Denny Dzerowicz first showed up on Morty's doorstep more than 20 years ago, in the glow of the high political Shulman years. Denny, a looming rough-voiced Ukrainian, in those days had bushy dark sideburns and all his hair. Although hardly a gut NDPer any more than Morty was, Denny announced he liked Morty's style, was ready to pledge fealty, could deliver a large pocketful of his West Toronto landesmann to the Morty box on the ballot and help him win his second sweep.

Denny was just the kind of fellow roisterer Morty liked. Many were the jolly outings and escapades the two got up to, while forging a fitful but fruitful political and entrepreneurial alliance on the side, Denny putting together a nice workable fortune wheeling and dealing in . . .

"What does Denny do?" chic Esther Sarick asks her husband Sam as they drive Morty out to Denny and Roma's. Gloria is not coming to the party.

"Denny makes displays," Sam explains.

"Makes displays . . . ?" Esther ponders.

"You know, for trade shows."

"Can you make money doing that?" wonders Esther; a moot point, since the Dzerowicz spread has plainly been built with a good deal of it.

There is a rambling house with a gym and media room, a two-acre backyard with a boardwalk leading from the deck to a man-made islet in the middle of a natural pond. There is Christofle silver and three different sets of crystal goblets a-twinkle on the banquet-sized dining table.

Bonnie and Clyde, the Dzerowicz mastiffs, the sort of over-leaping behemoths whose owners assure you are just pups who would not hurt a fly, do not try to overpower the visitors this afternoon.

Indoors, the circle mill and greet with affectionate kisses. The men tend towards jackets and ties, the women are beautifully made up and outfitted in coordinated couturier ladies-who-lunch ensembles worthy of a high noon shopping break in Yorkville.

All are drinking champagne poured into slender flutes by a smiling young woman with a lightly mustached upper lip and a purple pantsuit. She and her bearded chef-hatted husband, caterers of the tribute lunch —asparagus *en croute,* fresh poached salmon, a six-tier opera torte — are the singing proprietors of an opera bistro in Rockwood. After the button popping lunch they will oblige the guests' request for an a capella rendition of "La Buona Notte," she a melodious throaty alto, he a fluting tenor.

The circle, three-quarters of whom are directors of Morty companies past, present and future, have grown to, for none of them was born to, savor the subtle delights of opera and the silken joys of extremely expensive wines, many of whose names they happily admit they cannot pronounce.

Arnie Fogle will sit through the aria with eyes blissfully closed. Arnie is a hefty shrewd-faced 59; is big and slick-haired, crag nose and plum silk bomber jacket. He is an ex trucker who carried a baseball bat in his teens, against thugs trying to extort protection money. Today, Morty tells you, 90 per cent of the fruit imported into Canada comes via Arnie's Ontario Tree Fruit Company: Chilean grapes, U.S. apples, oranges, you name it; kiwis from Australia.

All through dessert Arnie is softly and melodiously singing along with Pavarotti, a Mortycircle favorite, as they sip the third fine wine from Morty's cellar; first a silken honeyed white, then a vintage Bordeaux and an icy-sweet *sauternes*.

Adele Fogle, Arnie's wife of 30-some years, looks and sounds like a Damon Runyon doll, blonde and bosomy and wispy voiced and never missing a trick. She fears nothing, flies her own plane. Closely questions, in that little girl voice, about the state of the economy; can explain in detail why the $25,000 fine slapped on Ontario Tree Fruit for polluting Six-Mile Creek and Lake Ontario is nothing but a crock.

Adele softly tells the assemblage Morty was an idol of her dad's. "Not that I'm saying he is very much older than me but, I can remember, there I am 15, 16, and my dad is coming home from the bridge club raving about the way Morty plays bridge."

The brunch is to mark two milestones.

The first is the news of Morty's impending induction, at last, into the Order of Canada.

The second is his final break with the company that he and Parkinson's built, the rift which, finally and inescapably leaves him on one side of the canyon and, on the other, Martin Barkin and Geoff Shulman.

From Morty two strictly-confidential documents have gone winging on the May 15 faxwires. The first is to Geoff Shulman:

Dear Geoff:

Thank you. It finally sunk in after our talk that Deprenyl is no longer mine, and I have nothing more to contribute that would be willingly received. A major problem is that for four years I ran the company by my own judgment and it took quite a while for it to sink in that it is over. So long as I am a shareholder I am afraid I will be looking at things thinking I could do it better.

I compounded the problem when I borrowed the money to buy the company's shares, and at that point when Barry Sherman reappeared on the scene, I automatically burst into battle (successfully) with him since no one else was doing so.

My situation — i.e., as a large shareholder with no say — is an impossible one for me, and I am going to sell my shares, repay the Deprenyl loan, and redirect my attentions.

If I am unable to conclude this by May 26, I am making sure that the loan will be one hundred per cent covered. You will have the 400,000 shares of Deprenyl Animal Health and if I cannot get sufficient DUSA freed up, I will assign you my net equity interest in my accounts at Friedberg (please see attached).

I am using those to margin my short Canadian dollar position but there is sufficient equity left over to cover the remaining amount I owe Deprenyl. I hope this is satisfactory, as the alternative would be difficult for everyone.

In any case, I intend to pay off the Deprenyl loan as quickly as possible.

I will make no further public comments about Deprenyl. Please ask Martin to extend the same courtesy to me. I shall not attend the annual meeting.

It is signed with a small stiff sad "Morton." Copies are indicated to Sam Sarick, Arnie Fogle and Stewart Saxe.

Chapter 10: The Bestowal

The second confidential document, dated May 5th, comes from The Chancellery, Rideau Hall, The Order Of Canada.

"I am pleased to inform you," writes Judith A. LaRocque, secretary to the Governor General and Secretary General of the Order, "that the Advisory Council of the Order of Canada has recommended to the Governor General that you be appointed an Officer of the Order of Canada. The Order was established in 1967 as a means of recognizing outstanding achievement, honouring those who have given service to Canada, to their fellow citizens or to humanity at large. . . ."

Ms. LaRocque and her colleagues "trust that you will hold this information in strict confidence until the official announcement is made."

Naturally, Morty has impressed upon all those he has told the news that it is strictly confidential.

Here at Roma and Denny's is a swaddling circle of warmth in which the public Morty is never seen. The tableful of updressed men and women raise the glasses of extremely good red of impressive vintage, warmth unquestionably genuine.

What is noteworthy about the circle, amongst which are some of those Morty considers his oldest and dearest friends, is that all the women are good-looking; all the men and almost all the women do business with Morty. And, none of them are his betters.

Vince Murphy, a good-humored blue-suited man with a receding ginger hairline and the build of a football player going to heft leads the toast. "For an honor long overdue, to recognize . . . singular man . . . great accomplishment in helping so many, bringing in Eldepryl," Vince Murphy says.

Gracefully he turns the Deprenyl break from dark to light. "We understand that you would have gotten this Order Of Canada long before but the association with that bunch of scoundrels at Deprenyl was holding you back. The Order was just waiting for you. Start something else, anything else worthy of you. . . ."

Eyes mist, crystal delicate as eggshells softly tinkles.

Morty speaks briefly of changes.

New beginnings, Morty. Not endings. A new beginning.

Morty asks Jim Kingham for his dark glasses, pops them on, cocks a pose. "I'll be back!"

"I shall return! Just like McArthur," expostulates Vince Murphy, who has just been laid off from the major downtown law firm where only a year past he was in line for a partnership.

"I should've grabbed him for Deprenyl," Morty says. "Helluva fine lawyer. Great sense of humor."

Morty, thin and gray and fragile today, is seated with a buffer cushion of women. He is beside Roma, at her right hand, frequently reaching a hand to touch her arm, leaving her left arm, braceletted with a charm circle of hammered gold cupids with eyes of diamond specks, to be stroked, for comfort, by master gambler Sammy Kehela.

On Morty's other side the lovely Adriane Murphy, all warm golden tones, ashen hair and tawny skin, dressed in a floaty golden frock bought on the Murphy's Key West vacation . . . with Morty. Ada, a teacher of gifted high school students, once so impressed Pavarotti himself with her beauty that he asked her to sit on his knee when she went backstage after a concert.

Beside Ada is the redoubtable Adele Fogle softly cashmered in sweatery red. Then Vince, who left university teaching —he taught economics at Fordham University — for the distressingly ephemeral security of law. Esther Sarick, small and sleek, hair in a dark smooth bun, tortoiseshell shades, Hermes scarf, a chunk of gold necklacery and braceletry. Beside her Sam, president of his own development company, round of face and belly, avuncuclar small man with deceptively sleepy eyes.

Roma and Denny at the head and foot of the table; Roma exuding businesslike gaminery, with her smooth cap of dark blonde hair, its elfin cut curving down her smooth brow, a linen suit of hard bright coral with a soft downcurving neckline. Denny, his bushy beard white, bald pate tanned, gentleman farmering in white collarless shirt with white on white suspenders.

Kitty corner, in Morty's direct sightline, is another statuesque pale Ukrainian, a member of the Barbados junket group, Anastasia Kingham. Like her husband Jim she is an ardent environmentalist; author of *Poison Stronger than Love*, about the blighting of Grassy Narrows native reserve. Arnie Fogle sits with arms loosely draped around the chairs of each woman beside him.

Arnie's other arm rests at the back of a stylish Anita, life-love of Sammy Kehela, the pensive philosopher and pro bridge champ, who still counts on regular matches at St. Clair Bridge to turn an intermittent few hundred.

"Sammy, tell me, what sort of money do you and Arnie play for which he never tells me about?" Adele is asking in the Miss Adelaide voice that does not bely the hundred per cent aware twinkle in her big blue eyes.

"Nothing, almost nothing, pennies."

"How much nothing, Sammy?"

"Pennies, a couple of hundred, maybe two fifty."

"So, there's no difference between pennies and two-fifty? And that's it, Sammy?"

"Never more than, the most would be seven hundred. Fifty. Tops."

Sammy is pale and a little stooped with worried spectacled eyes and uneasily frizzed hair. He was born in Baghdad, after his Iraqui-Jewish family was summarily bundled out during the pre-war pogrom atmosphere of pre-World War II. There were tumultuous periods in India, Jamaica and L.A. before Sammy decided to make Toronto his home base in 1970, and championship bridge his uneasy livelihood.

Beside Anita, Jim Kingham, Morty's newest scientific guru. Kingham is neatly gray, has the crisp mustached look of a clear eyed flying officer, one ready and able to guide the potent ALA abortafacient cream-missile safely to target market.

Kingham, who is in his mid-50s, studied physics, biochemistry and genetics. He is a judge in Peel County, "on the garbage circuit," Morty says. Kingham's love is saving the planet, which activity brought him in contact with Morty's daughter Dianne, environmental lawyer, years before he met Morty. His real love, after the environment, is porphyrines, a blood element on whose indispensability to human life he will happily discourse for as long as the listener likes.

It was Jim's eagle eye that flew to the porphyritic element in 5-ALA; it is Jim who alerted Morty to all those potentially fantastic but ultimately non-exercisable uterine applications.

There are to be always, so it seems, these gatherings in Morty's life, variegated and varying groups of the faithful and the hardy and the hopeful.

Not your average expected bunch: a lot of self-made money, the rough raising Roma's crystalware next to therefined; chunky gold jewelry indoors and plastic yellow lawn pinwheels on the grass outside.

Although it's a treasure of a shining sunny May morning, the group never ventures out of the house. It's hard to amble through the back forty in suede high heels.

After lunch there is an ad-hoc partial board meeting downstairs in the gym. Arnie, Kingham, Morty: Arnie wants to know if Safety Corp. is going to be in competition with Deprenyl. He also wants to know just where Safety Corp. is at.

Sam Sarick stays at the table, where the golden *sauternes* shimmers in the glasses, nodding and seeming to doze, and missing nothing.

There are dragons to be slain, wicked witches and wizards to be overcome. On the drive home Morty is hyped, up and down.

Viola McMillan, whom he once dubbed the Boadicea of mining promotions, one of his targets in the Windfall mining scandal of the '60s, has breathtakingly transcended a 1967 conviction for stock skulduggery and received an Order of Canada, too, at the spring ceremonies just past. They moved the date of the presentation to April 21, to coincide with her 90th birthday, April 21.

As a confidential OC-to-be, Morty is roused at this deification of a doyenne of the multi-million dollar Windfall Oils and Mines brouhaha. Charged with manipulating shares, McMillan was convicted of wash trading, which means setting up fake accounts to create the appearance of heavy trading and drive the share price up. She was sentenced, at the age of 64, to nine months in the lockup, and said to have served seven weeks. In 1978 she received a pardon. In 1991 she was inducted into the Mining Hall of Fame, hailed for "her driving commitment to transforming the Prospectors and Developers Association."

Thus do laurels wreath the brows of those who make markets.

"She was supposed to spend nine months in prison; I swear she never spent a day! I railed against her in the Legislature, I went to see her in prison and I couldn't find her; they took her in the front door and out the back. It was an unbelievable scandal."

Will anyone, anyone at all listen?

Sam focuses serenely on the highway, seems not to be paying attention, until Esther pricks up at something Morty has just said: medication smuggled from Canada and abroad, for illegal resale in the States; imminent rack, ruin for the generic king . . .

"Does Martin Barkin know about this?" Esther asks.

"Martin won't talk to me," Morty says.

"Martin won't talk to you? Oh, nonsense. Whatever gives you that idea? Everything has been taken into account." Sam has been listening, after all. Morty twitches his shoulders, turns to the window his wide and watering eye.

"Nothing will be done. Won't make any difference," he mutters.

Before Sunday is through most of Morty's friends get one more phone call. He has to impart new strictly confidential information to clarify the original strictly confidential information about the Order of Canada; strictly confidentially.

"Did you realize I'm being made an Officer of the Order of Canada? I thought it was just a Member! I just reread the letter. Everybody read the letter and nobody picked it up! Member is lowest, Companion is highest, Officer is second highest! I can't believe it. It's supposed to be strictly confidential."

Viola MacMillan only became a Member; the level reserved for those who have merely made "outstanding contributions at the local or regional level." On the other hand, she has a gallery bearing her name in the Canadian Museum of Nature in Ottawa, to which she donated $1.25 million for a mineral collection.

The endowment to Toronto Western Hospital's Gloria and Morton Shulman Wing amounted to $3 million, from Morty's personal Deprenyl stock profits

But hey: How many people are gonna see a person's name in a gallery full of rocks?

Postscript

FROM: Sylvia Fraser
      701 King St. West, #302
      Toronto, Ont. M5V 2W7

TO: The Advisory Council for the Order of Canada

I wish to nominate Dr. Morton Shulman for the Order of Canada. I believe him to be a worthy recipient, for the following reasons.

From 1963 to 1967, Dr. Shulman was the Chief Coroner of Metropolitan Toronto. During that period, he was seldom out of the news because of his intolerance for negligence, leading to unnecessary deaths.

As a direct result of Dr. Shulman's caring efforts, guard rails were installed on the Don Valley Expressway and other major provincial arteries, thus eliminating the lethal spear-ends on which victims were all-too-regularly being impaled. Regulations were devised for the counting of surgical instruments before and after operations. Safety procedures for the care of children during and after tonsillectomies were also implemented in Toronto Hospitals, preventing perhaps a dozen needless child deaths a year; these procedures have since become standard in hospitals throughout the country. Dr. Shulman also made available the pituitary growth hormone for children lacking it, enabling them to achieve normal height.

In sum: during the four years in which Dr. Shulman was Metropolitan Toronto's chief coroner, he radically redefined his job as preserving life rather than documenting death. Two decades later, his life-saving changes are a gift that keeps on giving.

From 1967 to 1975, Dr. Shulman was the NDP member of the Provincial Legislature for High Park Riding in Toronto. As a result of his eight years of feisty opposition, changes were made in the practices of the Workmen's Compensation Board, assuring that accident victims would receive full benefits until able to resume employment. Previously, when a worker was half better, the payment was cut in half even though work could not be resumed, adding a punitive quality to the painful process of convalescing. Dr. Shulman was also responsible for instituting pensions for the disabled in chronic-care hospitals — again, a permanent change enabling the handicapped to live in dignity.

Indicative of the range of Dr. Shulman's activities was his successful agitation for revision of Ontario's liquor laws so that legislation, proclaiming it illegal to drink standing up in some places and illegal to drink sitting down in others, was reshaped with due regard to common sense. Such revision eliminated a pocket of foolishness where the law was open to ridicule.

From 1973 to 1988, Dr. Shulman was a twice-weekly columnist for The Toronto Sun. He also spent eight years — from 1975 to 1983 — as a talk-show host for City TV. In these capacities, he continued to adopt causes, issue challenges, prick pomposity, skewer the guilty. Typical of his concerns was an incident in which the giving of wrong-type blood to a patient in a Toronto hospital resulted in death. Convinced this tragedy was due to slack hospital procedures, Dr. Shulman wrote twenty columns of attack. Though a bitter controversy with the College of Physicians and Surgeons persuaded him he had lost this fight, a year later the province assumed administration of the hospital.

Epilogue: Postscript

The year 1987 marked Dr. Shulman's professional debut onto the world stage. The impetus was personal tragedy: in 1983, he had been diagnosed as having Parkinson's disease, an incurable and progressive impairment of the central nervous system. For four years he managed to maintain his extraordinarily active life supported by drugs; then, in 1987 his program failed. Faced with gross disability, Dr. Shulman went international in his search for treatment. In Hungary, he found what he needed — a drug called deprenyl which, in its effects on him was equivalent to resurrection. However, not only was this drug unavailable in North America, but a U.S. company had already spent eight years and ten million dollars in a failed bid to convince the U.S. government to allow importation.

In 1987, Dr. Shulman established his own drug company, which became Deprenyl Research Limited (DRL), for importation and distribution of this drug, subject to governmental approval. Though the situation looked hopeless, he was spurred on by an inconvertible fact: his life was hell without deprenyl; with it, he was able to wrest precious daylight hours of normalcy from an affliction which continued to overwhelm him every night. Though he himself could afford the cost and inconvenience of acquiring the drug from foreign sources, thousands of others across North America — equally afflicted, equally humiliated by Parkinson's — could not.

Through his forceful personality and the justice of his cause, Dr. Shulman persuaded the Canadian Minister of Health to allow him to import and sell deprenyl on compassionate grounds. During February of 1988, he sold a hundred pills from a box, informally kept in his secretary's desk drawer. Word got around. Sales rocketed.

During the next four incredible years, Dr. Shulman convinced the Canadian government, based on well-documented studies, to fully license his company for the importation and distribution of deprenyl. He also expanded its staff of two — himself and his son Dr. Geoff Shulman, a dermatologist — to thirty-eight. Today DRL — founded with a capital of $1.4 million U.S.

287

raised by Dr. Shulman and a half-dozen friends — has sales of over a million dollars a month in Canada alone. As the largest entirely Canadian-owned pharmaceutical firm, it distributes three drugs for Parkinson's under full government regulation: Eldepryl, which is the trade name for deprenyl, making up ninety-five per cent of its sales; Prolopa, and Apomorphine. The latter, for advanced Parkinson's patients, is distributed free by his company to five hundred people in Canada, as a public service.

In addition, DRL has licensed Alzene for restoration of memory in Alzheimer's patients, which it sells for compassionate use in Canada and for export to individual patients; Doral, a non-habit-forming, non-toxic sleeping pill, which is also under application; and 1 alpha D-2, to counter osteoporosis in women, now in the testing stages. ALA

With the aid of his son, Dr. Shulman created this miracle of productivity in only four years, while he himself was suffering — often cruelly — from the disease his drugs help to alleviate. He did so by focussing four brands of expertise: medical, financial, political and administrative. He did so out of zest for the enterprise, but also knowing that every pill sold eased the suffering of a Parkinson's victim like himself.

Certainly, Dr.Shulman's generosity is legendary. Publicly, he and his company are in the process of donating up to five million dollars to the Toronto General and Western Hospital Foundation for research into the treatment of Parkinson's and related disorders.

As an art connoisseur, Dr. Shulman — the author of seven books on such topics as art and finance — has also made generous donations of cash and rare artifacts to museums and art galleries across the country, especially to The Royal Ontario Museum in Toronto and The National Museum of Civilization in Ottawa.

Yet, through all of these activities — each of which would have been a full-time career for a less versatile person — another runs like a spine, providing cohesion and grounding. Since 1950, when Dr. Shulman opened his medical office in a modest working-class district in Toronto, he has been a general practitioner.

Though he stopped accepting new patients seven years ago, even today he sees a limited number, six days a week. Most are aged; some are among the hundreds of children he himself delivered, a few are children of children.

Recently, on a Saturday afternoon, I received a phone call from Dr. Shulman: a young woman, whom he had delivered was consulting him over a matter of sexual abuse. Though she had long since moved out of his neighborhood, and was a teacher with many contacts in her own community, Dr. Shulman was the first person she thought to turn to in her despair. Quite appropriately and typically, he phoned me personally and on-the-spot because he knew I could provide the information she needed.

Over the years, Morton Shulman has been a thorn in the flesh of the powerful — a role he has relished. He has been quick to use the media rather than the expected channels of authority. He has never been a team player, and his acutely honed sense of the ridiculous has sometimes overcome what others might call sober judgment. Though these quicksilver qualities have occasionally earned him the rebuke of dilettantism, his public career has had great moral consistency: he always fought for the under-dog; he was always available to any member of the public who felt he/she had a grievance; no matter how successful he became, he never identified with the Establishment; he never considered the professional consequences of fighting with peers and employers; he specialized in causes to which he could bring personal and professional experience; while he showcased the striking individual case, he pursued it to its common structural cause, instituting and demanding reform.

To review Dr.Shulman's public career is to review the life and times of Ontario. In galvanizing attention for one cause or another, he made everyday doings of the city and of the province dramatic and fun to a wide spectrum of ordinary peo-ple, who believed governments and institutions to be grey, priv-ileged, self-serving and remote. For them, Morty was a ticket to a ballgame. He was their Crusading Coroner, inspiring the acclaimed TV series "Wojeck." He was the man who could fight city hall on their behalf, and win. They could read him in their newspapers. He was as close as their television screens.

In his last ten years, Dr. Shulman's public role is one he would not have chosen: as an all-too-aware spokesperson for Parkinson's. Only those of us who are privileged to know him well can guess how much it cost this man — whose hallmark is his zest for life — to go public with this debilitating disease. Only those of us who know him well can guess the courage and tenacity that it takes, day by day, to turn the crises of running a small drug company, in treacherous international waters where the sharks run fast and the stakes are high, into off-the-cuff anecdotes, brimming with self-deprecating good humor. More candidly: even after a friendship of thirty years, I could never have anticipated the spiritual transformation that affliction has drawn from this remarkable man. The more restricted his life has become, the more he revels in the pleasure of his family and friends, and the more he appreciates the joys that each day brings. Even now, after some small event, such as a birthday party, he will exclaim that this day has been the best day of his life — and mean it!

Morty is a bone fide hero, and he is a well-loved one. After ten years outside of the public glare, he is still approached everywhere he goes by waitresses and cab-drivers and sales clerks who want to acknowledge him, or thank him, for something he may have long forgotten. They do so in full confidence of his caring and compassion.

Though this letter is a long one, it only sets out the bare bones of a life fully lived, with continuous dedication to public service. In Dr.Shulman, the Advisory Council has a candidate with unusual grassroots' support, combined with a solid record of accomplishment in many fields. His name will add lustre to the awards, by enhancing their relevance for many Canadians.

Sincerely,
Sylvia Fraser

Postscript II

"Morty, A First-Class Grandfather"
by Rebecca Saxe

November 22, 1992

There aren't many people who can say that they are Morton Shulman's daughter's child. Only 3, in fact. I am one of those lucky few.

Ever since I can remember, Morty and Gloria (never Gramma and Grampa, because that sounds "old") have lived in the castle at 66 Russell Hill Rd.

When I was really little (up until I was 3 yrs old) my parents, Dianne and Stewart, or Mommy and Daddy, depending on your point of view, and I lived way out in the country, but every Friday night we came down to the heart of Toronto to have Shabbat dinner with Gloria and Morty. Meals there were and still are huge affairs. Gloria's attitude towards food is a family joke. For the 8 of us, including Uncle Geoff, Auntie Dianne, and Great Bubbie, there was always enough food on the table to feed an army, and more waiting in the kitchen. I have never yet managed to leave that house without having had something to eat.

When we moved from the country just before my brother was born, we moved into 248 Russell Hill Rd., where we still live. Our house is just a block north of theirs, so the whole family would troop down, usually with a few of my friends in tow, to swim, or talk, or eat. Usually all 3.

One of our earliest home videos is of Mom, a group of my friends and I walking down the street to Gloria and Morty's

---

291

house, all dressed up, for my fifth birthday party. Gloria and my 3 great-grandparents were waiting for us and cheering as we came into sight. From behind their chairs, Morty was waving and cheering harder than all four put together, a huge grin stretching from ear to ear.

I remember once when I was in grade 2 or 3, Morty promised me that he'd take me shopping after school for some things for my doll house. Imagine my surprise and delight when at 4 o'clock, in front of my school, Morty was waiting for me in a white stretched limo, with a chauffeur to open the door for me and everything. I had never been in one before, and I felt exactly like Cinderella. I think I had more fun exploring the car (it had a T.V. and a phone and all sorts of neat stuff!) than shopping for the dolls.

When I was in grade 3, Morty took me with him to Miami. I don't remember that much about the trip, but I do remember 2 things. The first is that we travelled first class, which I absolutely adored. My seat was enormous, and I was tiny which was a very comfortable combination. The other thing I remember is that I had a room of my own, another first. My bed was a round, queen-sized water bed. I even had my own porch, with a round hot tub which I never used, but was fun to have sitting there.

Gloria always used to have one of the Seders at her house. Mom would run and lead the service, while Daddy and Morty sat together at the opposite ends, making funny comments and generally trying to annoy her. Morty hid the afikomen, and usually got as excited about it as we did. After we had found it, my brother David and I use to have to fight hard in bargaining against him for a good deal. However, after a few minutes of tough bargaining, we always ended up with a silver dollar or a 5 dollar coin, and sometimes even a 10 dollar coin for whoever had actually found it (usually me, being the oldest and having the longest legs).

While looking through my mom's bookshelf for anything

readable, I came across one of Morty's books, "Coroner". I sat down with it on the basement floor and read it until dinner. I read some more after dinner, and then finished it the next day. Of course I've heard all about the T.V. show, being a coroner and then a MPP, but it's always hard to believe that that person was the same person as my grandfather, who always has a hug and kiss for his grandchildren whenever they drop by. All the documentaries, and newspaper headlines seem so unbelievable, even though I know that they're true and they're about my very own Morty.

I don't understand the stock market in the least, although Morty has tried many times to explain little bits of it to me. What I do understand is good news, so I cheer him on whenever I can, and read many of the articles about him, and hope for the best, which is usually what I get.

When we were on our way to Palm Beach, 4 strangers stopped us in the airport to ask if he wasn't Morton Shulman, and of course each one of them had watched his show and read his columns regularly, and missed them terribly. Whenever I mention to my friends' parents or my teachers that I am Morton Shulman's granddaughter, a new respect comes into their eyes as they ask "Morton Shulman?! 'The' Morton Shulman?!" Yes, the Morton Shulman, the one and only Morton Shulman, my grandfather.